Cultural Encounters in the Early South

Cultural Encounters in the Early South

Indians and Europeans in Arkansas

COMPILED BY

Jeannie Whayne

THE UNIVERSITY OF ARKANSAS PRESS

Fayetteville 1995

99   98   97   96   95   5   4   3   2   1

Designed by Gail Carter

⊖ The paper used in this publication meets the minimum
requirements of the American National Standard for Perma-
nence of Paper for Printed Library Materials Z39.48-1984.

Library of Congress Cataloging-in-Publication Data

Cultural encounters in the early South : Indians and
    Europeans in Arkansas / compiled by Jeannie Whayne
        p.   cm.
    Includes bibliographical references (p.   ) and index.
    ISBN 1-55728-394-X (cloth : alk. paper)
    1. Indians of North America—Arkansas—History.
    2. Indians of North America—First contact with
    Europeans—Arkansas. 3. Arkansas—History.
    I. Whayne, Jeannie M.
E78.A8c85   1995
967.7'00497—dc20   95-20274
                                              CIP

Contents

Contributors   vii

Preface
    JEANNIE WHAYNE   ix

Introduction
    CHARLES HUDSON   xi

The Expedition of Hernando de Soto:
A Post-mortem Report
    DAVID SLOAN   3

Living in a Graveyard:
Native Americans in Colonial Arkansas
    WILLARD H. ROLLINGS   38

Protohistoric Tunican Indians in Arkansas
    MICHAEL P. HOFFMAN   61

Rituals of Encounter:
Interpreting Native American Views of European Explorers
    GEORGE SABO III   76

Almost "Illinark":
The French Presence in Northeast Arkansas
    GEORGE E. LANKFORD   88

Between a Rock and a Hard Place:
The Indian Trade in Spanish Arkansas
    GILBERT C. DIN   112

The Significance of Arkansas's Colonial Experience
    MORRIS S. ARNOLD   131

Indians Signs on the Land
    SAMUEL D. DICKINSON   142

Endnotes   159

Index   197

Contributors

MORRIS S. ARNOLD is United States Circuit Judge for the Eighth Circuit. The French government has named him a *Chevalier de l'Ordre des Palmes Académiques* in recognition of his books and articles on the subject of colonial Arkansas.

SAMUEL D. DICKINSON of Prescott, Arkansas, is a retired newspaper editor who prepared himself to be an archaeologist. Besides his newspaper editorials, he has written four books and numerous articles that have appeared in archaeological, historical, and folklore journals.

GILBERT C. DIN is professor emeritus of history from Fort Lewis College, presently living in Olney, Maryland. His research interest is the Spanish period in the eighteenth-century Mississippi Valley. He is the author of several books and numerous articles on the subject.

MICHAEL P. HOFFMAN is professor of anthropology at the University of Arkansas and curator of anthropology at the University Museum. His research interest in Arkansas Native Americans during the protohistoric and colonial periods have resulted in the coeditorship (with Gloria A. Young) of a book, *The Expedition of Hernando de Soto West of the Mississippi, 1541–1543* (University of Arkansas Press, 1993) and several articles during the last five years.

CHARLES HUDSON is Franklin Professor of Anthropology at the University of Georgia. He is the author of several important works on Indians and Europeans in the early South and is currently finishing a book on the de Soto expedition.

GEORGE E. LANKFORD is the Pauline M. and Brooks Bradley Professor in the Social Sciences at Lyon College, Batesville, Arkansas. As a folklorist and regional historian, he has published a book and several articles on Native American and Ozark traditions.

WILLARD H. ROLLINGS is associate professor of history at the University of Nevada, Las Vegas. His work has focused on Native Americans of the southern prairie-plains. He is the author of two ethnohistorical books on the Comanche and Osage people. Rollings is currently at work on a book examining Osage cultural resistance to early nineteenth-century Christian missionaries.

GEORGE SABO III is associate archaeologist at the Arkansas Archeological Survey and associate professor of anthropology at the University of Arkansas, Fayetteville. His current research is on the prehistoric and historic evolution of Native American cultures in the Trans-Mississippi South.

DAVID SLOAN is associate professor of history at the University of Arkansas, Fayetteville. He is currently engaged in a comparative analysis of the creation and perception of communities in the Spanish, French, and British empires in the Western Hemisphere.

JEANNIE WHAYNE is assistant professor of history at the University of Arkansas, Fayetteville, editor of the *Arkansas Historical Quarterly*, and has written extensively on the Arkansas Delta, including articles in *Agricultural History*, *Forest and Conservation History*, the *Mississippi Quarterly*, and *Locus*. She has written, edited, and coedited books on Arkansas topics.

Preface

JEANNIE WHAYNE

Although the protohistoric and colonial periods in Arkansas have attracted relatively little scholarly attention, several enterprising and perceptive anthropologists, archaeologists, and historians have devoted their considerable analytical skills to research in this rich but little understood era in Arkansas history. Recognizing the paucity of literature devoted to protohistoric and colonial Arkansas, the *Arkansas Historical Quarterly* invited four scholars to contribute essays to its Spring 1992 issue. The popularity of the issue encouraged the editor to commission four additional essays, which together with the four published in the journal make up this volume. Charles Hudson, who has recently received attention for arguing that de Soto took a different route in his infamous sojourn into Arkansas, provides a provocative introduction.

While the contributors to this volume have broken new ground in the field of colonial and protohistoric Arkansas, several of them have also entered heated debates, sometimes against each other, concerning aspects of the preterritorial era. Willard Rollings and Gilbert Din, for example, have very different views of the Osage; these opposing perspectives are inherent in their interpretations of the Osage experience in Arkansas and are reflected in their respective chapters. Morris Arnold's position, meanwhile, posits a thesis challenged elsewhere concerning the influence of the colonial presence in shaping the history of Arkansas as a territory and state. Samuel Dickinson employs both linguistic and historical evidence to discover the origins of Indian place names in Arkansas and thus implicitly suggests that there is a colonial legacy of sorts. David Sloan perceptively explores the question of the de Soto route, and George Lankford's chapter details for the first time the considerable population of the French beyond the settlement of Arkansas Post in what is now Arkansas. George Sabo's intriguing chapter illuminates the distinctive social and cultural patterns of the Caddo and Quapaw, while Michael Hoffman makes a strong case for the existence of the Tunicans in Arkansas, a presence disputed by other anthropologists.

The authors and compiler are indebted to numerous individuals and institutions. The compiler wishes to thank Willard Gatewood for his support and encouragement, Mary Kennedy for her willingness to generate the marvelous maps appearing throughout this volume, and Gretchen Gearhart for her endless patience and perseverance in attending to the many details necessary in such a project. Michael P. Hoffman is grateful to Dan Morse and Marvin Jeter of the Arkansas Archeological Survey for their intellectually stimulating ideas about the protohistoric period in eastern Arkansas. George Sabo acknowledges the support of the Newberry Library Columbian Quincentennial Program and the National Endowment for the Humanities. Samuel D. Dickinson gratefully acknowledges the data on Quapaw names provided by Robert L. Rankin of the University of Kansas, and the *Jefferson County Historical Quarterly* for permission to publish a revised version of his essay which originally appeared in that journal. Morris Arnold wishes to thank the compiler for honoring him with an invitation to participate in this endeavor. David Sloan thanks Robert Finlay and Jeannie Whayne for critical appraisals of earlier versions of his contribution. Willard Rollings thanks his wife, Barbara Williams-Rollings, a skillful editor who spent many hours reading the manuscript and making thoughtful, wonderful suggestions. George Lankford wishes to acknowledge the many people who assisted in searching out little bits of information hidden in historical documents, and would like to give special thanks to four scholars who read the manuscript and caught some errors: Judge Morris S. Arnold; the late Marion Craig, M.D.; Nancy Griffith, archivist at Lyon College; and Scott Akridge, White County teacher and archaeologist. Among others who assisted in the preparation of this volume are Elliott West, Gretchen Gearhart, Mary Kirkpatrick, and the staffs of the University of Arkansas History Department, the University Museum, and the Special Collections Division of Mullins Library, University of Arkansas, Fayetteville.

It is the hope of the compiler and contributors to this volume that *Cultural Encounters in the Early South* will serve as a starting point for a revived interest in early Arkansas history.

Introduction

CHARLES HUDSON

The problems of writing the history of early America are formidable. Wherever one strikes one's historical spade—in Arkansas, for example—the deeper one digs, the more insubstantial the soil becomes. As one delves into the past, the documents eventually give out, and one enters the realm of the archaeologist where the only testaments of human activity are the remnants of the things people made and the disturbances they made in the soil; and archaeologists dig these out using real spades, not metaphorical ones. Some have termed this temporal zone "protohistoric," where history and archaeology meet and where documents and artifacts play roughly equal parts.

The protohistoric era in Arkansas—from about 1541 until 1700—is frustrating for both historians and archaeologists. For historians, their standards of proof can rarely be met. Documents from remote times are scanty, leaving many areas in total darkness. Where evidence does exist for a particular event or phenomenon in the past, it may be limited to a single document—and even that may be extremely problematic—so that the corroboration historians require may be impossible. Archaeologists examine material remains from the past and, using elaborate chains of inference, seek to reconstruct patterns of behavior—the day-to-day repetitive actions of people in society. They are discomfited when history, with its individual actors and unique events, enters their realm. To archaeologists, such individuals and events are uninteresting, almost beside the point. Neither historians nor archaeologists feel at home in protohistory.

But this era cannot simply be avoided. Without some grasp of who lived where in protohistoric Arkansas and of what sort of people they were, how can one understand the historical processes that helped produce the societies of later times? In Arkansas, as in many parts of the Southeast, protohistory begins with the expedition of Hernando de Soto. That is the subject of David Sloan's chapter. As he shows in his "post-mortem," the de Soto expedition produced the most documents of all the sixteenth-century Spanish entradas into the Southeast. But scholarship on the expedition remains bedeviled by serious problems and questions, including the extreme difficulty in reconstructing de Soto's route and four centuries of fanciful, grandiloquent, romantic storytelling and poetizing about the expedition.

Surely the difficulty in determining where the de Soto expedition went has been the major impediment to securing its appropriate place in early American history. Using documentary sources alone, it is not possible to accurately reconstruct the route. However, archaeological research during the past fifty years has put within reach a solution to the perplexing problems of the de Soto route through the Southeast. The commission appointed by Franklin Roosevelt in 1935 and headed by John Swanton made a prodigious attempt to reconstruct the route from beginning to end; their failure to do so was largely because American archaeology was then in its infancy. In association with several others, the present author has spent many years in developing a reconstruction of de Soto's route (as well as the routes of Tristán de Luna and Juan Pardo); time will tell whether he has come closer to the mark than did John Swanton and his collaborators.

As horrendous as the military actions of de Soto were on the native peoples of sixteenth-century Arkansas—particularly the people of Anilco, where de Soto ordered a surprise attack on the general population to incite terror throughout the region—the effects of the diseases the Europeans brought with them were far more devastating. That a very great population collapse occurred across the Southeast beginning in the second half of the sixteenth century is now beyond serious challenge. The only questions that remain have to do with which illnesses struck where and when. Did de Soto's people unwittingly infect the native population, or had Old World diseases reached the Southeast before the entrada? Were any areas in the region given a reprieve for a while? One of the ironies in early Arkansas—as Willard H. Rollings shows—is that what was bad for the native people was good for the animals, at least for a time. As the big chiefdoms collapsed and the landscape was littered with human corpses, deer, bear, and (in the west) bison, swelled their numbers. In the course of time, Arkansas became a hunters' paradise.

One of the most important problems in the social history of the early Southeast is to describe and explicate the way in which the descendants of the surviving chiefdoms made it into the eighteenth century. To de Soto's chroniclers, the chiefdoms of Arkansas were the most populous in all of La Florida. One hundred years later, Arkansas was virtually a wilderness. As Michael P. Hoffman shows, Tunican-speakers appear to have occupied a much larger area of eastern Arkansas than was previously thought. But by the end of the seventeenth century, these Tunican-speakers had been reduced to a few small towns. The pivotal native players in eighteenth-century Arkansas were some Caddo-speaking people in the southwestern corner of the state, the Siouan-speaking Osage on the western fringe of the Ozarks, and the Siouan-speaking Quapaw at the mouth of the Arkansas River.

Both the Osage and the Quapaw appear to have been newcomers to Arkansas. The problem of where the Quapaw came from is particularly difficult. The main question is did they wholly originate outside of Arkansas, or were they at least partly composed of remnant Arkansas populations? The Quapaw spoke a Siouan language, and there is no clear evidence that any of the people de Soto encountered in the Southeast were Siouan-speaking. Yet, it seems incredible that the chiefdoms encountered by de Soto in the Central Mississippi Valley could have disappeared leaving no survivors. All of this is perhaps beclouded by a Quapaw oral tradition that they came from the north, moving down the Mississippi River to the mouth of the Arkansas River. But how far downstream did they move? Did they come from the Ohio Valley, or were the people of sixteenth-century Arkansas more complex linguistically than we presently imagine?

Certainly considerable linguistic and social complexity existed in the sixteenth century in the eastern margin of the Southeast (in present South Carolina and North Carolina). At least three different language families—Muskogean, Catawban, and Iroquoian—were present, as well as a paramount chiefdom and several lesser ones. But out of all this diversity, the Catawba Indians were the only ones in the Carolinas to have survived into the present day. Well into the twentieth century, scholars believed that the Catawbas were a unitary linguistic and cultural entity whose history stretched in simple linear fashion back to the de Soto and Pardo era. We now know that in Pardo's day they were a single town of Indians who were not very important in the larger scheme of things. We also know that in the eighteenth century "Catawba" came to be applied to a long list of remnant populations from the Carolinas who coalesced to swell their numbers. In retrospect it seems almost accidental that the Catawba language became the dominant means of communication among these people, displacing all the others that were spoken. One has to ponder whether a similar scenario may apply to the ethnic formation of the Quapaws.

One of the greatest deficits in writing the social history of the early Southeast is that we have so little access to the inner world of the Indians. The Europeans produced the documents, and we therefore have access to *their* thoughts, schemes, explanations, and rationalizations. But when we attempt a similar investigation of the Indians, we find that early European observers rarely tried to grasp things from the natives' point of view. The best we can do is to read European accounts of Indian actions (whether practical or ritual) and try to infer the deeper meanings. And to this, anthropologists can make judicious use of information collected by more disinterested and less ethnocentric observers of these and related people from later times. This can be enhanced by drawing upon theories that anthropologists have developed from doing first-hand fieldwork with comparably simple societies in other parts of the world.

George Sabo seeks to show that La Salle and his comrades encountered greeting rituals that were animated by two contrasting principles. That of the Quapaws was based on the principle that all parties in society are on an equal footing; all are equal. But the practice of the Caddos was based on the principle that people in society exist in a hierarchical order; all are unequal.

Such differences may be cultural, as Sabo implies. But it is also possible that these rituals were aspects of larger historical patterns in the protohistoric Southeast. That is, there appears to have been two basic organizational patterns discernible in the post-chiefdom collapse. The first of these might be called traditionalist, that is, people like the Caddos, Natchez, and, to some degree, the Apalachees who attempted to sustain some elements of the old hierarchical order. The second might be called egalitarian, that is, the organizational approach of such people as the Quapaws, Creeks, Chickasaws, and presumably the Catawbas. Both the traditionalists and the egalitarians absorbed populations from shattered, decimated societies, but they did so according to two different plans. It makes sense to think that each was sustained by different patterns of ritual and religious belief.

It is striking that at the time of the de Soto expedition, what is now the state of Arkansas was one of the most highly "developed" parts of North America, while from 1700 to the present day this same area has been relatively "undeveloped." The same lands that were so bountiful for the protohistoric native horticulturists—the flood plain of the Mississippi River—were seen by early European colonists as sandy and subject to flooding and therefore undesirable. The crucial difference in the two agricultural systems was that the native farmers only wished to raise enough food for subsistence, and the small but immensely fertile levee ridges scattered throughout the region were sufficient. Additionally, the Indians were willing to put up with the river swelling out of its banks, creating the small and large floods that periodically covered their houses and towns. The Europeans, in contrast, practiced plantation agriculture in vast open fields for a world economy, and they had too much invested in buildings and infrastructure to tolerate flooding.

In the eighteenth century Arkansas became marginal to early America, a wilderness where only the simplest kind of extractive economy existed— the harvesting of animal products (i.e., skins, meat, tallow, and oil). Gilbert C. Din shows that Arkansas Post was the center where trade was conducted, and this selfsame trade was used to control the Indians, though not always successfully. Just as difficult to control were white hunters. Many of these hunters were French subjects who fled the English takeover of the eastern side of the Mississippi River in 1763, and later the American seizure of the French colonial towns in the 1780s. These white hunters were few in number. They left no enduring architectural remains, and even precious little archaeological evidence. George E. Lankford, however, succeeds in his chapter in this volume in giving us a glimpse of these French frontiersmen in northeastern Arkansas. And Morris S. Arnold provocatively argues that Arkansas Post was to modern Arkansas what Philadelphia was to modern Pennsylvania: that is, the underdevelopment of modern Arkansas may have roots that reach back into the eighteenth century.

It is a pity that the protohistory and early history of Arkansas has left so few material monuments to the past. Mainly through the efforts of Arkansas archaeologists, some of the mounds from the protohistoric still stand, though many more have fallen victim to the plow and to earthmoving machines. Scatters of native artifacts exist in many parts of Arkansas, and in a few places Spanish, French, and English artifacts may be found. Beyond this, there is little more than those place-names that visitors to Arkansas have trouble pronouncing. These are listed and discussed by Samuel D. Dickinson.

There is much more to be learned about early Arkansas. The information is suffused in objects in the soil itself, for the archaeologists to dig up and to run through their inferential wringers for meaning, and the information is in the archives, where historians can perform their own labors and search for their own meaning. It is to be hoped that this present volume will serve as a catalyst for research on protohistoric and early historic Arkansas that will not only produce learned papers and monographs, but also popular histories and, even more, chapters in textbooks.

Cultural Encounters
in the Early South

The Expedition of Hernando de Soto

A Post-mortem Report

DAVID SLOAN

In the late spring of 1539, the largest, best organized, most carefully planned of the sixteenth-century Spanish expeditions, under the command of a man whose experience in this business could be matched by no other, landed on the Florida coast. Over four years later, the survivors—half-starved, recognizable as Europeans only by their speech—wandered into a small Spanish settlement on the Rio Pánuco, sixteen hundred miles away on a direct land course (which was certainly not the route they had taken). Their commander was no longer among them. Wrapped in shrouds and stuffed in a tree trunk, he was going down the Mississippi River alone, pulled along the bottom by the currents.

The de Soto entrada stands as an extraordinary episode, even in an age when a prudent person expected the bizarre and often got no less. It left a large body of documentation, relative to other Spanish expeditions, and was a preoccupation of the generation of historians nearest in time to the event itself. Yet after four and a half centuries, even the most basic of questions have either remained unanswered or have been answered in disputed ways. What was the purpose of the expedition? Why did it go where it did? Where *did* it go?

Why do so many questions remain? One way of approaching this problem is to review the literature on the expedition. Turning first to the original documentation, upon which all subsequent accounts would be based, one confronts a body of evidence that is both informative and perplexing. To a degree this is simply because the earliest accounts conflict with one another— a problem for the historian of almost any subject. But there is added a further and more unusual complication, to which we shall soon turn, that had the power to shape the nature of interpretations for a very long time.

The documentation comes mainly in the form of eyewitness reports, with official communications providing some sparse supplementation. Two eyewitnesses left independent testimonies. The first to gain wide attention was that of the "Gentleman of Elvas," so named because he was of a contingent of Portuguese who joined the enterprise from the small town of that name near the border city of Badajoz. Little was known about him at the time; not much has been learned since. His *Relaçam verdadeira* first appeared in 1557; Richard Hakluyt, England's most avid promoter of transoceanic expansion, had a translation out by 1609, and a second edition two years later.[1] Elvas's lengthy report is a curious document. It contains little of the specific detailed information that would suggest constant reference to a diary, yet it does not draw its bulk from the imaginative embroidery that often characterizes recollections without such a mooring. Absent, too, is the dramatic framework so common to conquest literature over the centuries. His main concern is getting the expedition from one place to another; observations, asides, and judgments play a distinctly secondary role, and the man himself, with a single exception, disappears into the events he describes. Whatever his reasons for leaving a record (and this remains a mystery), self-justification may be ruled out.

Through his eyes one watches the expedition chart a bloody course, a bloodier account than that of all but one of the other eyewitnesses:

> All the rest he ordered to be punished by being fastened to a stake in the middle of the plaza and the Indians of Paracoxi shot them with arrows; . . . The governor ordered one of them to be burned; . . . and the Indians whom they took along in chains roiled the water with the mud of the waters, and the fish, as if stupefied would come to the surface; . . . [when] thirty Indians came with fish, he . . . ordered their right hands cut off. . . .[2]

Such reports fill his pages, all laid down with neither judgment nor emotion. When at one point Elvas suddenly cries out against the butchery of women and children that his captain had wished to spare, one is startled by the display of feeling.[3] And it is no different when he writes of Spanish travail. "The Christians were become so demoralized," he notes of the battle of Chicaça, an especially bloody moment for the expedition, "together with the lack of saddles and weapons, which had been burned, that if the Indians had returned the second night, they would have routed them with little trouble."[4] He speaks of near-annihilation as he speaks of the weather.

Similar to Elvas in tone, but with a brevity that precluded almost any elaboration, is the account of Luys Hernandez de Biedma, the King's factor. Biedma presented his report, the only one that still exists in manuscript,

Portrait of Hernando de Soto which appeared in many of the works
considered in this chapter, but without the border depicting Amerindian
labor in the mines that accompanied the portrait when it first appeared
in the early seventeenth century. When the drawn sword is juxtaposed
with the Dantesque images, the visual message becomes considerably
more ambiguous.

Reproduced from Manuel Lucerra Salmoral, ed.,
Historia General de España y América, vol. 7.

to the *Consejo de Indias* in 1544, but it did not become available in published
form until the mid-nineteenth century, first in a French translation of 1841,
then in English translations of 1850 and 1851, with yet another in 1866.[5]
The factor was a miser of words and had few positive ones for de Soto. The
sourly laconic flavor of his account is epitomized by his description of the
commander's death: "The Governor, from seeing himself cut off and seeing

that not one thing could be done according to his purpose, was afflicted with sickness and died."[6]

Nor does de Soto get high marks in the eyewitness account provided by his private secretary, Rodrigo Ranjel, to the *audiencia* on the island of Hispaniola in 1546. Here another complication appears. One can find the Ranjel report only in transcription, embedded in a massive general history prepared by the sixteenth-century Spanish adventurer, colonial administrator, and scholar Gonzalo Fernández de Oviedo y Valdés.[7] Why this would create difficulties appears immediately: Ranjel begins his account (which ends abruptly and without explanation at the third winter encampment at Autiamque) with a criticism of de Soto's insistence upon being a part of the risky search for a port on the mainland—better, thought Ranjel, to leave such tasks in the hands of lesser, more expendable men. The critical stance thus established is maintained throughout, making the Ranjel version easily the most hostile toward the expedition and its commander.[8] Captured Indians enchained in coffles appear constantly, often accompanied by indignant commentary, and only here is it charged that the Spanish expected females for prostitution.[9] Conversely, Ranjel is full of praise for the aboriginals, especially regarding their courage,[10] and sharply condemns the expedition for attending so poorly to the conversion of a people whose capacity for faith "would have been greater than that of the conquistadores, if they had been instructed."[11]

How much of this is Ranjel, and how much Oviedo? Does it have any credibility as a primary source? This is an important question, for information critical to many matters hinges upon it—the expedition's experiences with, and attitudes toward, the aboriginals is but one example. The answer is not simple.

There are some clues. Recall that by the late sixteenth century, the great debate sparked by Bartolemé de las Casas over the morality of the conquest was well under way. Oviedo, though he took the position that the benefits— to crown, church, and aboriginal—outweighed the costs, remained deeply distressed about abuses, both of people and of office. Further, he knew the conquistadors, having spent decades in their company. Such first-hand experience, as Alberto Salas has noted, set poorly with fantasies of chaste and selfless heroes. Indeed, his *History* was written in part to empty other heads of such clutter.[12] On the other hand, Ranjel, whose own life and reputation was to an extent bound up with that of his employer,[13] might have been disgruntled and disappointed, but would hardly have been so disapproving. Passage through three years of a hell unfolding might generate the line, "This Governor was much given to hunting and killing Indians,"[14] but surely we must be hearing pure Oviedo in the more extreme reproaches—such as a portrait of de Soto that begins with, "this ill-governed Governor, instructed in the school of Pedrarias de Avila [de Soto's father-in-law, and a special enemy of Oviedo] in the dissipation and devastation of the Indians of Castilla de Oro, graduate in the killing of the natives of Nicaragua and canonized in Peru, according to the order of the Pizarros."[15] Still, evidence from elsewhere in the *History*, where the texts from which he drew are extant (such as the Cortez letters), show a regard for accuracy considerably in advance of the standards of his time.[16] So there is at least some assurance of reliability, and from that one might safely conclude that much of the Oviedo/Ranjel narrative *is* directly from Ranjel, and that he emerged from his experience without the rancor of Oviedo, but also without much enthusiasm for the expedition or its management.

The problem of sources becomes even more complicated with the appearance of the next contribution, one that has had more influence upon later accounts of the expedition than any of the preceding three, even though its credentials as a primary source are the most suspect. It is the long narrative, *La Florida del Ynca*,[17] by yet another of the literary masters of the sixteenth century, Garcilaso de la Vega, "El Inca." Garcilaso—the product of a union between Pizarro's associate Don Sebastian Garcilaso de la Vega Vargas and Chimpa Ocllo, daughter of the Inca ruler Huayna Capac—spent a lifetime within and between two worlds.[18] He was both equipped and compelled to write the history of the conquest of the Americas, as he was surrounded by people directly involved in the event and, of necessity, deeply interested in what is now called acculturation. Working in the late sixteenth century, he built *La Florida* around a number of eyewitness accounts, none of which has survived elsewhere: that of Alonso de Carmona, who, according to Garcilaso, prepared an account entitled *Peregrinación*, which he never intended to publish;[19] that of Juan Coles, about whom the author offers almost nothing; and possibly others too, as Garcilaso claims a familiarity with some who drop in and out of his narrative.[20] However, the bulk of his information comes from another individual whom Garcilaso never identifies, but who is almost certainly one Gonzalo de Silvestre: Garcilaso punctuates his story with the great deeds of this man (most of which escaped the attention of the other chroniclers—with suspicious regularity) and describes events for which Silvestre seems to have been the sole witness, or nearly so.[21]

The account he constructs is by far the longest, as well as the most detailed. To what extent is it reliable? There are a number of possibilities. The first, obviously, is that it is a complete fabrication. If so, it certainly stands as a marvelous one. But it seems unlikely that so elaborate a hoax could have gotten through its own generation, and no suspicions were raised at the time, either toward the book or its author. Also, it would be difficult for even the most skeptical to read it through without becoming convinced that whether or not the descriptions are accurate, its author is thoroughly conversant with accounts of the expedition. The description of the great battle at Mauvila is a case in point: in his reconstruction of this blood bath, seen by all (including Garcilaso) as *the* disastrous turning point for the expedition, he painstakingly compares the memories of all three of his informants.[22] Its accuracy is still a problem, but the result strikes one as honest.

Is it accurate? Parts of the description, it would seem, simply could not be. How could his discussion of what went on in Tascaluza's council of war before Mauvila be anything but guesswork?[23] Another example is his elaborate description of the huge weapons storehouse found at Cofitachequi, so overwhelmingly grand that a single chapter of description will not do. Eight rooms, each filled with a different type of weapon—one with pikes, maces in the next, then battle-axes and broadswords, on to truncheons, bows and arrows, and finally two rooms of shields, one for the oblong variety, another for the round. "The eight rooms were filled with all these offensive and defensive arms, and each one of them contained so many of the particular kind of arms that were in it that the governor and his Castilians marveled especially at their number, besides the neatness and perfection with which they were made and arranged in their order."[24] How the others, all military men, could have missed this is difficult to understand and yet, in a description perfunctory enough to be overlooked on a cursory reading, only Ranjel takes any notice.[25]

Still, this could be merely a problem of exaggeration for which allowances might be made. Its presence is less disturbing than that of another, much more fundamental problem; one for which it is more difficult to find a mode of correction. Garcilaso had the zeal of a convert for European culture, which seems to have pushed him toward casting the expedition into a mold of great deeds "much nobler than those of the Greeks, Romans and peoples of other nations"[26]—the world of his Spanish education, for which conquest of the land of his ancestors had to have been a part. Though he was a declared "enemy of such fiction as one finds in books of knighthood and the like, good poetry excepted," there are evocations of El Cid, Antony and Cleopatra, and Hercules; and there are Indians who demand single combat, handle the broadsword without training, and speak in the cadences of the great classical orators.[27] There is throughout the work a tendency to move toward the fanciful, and it is hard to determine how much movement has taken place at any particular time.

With the exception of an as-yet-unidentified account in the history of Antonio de Herrera y Tordesillas,[28] *La Florida* ended for many years the list of direct observations. It is out of these that subsequent histories have been fashioned, and it is in large part because of their peculiar nature and the sharply differing perceptions that emerge from them that later histories have taken the forms they have. When one finds the sources deposited not in archives but instead in the earliest histories of the event—histories written by literary giants of the age who were personally and passionately involved in imperial expansion—not only is it difficult to separate the one from the other, but also to avoid becoming an emotional captive in the process.

As few have wished to cast aside either Oviedo or Garcilaso, they have remained important sources. Their continued use has tended to push later interpretations in one of two directions. Both encourage a fundamentally Eurocentric view, an attitude they shared, each in his own fashion, with most who would take up the matter in the centuries thereafter. Beyond that they diverge into diametrically opposed points of view: the expedition was merely a looting party, or it was a more multifaceted affair with an interest in planting and spreading a culture believed at the time to be a boon to those who would receive it. Certainly there would be room for variations upon either theme, but so long as history was defined as a narrative—a story—and without new evidence (or more innovative ways of reading the available evidence), these would remain the approaches. In one way, this was very restrictive. Yet it could be oddly liberating, too, for it meant that if one wished to turn the events of the sixteenth century to presentistic ends, one could pick and choose one's weapons from two well-stocked arsenals. That is precisely what happened.

Because interest in the de Soto expedition did not sustain itself, much of the influence of these early eyewitness/commentary hybrids would not become apparent until far into the future. The Spanish, understandably, became preoccupied with those parts of the empire over which they maintained more than a tenuous diplomatic claim. As the Hispanic empire expanded, first over South and Central America and then into the southwestern reaches of North America, the consequences of the *conquista* in that huge area were more than enough to explore and ponder. The French showed some interest, as they pushed their inland empire from its St. Lawrence base down into the Mississippi Valley. But circumstances prevented them from becoming *too* interested, as publicity for early Spanish activity might validate Spanish claims to an area the French hoped to control. The *Journal Historique* of Jean-Baptiste Bénard de La Harpe, who explored the Gulf Coast area for the French in the early eighteenth century, suggests a deliberate downplaying of earlier Spanish activity: in a dismissive first sentence he covers all early Spanish explorations, the de Soto expedition included (and misdated), judging them to be both isolated and ephemeral.[29] The French Jesuit Pierre de Charlevoix, who traveled into the region as a royal envoy in the early 1720s, gave de Soto the same treatment, barely glancing at the expedition in his *Histoire Generale* and in his travel letters.[30]

Thus, the subject became primarily an interest of the Anglo-American world. Signs of an appetite for information had appeared almost immediately with Hakluyt's translation of the Gentleman of Elvas, but that proved to be a hunger quickly appeased; here, too, the concentration would for many years be more parochial. Those areas where England was having success in planting populations received the bulk of historical attention. Englishmen always had translations of Las Casas before them (in the unlikely event that their hispanophobia would need freshening) but they would find no more in there on the "Tyrant [of whom] we have had no news these three yeares" than the friar's spare, harsh comment: "If he be alive, most assuredly he hath destroy'd an infinite number of people, for he among all those who have done most mischeife in ruining both Provinces and Kingdoms, is famous for his Savage fury; wherefore I am apt to believe that God hath put the same end to his life, as to the others."[31]

William Roberts's *An Account of the First Discovery, and Natural History of Florida . . . ,*[32] a short information pamphlet on the territory just ceded to Great Britain by Spain, did feature the expedition in its review of prior exploration (and in a surprisingly non-judgmental way, though the general introduction is vehement on the Spanish). Yet far more important was the attention it did *not* get elsewhere: one finds not a word on the enterprise in the most influential work on the Americas—not only for that generation but for generations to come—the magnificent *History of America* by the Scottish scholar William Robertson.[33] Partly, this was because the American Revolution stalled Robertson's plans to deal with North America, and he never found time to return to the subject (his son incorporated what little he had written into a "Posthumous Volume" for later editions); but that was not the whole of it. What had happened farther south was, in Robertson's revealing phrase, "the most splendid portion of the American story."[34] Generations on both sides of the Atlantic would inherit this emphasis, through new editions of Robertson (yet another, this one complete with a "Questions for Students" section, appeared in America just before the Civil War),[35] and then through William H. Prescott's monumental histories of the conquests of Peru and Mexico, which would capture the public imagination upon their appearance in the 1840s.

Interest did not really gain momentum until the nineteenth century, when de Soto studies became a minor literary industry. First into the field was the full-length study by Theodore Irving,[36] nephew of Washington Irving. The family connection is important, for the elder Irving was the country's leading hispanophile in the early nineteenth century. Through his *Tales of the Alhambra*, as well as in his scholarly histories *Columbus* and *Companions of Columbus*, Irving crafted a version of the Spanish past quite foreign to an Anglo-American world nursed in a contempt and hostility for things Iberian (going back to the Armada). His nephew stayed with him in Spain, helped in his researches, imbibed his love for the country, and eventually joined the force.[37] The younger Irving drew upon the Gentleman of Elvas, Herrera's work, and a French translation of Biedma for the revised edition, though he dismissed the latter as "a confused statement by an illiterate soldier."[38] But throughout the book the watchword is always, "We follow the Inca."[39] The author was convinced that Garcilaso's account, in its detail and its interpretation, best captured the nature of the expedition, pulling back only when the Inca is "evidently inclining to magnify."[40] Unsurprisingly, the picture that emerges is very similar to Garcilaso's: here we have a de Soto driven by a lust for gold (as were they all) but with grander dreams, too—an "agent of conquest *and* colonization," at least until the disaster at Mauvila, when melancholia and the challenge to his authority induced the aimless desire to "finish his existence" that reversed only temporarily at the third winter encampment.[41] This is a brutal de Soto, but brutality, Irving reminds his readers, was a part of the age, and he compares the commander favorably with his successor Luys de Moscoso (whose atrocities included chopping off the hands of thirty Indians).[42] Irving's sympathies are with those whose lands were and would be invaded—he observes in the Indians of the Florida wars of his own day "the same proud and unyielding spirit" of the ancestors that de Soto had confronted—but here the author holds up a balance sheet that so often served in the nineteenth century to turn a moral question into a romantic tragedy: one's revulsion at the slaughter should be tempered by the remembrance that most of the Spanish invaders died too.[43]

But if Irving stands at the beginning of the modern romantic tradition in de Soto interpretation (a term he himself accepted when he called the object of his study a "romantic enterprise"),[44] he nevertheless had a concern about the more mundane aspects of the expedition that evidences the spirit of modern anthropologists (whose work we shall come to later). He studied his documents carefully for any hints about the exact path the expedition might have taken, maintained a healthy skepticism about the bustling "artifact" industry (quoting with approval a comment from the Smithsonian Institution that building even a tenth of the "forts" attributed to it would have left the expedition almost no time to do anything else),[45] and introduced to a larger public the work of many local scholars.[46] It was in some ways the best history of the expedition that the nineteenth century would produce.[47]

But it did not have the field to itself for long. William Gilmore Simms, by that time well established as both novelist and historian, had thought considerably about the subject and how it might best be treated. A figure of transatlantic intellectual interests, Simms had become fully absorbed in the evolutionary nationalism of the European romanticists and just as thoroughly repelled by the cautious, fact-bound approach of Barthold Georg Niebuhr's German school. The great Livy, Simms maintained, had reawakened Rome through the power of his imagination, but Niebuhr, with the "sleepless research of the coldly inquisitive man," had entombed it again.[48] Simms had lightly touched upon the expedition in his *History of South Carolina*,[49] had worked on a fictional treatment of the expedition in the 1830s, and had written an essay on its dramatic possibilities.[50]

Convinced that the "sterner muse" had carried its charge to the point of sterility, he determined to infuse the story with "a vitality which fiction only can confer." The result was his novel, *Vasconcelos: A Romance of the New World*.[51] Simms is concerned with two matters. First, he uses this historical event to show how the genius of a people prepares the stage for the next advance. He had done so in earlier works with the American Indians;[52] he does so here with the Spanish: "strife, blood, conquest, glory, and personal prominence," are the forces driving them to be "the pioneers for other races, who shall more securely enjoy what they neglect and despise"—why condemn them for playing their historical part?[53] Second, he puts before his readers a primer on codes of individual conduct, a subject in which he was far more interested. It was a full program with little room either for the expedition—it does not get to Florida until the novel is three-fourths through—or for any serious attention to the author's pious commitment to respect the "*material* resources of the Historian."[54]

Briefly, the story: the title character, a Portuguese whose truly chivalric values Simms throws into contrast with the rather shabby ones of de Soto, becomes so disgusted with the behavior of his fellows that he helps the Queen of Cofitachequi (Coçalla is Simms's name for her) escape her kidnappers. For this he is stripped of his knighthood and left to die, but is saved by Coçalla, whose heart is his forevermore.[55] This further complicates things for the lovelorn Castilian noblewoman who somehow has been going undetected as his page; but not for Vasconcelos, who single-mindedly pursues the agent of his humiliation. Commanding with Tascaluza the ever-growing army of an Indian confederation spanning the entire Southeast,[56] Vasconcelos becomes de Soto's nemesis until the Spaniard, stripped of power, resources, and hope (and any factual ground on which to stand), goes to his grave.

Simms erased the line between history and fiction in his effort to redraw it, but that should not divert our attention from the point that his enterprise was considered to be a valid one, and not only by Simms himself. That he had a *choice* between the two modes of expression, with one having no advantage over the other in bringing the past to the present, was a position that many of his contemporaries would not have questioned. A novelistic treatment would not be treated pejoratively by the public; for many, Simms would be just as valid as Irving, and as likely to shape opinions on this aspect of the past.

The blurred line would certainly not be brought back into focus with the publication of another book, this one by the newspaperman Lambert A. Wilmer.[57] He seems to have had no particular scholarly qualifications for entering the field, but Wilmer had other reasons for being there. He had no use for Spanish historians (or for the Spanish in general, or for *any* foreigners, as becomes clear) whose "taste for self-glorification, or rhodomontade, which is presumed to be one of their national characteristics, has, in this instance, been indulged to an unlimited extent. . . ." He thought no better of Irving, whose supposed claim that the historian should "illustrate the glories of his nation" he found offensive, or of Prescott either. There are dark hints in his introduction about both authors (and he had to deal with both, since Irving had covered only the North American part of de Soto's life), suggestions that they had been given access to private sources, secret materials denied to him. Worse, they had used them poorly.[58]

Wilmer's corrective to all this previous misinformation turns out to be the finest illustration of one important reason why interest in the de Soto expedition was so high: discussed in a certain way, the expedition could work wonderfully well as a vehicle for the expression of anti-foreign, and especially anti-Catholic, attitudes. This was the moment in the nineteenth century when the first great wave of nativism crested; this particular decade was the one in which the American ("Know-Nothing") Party became a serious political force in many states. There were already plenty of propagandists in the field, and Wilmer himself would contribute in that way too; but for the moment he had another, less obvious way of making the point. No modern reader of Wilmer's book would know of this, for Wilmer's *stated* agenda had nothing to do with nativism. His contribution (in addition to correcting the mistakes of previous writers) would be to offer a study in personality development: to solve the puzzle of why the morally upright man (de Soto I) can engage in immoral acts (de Soto II), "the magnitude and boldness of which can offer no excuse for their cruelty and injustice." One does this, says Wilmer, by isolating the "critical moment" that conditions all that follows. For de Soto, it was not the brutalizing process of the Pizarro campaign (de Soto had had his qualms, Wilmer grants, but they did not stop him from following that "Machiavellian bastard"), nor even the time spent in Central America prior to that; instead, it was the rejection— the *contemptuous* rejection—by Pedrarias de Avila of his request to marry Isabella de Boabdilla. "He discovered," argues Wilmer, "that *poverty* was the only obstacle to his happiness and respectability; and having pondered on this discovery with much bitterness of feeling, he determined at last— regardless of all hazards and sacrifices—to become rich"—a resolve based upon love (that "idolatry of women" so characteristic of chivalry), but no less destructive for being so, as it could (and here did) eliminate "the restraints of reason or religion, honor or humanity."[59] To clinch his point, Wilmer produces a long letter from de Soto to Isabella (the original copy, "said to be in the cabinet of a Spanish gentleman," he had not seen—nor has anyone else, to my knowledge);[60] its contents fit his case remarkably.

All of this produces a satisfactory degree of drama and also introduces a love angle—always a scarce commodity in the de Soto story. Wilmer further heightens the dramatic tension by developing a poisoning theory to explain the demise of the *Adelantado*.[61] But readers brought in by all this are to be taught another lesson as well, one of urgent relevance, in Wilmer's opinion, to their own time. Hints of a hidden agenda have been dropped all along the way, but the hand is not shown until very near the end when Wilmer begins to summarize what went wrong. Why, he asks rhetorically, did the Indians, habitually so receptive to the strangers (!), ultimately turn on them? Because de Soto and his men could never get it through their heads that they were *foreigners* who "can have *no* rights in any country except those which are conceded to them by the natives of the soil." And why could they not understand this? To Wilmer the answer is simple: they were blinded by Catholicism, a foreign perversion of the true—the *American*—faith. De Soto could never break free of the delusion that "the heirs and assigns of St. Peter had legally authorized him to play the tyrant . . . ; had the religion of Christ been presented . . . in a more engaging form, undistorted by bigot zeal, and unperverted by fanatical violence and dissembling avarice, no people in the world perhaps would have been more apt to receive and cultivate the truth of the Gospel. . . ."[62] One is therefore not surprised to find at the end of the book an advertisement for yet another Wilmer effort, *The Press Gang; or, The Complete Exposition of the Corruptions and Crimes of the American Newspapers*, in which the author promises a thorough exposé of papers that incite "adopted citizens" (his invidious phrase for Catholic newcomers) to demand more than they deserve.[63] There is one other feature of Wilmer's book worth noting: the large number of engraved illustrations. Undoubtedly, these helped to account for its popularity;[64] they may also be a rough measure of the publication's regard for accuracy. The images reinforce the anti-Spanish message of the book—"Spaniards shooting Indians," "Spaniards hunting Indians," and "Burning a Peruvian" are typical captions—but they also show a wild disregard for geography. Hot Springs, Arkansas, is put deep into the tropics, and the Rocky Mountains find themselves hundreds of miles from their usual location. Perhaps these anachronisms left Wilmer's readers undisturbed (and maybe modern readers, too—the Rockies have appeared there once again, when the late John Wayne rode in after Lucky Ned Pepper and an Academy Award in *True Grit*); that they did not disturb the author says much, none of it good, about his concern for accuracy.

One finds the same willingness to use the de Soto expedition for presentistic ends in the biography prepared by John S. C. Abbott, a Congregationalist minister from New England who gave up that calling to write an endless number of books.[65] His work is thoroughly derivative, drawing upon both Irving *and* Wilmer with no hint to the reader of the incompatibility of the two, but three points do deserve consideration. First, Abbott seems to have committed himself to the notion that the subject of one's study must be fundamentally moral, as if the discovery that this was not the case would somehow diminish both subject and biographer. Thus we enter Florida with a man whose "career thus far had shown him to be by nature a kind-hearted and upright man, hating oppression and loving justice. . . ." Deviations, such as those in Peru, must be explained away by the "terrible power" of military discipline, or the influence of bad company, or simply by the nature of the age.[66] Such a man must have a conscience, and so when de Soto does something morally incomprehensible—kidnapping the "Indian Queen" of Cofitachequi, for instance—Abbott invents the proper qualms: "he felt constrained to do that which his own conscience told him was unjust."[67]

Second, Abbott is very concerned—more so, even, than Wilmer—about making sure that Christianity of the wrong kind takes its lumps for its role in the conquest. He is severe with those who made a "career of spiritual conquest, with its pecuniary accompaniment"—that is, those who followed "the religion of the Spaniards."[68] This leads him to a consideration of the nature of the population waiting to be converted to the *right*

"Spaniards drinking from the Hot Springs in Arkansas."
Reproduced from Lambert A. Wilmer,
*The Life, Travels and Adventures of Ferdinand De Soto,
Discoverer of the Mississippi.*

variety of the faith. Third, ruminating upon the words of the Indian leader
Ucita, Abbott notes how refreshing it is to see a hint of "that nobility of
character" that existed there, not only before the penetration of Europeans
(a common enough observation), but "before the fall."[69] Abbott expresses
in an unusually extreme form an attitude quite common to these studies. It
is one that purports to admire the New World population but is nevertheless expressive of the deepest sort of condescension: in some way, usually
vaguely defined, life before the Columbian contact was preferable to what
followed. It is not accompanied by the suggestion that Amerindian behavior
is the result of having passed *through* earlier developmental stages (in one of

"De Soto encamped at the foot of the Rocky Mountains."
Reproduced from Lambert A. Wilmer,
*The Life, Travels and Adventures of Ferdinand De Soto,
Discoverer of the Mississippi.*

which, the implication would be, the Europeans and their heirs are still locked) from which such behavior has been experientially derived, but instead as having come *before*. The Fall, to Abbott, is clearly not to be understood as the beginning of the search for knowledge, nor is Indian behavior to be so understood. Thus, however admirable their previous situation, their present one demands that they willingly receive what the best of the

European heirs (read Protestants) are able to give them. It was a handy means of rebuking past behavior while retaining the right to manage and manipulate others in the present.

Following Abbott into what must have been an inviting market (judging from the number of vendors) was the New Orleans author Grace King. Her writings on the French colonial period (together with a personality so charming and witty that even Mark Twain found it irresistible) had made her a well-known figure by the time she turned her attention to the Spanish conquest.[70] Her contribution begins with an analysis of the sources in which she cautions the reader about the exaggerations of Garcilaso. King even concedes the possibility that Garcilaso had seen the account of the Gentleman of Elvas, constructed his narrative around it, fabricated all of his authorities, and embellished from what he had heard by word-of-mouth.[71] Despite this, Garcilaso is the source of choice and the book becomes essentially one long paraphrase of his work; the stupendous weapons cache at Cofitachequi, the staggering casualty figures at Mauvila, the unrelieved anguish at the death of the leader—all are pure Garcilaso, all evidence of the enduring power of that account.[72]

It is a great esthetical distance from Abbott and King to the next student of de Soto, Robert Bontine Cunninghame Graham.[73] He is a forgotten figure now despite constant efforts to revive his work. But in his own day, his wildly improbable life—full of eccentricity, adventure, probable lies and even less probable truths—made him the standard by which personality was measured among *fin-de-siècle* Britishers. Before he turned eighteen he had already traveled into a revolution in Argentina. By the time he fastened upon de Soto, he had squandered the family fortune on four continents and been jailed twice: first in Morocco for impersonating a sheik, then in England for assaulting a policeman (in the cause of Socialism—Graham was the first such in Parliament). In the idle moments, he had written nine books. For these and other accomplishments he had become the idol of Joseph Conrad, George Bernard Shaw, Frederich Engels, and many others whose reputations would far outlast his own.[74]

As a committed, if idiosyncratic, radical, Graham had nothing but sarcastic contempt for his own generation's misguided sense of mission ("which a wise providence has laid upon us, against which it would be impious to rebel, and cowardly . . .").[75] To write of its parallel in the sixteenth century might be a good way of administering a dose of self-realization. One does not have to read far to see that he knew he was bound to fail, but clearly he relished the hopeless errand. What better source could there be for such a history than Garcilaso, whose "interludes" grant "a colour of reality even to sordid facts," whose accounts "contain much of the much-bepraised sweet reasonableness to which rude facts so often give the lie," and whose discrepancies are "as it should be, and only [serve] to invest history with greater dignity."[76]

This light-hearted approach to historical accuracy was for Graham a way of mocking a generation of scholars committed to the proposition that history could be scientific—that facts would speak for themselves, given a proper chance. But twitting scholars was just an amusing diversion. The heart of his project was the deeply serious business of unmasking the hypocrisy of European, particularly English, imperialism. "Motives," says Graham, in his typical blend of humor and the knife, "are quite unfathomable; but still, in spite of all their greed for gold, zeal for the propaganda of what they thought the one religion in the world, and, above all, their simple piety and faith, neither of which, of course, as is quite natural, influenced their conduct in the least, places the Spaniards . . . upon a pinnacle of virtue compared to the *conquistadores* of the present day. . . ."[77] The sixteenth-century Spaniards may have been deluded in their faith (and Graham is merciless on the subject of Christianity, of whatever variety), but they believed it nonetheless, which by Graham's measure gives them a moral edge on his own pillagers of Africa, "whom no man can accuse of being blinded by belief in anything but gold."[78] Graham's crusade being twofold—erase from the minds of Englishmen three centuries of misinformation on the subject of Spain, and educate Europe on the subject of other peoples[79]—he finds himself caught in a contradiction difficult to resolve. He must explain how "good" conquistadors (de Soto) differed from "bad" ones (Pizarro)[80] and then praise the aboriginals for refusing to make the same distinction—indeed for giving de Soto a hotter reception than Pizarro ever got. Graham does not resolve the contradiction; ultimately he drifts toward the same Edenic idealization of the Amerindians that one finds in more pedestrian works.[81]

If by most measures Graham advanced de Soto studies no more than did either Abbott or King, he certainly raised the literary level. Whether because of his intimidating prose, or for some other reason, the biographical approach so popular in the nineteenth century dwindled in the twentieth. Fictional accounts continued to appear, including an enormous epic poem by the Mississippi jurist Walter Malone and an inventive novelistic treatment by the Englishman Dominick Daly,[82] but nonfictional interest was slight. There would be nothing beyond a listless account by Frederick Ober[83] (a sometime ornithologist and writer of juvenile books), an American edition of Graham, and reprintings of King, until 1930 and Theodore

Maynard's *De Soto and the Conquistadores*.[84] A convert to Catholicism, Maynard first entered Dominican training but dropped that vocation to become a professor, teaching at Georgetown University when his book was published.[85] The work was looked upon as something of a departure at the time of its publication. Maynard certainly saw it that way. His task, he said, was a revisionist one: that of bringing to the public an account of the whole of de Soto's life, free of the corruptions of Irving, Wilmer, and King. James Robertson, one of the most prestigious scholars of his day, saw it that way too, calling it the best work available in English.[86] Yet it is difficult to reconstruct why it would have been looked upon in that way, for now it seems more to extend an earlier tradition than to create a new one. Maynard pays attention to scholarship on the aboriginal environment and is up to date on controversies over the route. The prose is less flamboyant, but that seems more a response to audience expectations than evidence of a new scholarly temper. It is a book that stands within—near the periphery, perhaps—what Alfred Crosby has called the "bardic tradition":[87] its evidence is essentially the same core of documentary sources in use for centuries; its concentration is upon personalities, which forces a Euro-American bias (given the lack of information on non-Europeans offered by settled methods of reading the available evidence); and it ignores the larger socioeconomic implications, whether by design, inclination, or (as seems to be the case here) by a simple lack of awareness of them. Such history could be very carefully done (and is in this case, though some might quibble about the lack of scholarly paraphernalia and the Thucydidean latitude the author grants himself when it comes to speeches); but the limits, being ones of conceptualization rather than execution, are rigid, and the similarities to Theodore Irving's work a century before are striking. Indeed, the most notable feature of Maynard's work is its demonstration of the ongoing power of the first generation—Elvas, Biedma, Ranjel, Garcilaso—to provide not only the factual information, but the contours of interpretation as well.

Without a reformulation of the subject itself, there was simply not much more to be said. Only by using the expedition as a point of departure for fiction, as many had done (and more would do) with results proportional to the imaginations of the author and the inclinations of the reader, or by manufacturing documentation, as odd Lambert Wilmer had done, could one avoid making a twentieth-century study a mere rehearsal of the work of Theodore Irving nearly a century earlier.

While Wilmer still walks alone down his own weird bypath, many have continued along the other road of fiction. Andrew Lytle, well known to a Southern audience and others as a member of the Agrarians, drew inspiration from the expedition (mainly—and this is true for almost all of the fiction writers—from Garcilaso) for his novel *At The Moon's Inn*.[88] In this moody, mysterious work, Lytle tests de Soto's ability to bear the weight of all humanity's hopeless struggle to command nature, creating an unforgettable aura for the expedition. There is also John Jennings's *The Golden Eagle*, hawked as a "big, lusty novel" at the time of its publication (and now interesting mainly as an illustration of how much more we demand of those adjectives than we did in the Age of Eisenhower).[89] There was yet another epic poem;[90] given the nearly invisible response to Walter Malone's try at one earlier in the century, a second comes unexpectedly. But the author was a person impossible to deter: Lily Peter, remembered in Arkansas for the marvelously idiosyncratic gesture of importing an entire symphony orchestra into the state for two performances.[91] There is plenty of bashing and battling in her poem:

> And they fought for their lives as they might, himself on foot
> fighting for four hours in front of his men, with lance
> and sword and five hours on horseback lancing his enemies.
> And many a brave man died that day

and no shortage of high emotion:

> Alas for the pitiful frailty of man!
> The doom
> of stone and salt that waits at the end of the headland!

but on the whole little to suggest a fate for it much different from that of Malone's effort.

More intriguing than the fiction has been a revived interest in the expedition in the Hispanic world. The absence of sustained commentary over the centuries from the society that spawned the entrada has been itself a notable feature of the subject; de Soto's journey was overshadowed by smaller expeditions that had more visible and more lasting results. His exploits were also diminished by the political fact that the territory through which the expedition passed soon fell out of the Hispanic orbit.

What makes this renewal of interest doubly absorbing, however, is the form that it has taken. The biographical approach, which was—as we have seen—a popular way of handling the subject in the English-language literature of the nineteenth century, has fallen from favor, with nothing major since Theodore Maynard's work of over half a century ago. But it has taken on new life in the Hispanic tongue. Both the timing and the form are puzzling, but particularly the latter. It is not at all what one would expect of a historiographic tradition that has in general been so heavily influenced by the philosophy and methodology of the French *Annales* school. This approach, which concentrates upon long-term changes in the structure of human social, economic, and political life, does so on the grounds that this is not only the most valuable part of the past, but also the single part that is truly retrievable: the closer one gets to the activities of individuals—to *l'histoire événementielle*—the tighter becomes the link between the observer and the observed, thus the more subjective the interpretation. If one's eye is pushed in this manner toward glacial change—the *longue durée*—then anything in the short term is suspect, and biography in particular becomes a practically indefensible enterprise.

Still, this is what we find. One first comes upon it in the work of F. Blanco Castilla, who contributed the initial full-length biography to this emerging Hispanic tradition. He justifies his *Hernando de Soto, El Centauro de las Indias*[92] with the statement that the man who was seen as the equal of El Cid in the United States had gotten but a single—and unsatisfactory— biographical treatment in his own tongue.[93] Blanco Castilla proposes to remedy this not with a customary biography, which could supply no more than a "silhouette," nor with a biographical novel, but something in between. He describes his book as something similar to that of Garcilaso, whose work, dismissed for many years as novelistic, had actually captured quite well the complex reality of the venture—"Sink roots in the firm ground of History, and spread branches in the voluble atmosphere of Literature" to reach beyond a learned minority to the larger reading public. This is a liberty one can take, and an opportunity one may seize, through biography, a *"historia menor"* that does not require the "scientific rigor" of the real thing.[94] The result turns out to be more conventional than the preface seems to promise. Occasional invented dialogue aside, it is a standard biography, set off from its many English predecessors only by an eccentric meditation on the "seed of the Spanish captain" that nearly collapses into a maudlin love-makes-the-world-go-round appraisal of the expedition.[95]

The approach did not end with Blanco Castilla; it was used even more vigorously in the work of the Ecuadorian author and diplomat Miguel Albornoz. His *Hernando de Soto, El Amadís de La Florida*[96] was greeted by one critic as a work that needed immediate translation into English, not only because its subject "in some measure belongs to English-speaking America," but also because it might help to erase in that world the "prejudice that continues to exist toward everything pertaining to the epic Spanish deeds in the New World."[97] Fifteen years after its publication, Albornoz's work was translated and published by a press that soon abandoned such literature in favor of the children's book trade. Thus the only recent work available to an English-speaking audience is a very hard title to find. This is not a great loss, for the translation had already misplaced much of what validated the original work. It was made a more conventional biography, as the translator chose to introduce an air of tentativeness and to delete many of the more imaginative recreations. The most telling example of the latter is the death scene of the commander, where Albornoz has de Soto's lieutenants ruminating about parallels between the life of their *Capitán* and that of Amadís as they drop him into the great river. None of this is found in the translation. This is unfortunate, because introducing the fanciful seems much more here than literary whimsy; its presence is at the heart of one method of confronting the entire enterprise of conquest.

The interest in biography is connected, one suspects, with the Hispanic effort to come to terms with the whole matter of empire. By the end of the nineteenth century, empire had become a matter that stirred great ambivalence, and often hostility. Its final destruction in the Spanish-American War was even celebrated by some—the so-called "Generation of '98"—as a positive force for the regeneration of Spain. Still, there was a lingering desire to pull *something* from it; that was the adventuring spirit of the conquistadors. Don Luis Villanueva y Cañedo, the earliest of de Soto's modern Spanish biographers, moved toward this emphasis in 1892. Perhaps the whole conquest period was bad for peoples on both sides of the water, but could not one salvage a balance out of individual displays of fortitude, nobility, and heroism?[98] Intentionally or not, he showed a way to distance the present from the past while simultaneously retaining it, or at least parts of it. Further, if one emphasized a thralldom to Amadís and the other medieval heroes, then the conquistadors could become at once more interesting and less threatening: one could study them (and even admire them), without seeming to applaud the enterprise itself.[99] An extension of the thought of Villanueva is what lies beneath the redefinition of biography in Blanco Castilla and the seemingly fanciful elements in Albornoz; unfortunately, the only opportunity for an English-speaking audience to observe it has disappeared through translation.[100]

Three centuries of English-language writing about the entrada had produced a mountain of redundancy. Beyond this, there was much more to be learned, but the path would be a difficult one, for to find where it began, paradoxically, one had first to decide where it ended. The search has been one of the most interesting intellectual ventures of our century.

Before following its course, however, it must be noted that it was a march that was largely of interest only to the marchers. We are offered, in an unorthodox way, a strikingly clear insight into the relationship that has arisen between the general public and de Soto historians. In 1928—a year that saw the publication of yet another novel on the man—Chrysler Corporation introduced the De Soto automobile, a powerful vehicle designed to capture the market at the upper end, between its Dodge and Chrysler models.[101] Why that name? Clearly it was selected because the marketers were convinced that the associations made by potential buyers, even the presumably better-read ones in the upper-middle-class, would be based on no more than a vague notion of who de Soto was or what he had done.[102] Advertising strategists must have banked on a subliminal progression involving power, forcefulness, and control; even a hint that buyers might associate the name with ending up dead in the middle of nowhere would have brought a quick end to the idea. The success of the car over the next forty years suggests that their estimate of public inattention was correct.[103] From this point on, general interest seems to have become inversely proportionate to scholarly enthusiasm.

By the turn of the century, an alternative approach to de Soto research stood ready to emerge into its full vigor. As far back as the early decades of the nineteenth century, while the biographers were getting the most public attention, other students of the expedition were taking a quite different tack. Illustrative of their approach and their interests was the work of Albert James Pickett, whose *History of Alabama* appeared in 1851. Pickett had been working for many years on his subject, but in a way radically different from his predecessors. His concern was not with the drama of the expedition, nor with the moral lessons that might be drawn from it, but instead with what appeared to be mundane questions: Where had the expedition been? What was its exact route? How did it get from one place to another? The answers to these questions engaged Pickett in careful readings of the sources, not for keys to individual or national character, but for clues that might lead him to geographical anchors and possible artifacts that could verify a presence, provide a point of reference.

The results might be condescendingly noticed by those previously discussed. One might mention (probably in a footnote) the work, but it was not the sort of "history" one would actually *do*. The most one could grant was that it was unimaginative or uncreative; as Simms would say, with Pickett's work specifically in mind, mere *chronicle*.[104]

Yet the work persevered, surviving the deadly charge of antiquarianism and gradually, steadily gained for itself an increasing measure of respectability as the romanticists' definition of the historian's responsibility fell from favor.[105] It also received a boost from the new discipline of anthropology.

Rejecting the older definition of what constituted useful historical knowledge was necessary if the expedition was to receive a reorientation, but the magnitude of the change would surely have been less without the birth of anthropology as a professional discipline. As it happened, there was a convenient convergent evolution at work. The new discipline was emerging, with its interest in an American past predating the European presence, its concern for a methodology that could reveal that past, and its passion for shedding itself of ethnocentric judgments.

One can see the difference in approach as early as the 1880's, in John G. Shea's detached and judicious analysis of sources in his contribution to the multivolume *Narrative and Critical History of America*[106]—itself, as the title implies, a self-conscious benchmark of the intellectual revolution under way. One can see it even more clearly as the new century opened, in Woodbury Lowery's *The Spanish Settlements Within the Present Limits of the United States.*[107] The work appeared in 1901 among a cluster of biographies, but the distinction in approach to subject matter is already sharp enough to demand classification as a difference in kind. Lowery deals with the expedition not as a separate, isolated event, but as part of the larger process of European intrusion. He stays well within the redrawn evidential boundaries of the new dispensation, and draws heavily upon the archaeological and anthropological work then under way.

Lowery was the future. As each year passed, the volume of work that shared his interests and views of what was important increased. As our concern is with the changing perceptions of the expedition over time, it would not serve our purpose to be exhaustive in examples. But one can gauge the magnitude of the transition by moving forward to a publication that both embodied the principles and concerns of the new approach and absorbed the work done under its standard: *The Final Report of the United States De Soto Expedition Commission.*[108]

Published in 1939—the quadricentennial of the expedition's landing— the *Final Report* summarized the results of a monumental research project carried out under the direction of John R. Swanton. Swanton was a perfect representative of the professionalization of the past: he obtained a Ph.D. at Harvard with a dissertation directed by Franz Boas, whose name was practically a synonym for scientific anthropology, and spent his entire career in the Smithsonian Institution's Bureau of American Ethnology. The project had as its goal the determination of the route followed by the expedition. It constituted one of the most exhaustive analyses of any historical moment. Swanton's research group sifted through virtually every extant

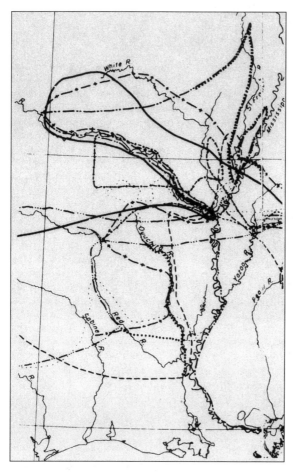

As this map shows, proposed routes of the expedition have been almost as numerous as students of the subject.

Reproduced from *The Final Report of the United States De Soto Expedition Commission* (1939; reprint 1985), 343c. Courtesy of the Smithsonian Institution Press.

document on the subject, reviewing each previous contribution that historians, ethnohistorians, anthropologists, archaeologists, and cartographers had made to the subject, supplemented with extensive field work.

The term "final report" applied only to the project, however, and not to the subject. Swanton himself denied that it was definitive. "No such finality," he reminded his readers, "will ever be attained."[109] He was certainly correct, at least in the case of his own work, for in the years since its publication, the "Swanton route" has been challenged over its entire course. Reviewing all of these criticisms would take us far beyond our scope, but looking for a moment at those in the area of the early trans-Mississippi passage will be expressive of the nature of the controversy throughout the route's course, for the problems confronted here are similar to those elsewhere.

First, the chance of pinning down the expedition's course with physical evidence—"artifactual diagnostics of De Soto origin," in Jeffrey Brain's phrase[110]—unlikely anywhere, becomes extremely remote in this region. The chances are greater of finding artifacts in the East, through which the expedition passed when it was young and well equipped. Finding remnants of the early sixteenth century in that area is not a problem, deciding who left them is the difficulty. Many Spaniards had been in and around the region by the time: the de Soto expedition itself came upon detritus from two earlier entradas—the catastrophes of Lucas Vásquez de Ayllón and Pánfilo de Narváez—during the course of its own wanderings; no one knows how many other contacts there may have been through shipwrecks, illegal traders, and slave or prisoner escapees.[111] Establishing something as certainly a de Soto remain is itself guaranteed to be problematic; even if that can be done, it still leaves the possibility of site transfer through Amerindian trade.

In the trans–Mississippi area the non–de Soto European presence was much thinner, not only before but also after the expedition's passage, making anything found more likely to have been from that enterprise. But by then the expedition's own artifact trail must have shrunk to near the vanishing point. Many months had passed without contact with the supply base in Cuba, and the military disasters at Mauvila and Chicaça had cut deeply into both manpower and materials. Carl Sauer's judgment[112] that it was now an expedition on the run may overstate the case—an expedition in that condition could have fled downriver immediately, rather than waiting another year and a half to do so. But it does suggest another reason why the difficulties of tracing the journey are now compounded. The army was short of everything, and de Soto's fateful turn to the north cut off any hope of resupply. After crossing the Mississippi River, the men spent long, dangerous hours taking the boats apart, board by board, nail by nail. So precious had even the smallest items become—a button, a torn piece of breast armor—that the chance of finding the dream artifact—a site-specific skeleton, buried in a style consistent with European rituals, wearing a religious medal (the one item that mourners would not appropriate) with identification on the reverse side—is perhaps as likely as finding other physical evidence; an optimist's way of settling with the unlikelihood of finding any physical evidence at all.[113]

Further, the eyewitness accounts are uniformly vague on the expedition's path from the disaster at Chicaça to the crossing point, and tend to evaporate in detail thereafter (with one, Ranjel, drying up completely). The march, after all, was now over two years old. What may have seemed worth

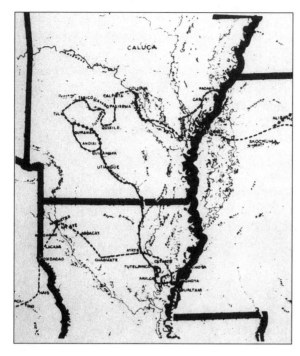

The Swanton
reconstruction of
the route in the
trans-Mississippi area.

Reproduced from *The
Final Report of the United
States De Soto Commission*
(1939; reprint 1985), 343c.
Courtesy of the Smith-
sonian Institution Press.

noting in the early days, when every sunrise brought the promise of Peru, surely seemed less so now, as few could have believed they were paralleling the trail from Cajamarca to Cuzco.[114]

Yet another complication is the matter of rivers. Crossing big rivers, like fighting great battles, is a difficult, complicated, memorable event, unlikely to be ignored in accounts. For that reason, rivers (in a metaphor admittedly uncongenial to their nature) anchor the expedition. The de Soto army found itself in a very well-watered area for much of its trans-Mississippi phase; still, there are a limited number of rivers that will qualify as those mentioned in the accounts. Three rivers, excluding the Mississippi, dominate the accounts in the first year after the Mississippi crossing: the Casqui, the Cayas, and the Coligua. By looking at a map, one sees that the likely candidates are, north to south: the St. Francis, the White, the Arkansas, and the Ouachita Rivers.[115] If one finds the point of crossing below the St. Francis, as Swanton did, one quickly shifts the march in a southerly direction. On the other hand, if the expedition enters above the St. Francis, then the southernmost point will become the Arkansas (and the Louisiana Department of Tourism has a problem on its hands). Which river becomes the Casqui will affect the expedition by moving it many miles to the north or south. The same rivers that might anchor the expedition can also set it adrift. All of them follow the lead of the Mississippi River, slipping out of one bed and into another, creating over millennia the great rich flood plains that drew the Amerindian populations toward them.[116] But what drew the Amerindians could also erase their presence through periodic flooding of their settlements. Even now, with all the technology of the twentieth century arrayed against it, the Mississippi's triumph may be just a matter of time;[117] in this earlier period, its whim was law. Since the expedition spent much of its time after the Mississippi transit following other rivers that behaved much like the great river, if on a smaller scale, the evidential problem repeats itself.[118]

Lastly, there is not much hope of solving the problem by working backward from later moments in the expedition. As Frank Schambach has commented, one must try—with fewer written sources than for any other period—to replot the course of a depleted army on the verge of starvation, exhausted, virtually leaderless, and with no plan beyond survival.[119] Nowhere along the route is an anchor point less likely to be found.

All of these problems led Swanton to observe, somewhat ruefully, that here not only did his "new" route essentially redraw the oldest—proposed by the French cartographer Guillaume de l'Isle in the early eighteenth century—but that it was necessarily tentative.[120] Still, as is often the case with interpretations, the passage of time created a mantle of authority for this one beyond anything claimed by its originators. It gathered authority, too, from the understandable desire of local interests to maintain the commercial value of the tourism created.[121] But in the years following the Swanton investigation, new methodologies produced new evidence, which in turn produced new possibilities.

Most significant was the expanding knowledge of Amerindian habitation produced by the patient work of a small army of archaeologists. The problem for the Swanton team was twofold: there was simply not much information available to it on aboriginal habitation, and there was no way of establishing with any precision a time frame for the settlements that were available. Modern techniques of fixing prehistoric sites in time are so familiar to us now that it is hard to remember that they have been developed so recently. Even radiocarbon dating, the one best known to the general public, has its origins later than the time of the Swanton work.[122] In sum, it is hardly too much to say that most of what is known *systematically* has been learned since the 1930s.

While the most intense controversy over this section of route is of recent origin,[123] challenges to it actually arose rather quickly. In 1951, Philip Phillips, James Ford, and James B. Griffin—engaged since the early

1940s in an archaeological survey of the entire lower Mississippi Valley—
questioned the route at its point of entry.[124] The report became a significant
benchmark, not so much as a proposal of a new route (for in fact its authors
did not settle upon one, confessing with amusing candor that "it is disap-
pointing not to be able to wind up with at least some tentative conclusions"),
but for two other, interconnected reasons: it cast serious doubt on the
Swanton report, and it did so by insisting that archaeological remains should
henceforth take pride of place as "best evidence." *If* the crossing had been
at Sunflower Landing, as Swanton had thought, and *if* the Indian village
described in the accounts as Casqui was in an area protected from the
ravages of the Mississippi, as Swanton had also thought, then the *absence* of
an appropriate site was fatal to the proposition that Sunflower Landing had
been the crossing point.

The archaeological focus of the Phillips, Ford, and Griffin report has
dominated de Soto studies since, and not only because of its position of
priority as evidence. It was symbolic of a vastly larger shift in focus for de
Soto studies: the transformation of the expedition from a *subject* into a *document*. The older, essentially Eurocentric questions regarding the nature and
purpose of the expedition could still be asked, but after four centuries the
chances of learning much that was new were diminishing. However, if the
subject became not the intruders but those intruded upon, then the expedition could take its place as a document singular in its importance.[125] Almost
everywhere else in the New World, from Jamestown to Tenochtitlán, the
European expansion was a continuing, expanding presence and pressure. In
the Mississippi Valley area, that was not so; the Europeans came, but did not
stay. In fact they disappeared for a very long time. Not until the Marquette/
Joliet and La Salle expeditions well over a century later would there again
be recorded observations of aboriginal life. The de Soto record, therefore,
becomes invaluable as the fundamental complement—the "base-line
data"—to the evidence in the ground. This new emphasis has liberated de
Soto studies. New questions could now be asked: What was the pattern of
Native American settlement at the time of contact? Where were the various
ethnic groups then? How numerous were they? What was their relationship
to one another? To what extent was their lifestyle affected by the expedition? If there are answers to these questions, they lie in part in the records
of the expedition. The treasure hunters, in one of history's wondrous turn-
abouts, have become the treasure.

With that new emphasis, the location—the *exact* location—of the expedition becomes a more important question than ever before. Charles Hudson
has explained why a person would spend some of the best years of an adult

life in what might appear to be the most myopically antiquarian of pursuits. It may look like "obsessive scholarship," says Hudson, but it is far more than that: it is instead an essential quest for an indispensable precision, "the more precise the reconstructed route the more the gains that may be made in understanding the native people of the sixteenth-century Southeast."[126]

However, asking new questions has been easier than settling upon answers, as a review of the matter of the new Hudson reconstruction of the route will demonstrate. Our concentration will be upon the attempt to extend the reconstruction into the trans-Mississippi area.

This route was constructed from the beginning with heavy emphasis upon a conformity of the path with known aboriginal sites—the area where knowledge had grown most since the time of the Swanton study. Applying the method to our area of focus, and simplifying it somewhat, the procedure is this: Of all the aboriginal sites in Arkansas, attempt to identify which ones are protohistoric, using the years 1400–1650 as the range for that term. Put each site (defined as "larger" or "smaller" on the basis of being more or less than one acre in size) into a computer which will then generate population clusters. Identify the sites where "probable mid-sixteenth century Spanish artifacts" have been located. Then construct a route that is consistent with this evidence.[127]

Hudson fastens upon one of the most thoroughly investigated sites in Arkansas, the Mississippian site of Parkin in Cross County, as the anchor point of Casqui. It was a crucial decision, for this means pushing the course of the entire expedition far to the north. From that point on, the expedition's course is controlled by its conformity with aboriginal sites (which it does perhaps too well: "*all* [known archaeological polities in Northeast Arkansas]," Phyllis Morse notes, "seem to have been directly visited by the de Soto expedition"),[128] and by the elimination of anomalies that would make the course an impossible one.

While the proposed route has not been the subject of debate so acrimonious as that which has occurred over earlier sections,[129] it is not without its problems or critics.[130] To an extent, an ongoing problem with this reconstruction is its vulnerability to the very methodological difficulties that it uses to discount other possibilities. Illustrative of this is what we will call the Hot Springs Problem, a point of attack for the Hudson supporters against the Swanton route. Hot Springs is perhaps its best-known point. However, if the Hudson route is to prevail, Hot Springs cannot be a winter encampment because it is too far south. Can it be eliminated as an anchor point?

The argument against it begins with the strong point that Hot Springs was never quite the anchor for the Swanton team that it has since become,

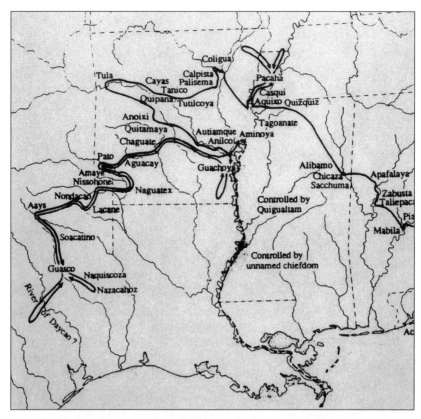

The Hudson reconstruction of the route in the trans-Mississippi area.

Adapted from a map entitled, *The Hernando de Soto Expedition, 1539–1543.*
Charles Hudson and Associates (March 1991). Courtesy of Charles Hudson.

the literary evidence having been too skimpy to support it. While supporters of the Swanton route continue to raise the point,[131] the Swanton investigation never made it central to that reconstruction (at least if the attention paid to it in the *Final Report* is representative),[132] probably for the good reason that the sources are indeed very thin on the subject. Elvas refers to a "very warm and brackish marsh" and the additional notes of Ranjel refer to "hot streams," but the former source is vague and the latter, if it does in fact refer to Hot Springs, is not time-specific—it could be something the Spanish had heard about, or it could be something they visited later during the western excursion after de Soto's death.[133] An expedition is not required to discover a natural wonder simply because it is now famous.

But what happens if the Parkin site is subjected to a similar line of

The Parkin Memorial Mound.

Reproduced from Phyllis A. Morse, *Parkin* (Fayetteville: Arkansas Archeological Survey Research Series No. 13). Courtesy of the Arkansas Archeological Survey.

critical analysis? It is a site now well known,[134] and conforms in general to the description; but did it for a few weeks in the summer of 1541? It is a truism of archaeology that it is excellent on space, weak on time. A computer print-out of all aboriginal sites dated to within a two hundred year period collapses centuries into a single instant of impressive density; but if one is dealing in weeks and months, it is an illusion. Whether the Parkin site even existed at the time of the European intrusion has been a point in question until quite recently.[135] While the point has been conceded, this would still seem to leave Parkin as no more than a strong possibility. The artifacts found there—a small brass bell and a glass bead—can be dated to the period, but, because of the possibility of aboriginal interchange of goods, not necessarily to the expedition itself (to have a compete *absence* of European artifacts at such a large population center would perhaps be the more curious phenomenon).[136] The Hudson inquiry did not simply end up at the Parkin gate; instead, the existence of the Parkin site led Hudson to rethink the possibility of a more northerly route for the expedition through Mississippi. This led to aerial surveys that revealed Indian trails on high ground through swampland that Swanton had dismissed as too vast to penetrate in the time allowed.[137] However, there can never be certainty without the indisputable anchor that site-specific artifacts would supply, and one is left with nagging uncertainty about whether the past has pressed Parkin upon the present or vice versa.

Still, the general tendency seems to be moving toward an acceptance of the Hudson reconstruction. It has been interesting over the past few years to watch the phenomenon of the gradual transplantation of the one route by the other. To raise the specter of Thomas Kuhn's *The Structure of Scientific Revolutions*[138] may seem rather grand for our modest discussion, yet it may be illustrative. Kuhn's point was that once a framework of understanding has been established, scientists then work within it, continuing in that fashion while anomalies gather. Eventually, the moment arrives when a new explanation is offered, one that escapes the old anomalies rather than continuing to attempt to work within them. But (and this is an often over-looked part of Kuhn's argument) the new framework will have anomalies of its own. Quite likely it will be less detailed in its explanation than the paradigm it tries to supplant, but will answer those questions that *now* seem to need a resolution. Something of this sort seems to be happening with the new route. Critics continue to challenge on many grounds: the lack of arti-factual evidence, the overreliance upon questionable written sources, and upon negative evidence—aboriginal sites that have *not* been found. But the momentum lies with the Hudson proponents. Clearly the most compelling matter for most of those involved is what the expedition may be able to say about the Amerindian life. This is their interest; the evidence on aboriginal populations is what the route must "fit." Thus, the strongest evidence against the Swanton interpretation becomes its seeming incongruity with what is known about population densities, while it is the best support for the Hudson interpretation.

But if all this work has been to the end of refocusing de Soto studies—to aim less at learning *incrementally* more about Europeans than to learn *substantially* more about Amerindians—it would appear that most of the rewards, if any, still lie ahead. The goal of this recent concentration upon the route was not to be more exact about one more thing that Europeans did at a particular moment in the sixteenth century, but instead to use this infor-mation to learn more about the new world populations; that is, to supple-ment and to clarify the evidence produced from archaeological work. However, it would seem that most of the supplementing and the clarifying is still going in the opposite direction: the evidence in the ground has been much more informative on the de Soto expedition than the Spanish writings have been for the artifacts. Archaeological work has provided what is, in the opinion of most, the best evidence in favor of the Hudson projection of the de Soto route; the literary evidence provided by the expedition has produced nothing that equally enriches the existing knowledge of native peoples. The work of Ann Early and Frank Schambach illustrates the point and the problem. Both have employed their archaeological findings in support of the Hudson route over that of Swanton. Early uses descriptions of native peoples in the accounts to place the expedition into an area known to be the territory of a Caddoan people; the native peoples locate the expedition, not the other way around.[139] Similarly, Schambach rejects Swanton's placing of Autiamque (the winter encampment of 1541–42) in the area around present day Camden because aboriginal populations there could not have fed such a large expedition for so long a period. This was not a land of "farmsteads and granaries" upon which the expedition had long been absolutely dependent. The Koroan peoples here could not have fed such a large group of intruders even if they had wanted to. Free from the constraints of settled agriculture that trapped other Indians in the path of the expedition, they could have avoided any contact. "Had the Spaniards tried to winter around Calion, or around Camden," Schambach concludes, "they would have perished within a month."[140] Again, one learns something new about the expedition, but nothing comparable about the aboriginals.

Even what would seem to be the most fruitful body of information, that about aboriginal populations contained in the accounts, has to this point not been as helpful as might have been expected. One illustration of this is the matter of depopulation. Many scholars have noted the obvious difference between the heavily populated land the de Soto expedition passed through and the almost empty land encountered over a century later by French expeditions. While problems with the evidence are obvious (the Spanish wanted large populations, because that was where the gold had been found by expeditions elsewhere, and may have inflated what they were seeing in a subconscious effort to avoid the depressing reality—there was nothing worth stealing—that had been their lot for over two years; the French may have simply missed the populations by staying on or near the Mississippi River, or they may have reduced what they did see, thinking that their government would be more receptive to news of small, non-threatening populations), it is hard to emerge from a reading of it without inclining toward the position that depopulation had taken place. If the European intrusion into the Americas brought a welter of diseases that ignited the greatest holocaust in human history—the debate over that now centers more upon questions of scale, pace, and responsibility than upon whether or not it happened—then one would expect the de Soto accounts to be invaluable sources of information on the subject.[141] As yet, however, having the expedition accounts as a starting point has not advanced our knowledge much beyond what could have been deduced from depopulation studies in areas where the evidence is more continuous. The accounts have not been helpful in determining either the rate of the die-off or the reasons for it. A recent educated guess of 75,000 at the time of the de Soto entrada and 15,000 by the time of the French arrival concludes that diseases accompanying the expedition were "undoubtedly responsible."[142] But the latter part of the statement is decisive and unsubstantiated in equal parts. Indeed, it would seem logical: this was a group of Europeans large enough to bring diseases, and it had been preceded by two other expeditions, one of which, the Ayllón expedition, included children. The likelihood of diseases in contagious stages among members of the de Soto expedition would lessen as time passed. Once introduced, though, they could be expected to transfer themselves into the interior, using natives as a traveling chain of host organisms. When the expedition moved toward the large congested populations where epidemics would be most obvious, it would have been difficult for the commentators to have missed the impact. But logic may be a false friend here. One finds almost no mention of disease. This is a notable omission, given the prevalence of commentary in accounts from other contact experiences—the Cortez expedition, for example, or the early colonial settlements in New England.[143] A recent paleodemographic study of aboriginal sites in Arkansas concludes that this was not simply oversight. "The evidence strongly suggests that the de Soto entrada did not bring epidemics with them [sic]," according to Barbara A. Burnett and Katherine A. Murray. "The major depopulation of this area occurred afterward."[144] If this view holds, then clearly the de Soto accounts may serve best as cautions against too facile an acceptance of the notion of immediate, sweeping die-offs.

It is convenient, then, that a somewhat chastened view of the potential of written sources to illuminate aboriginal societies has simultaneously emerged. Much that was of fundamental importance, as Bruce Trigger was among the first to observe, would not have been seen by even the earliest European observers, no matter how acute their vision. The entire European package, from diseases to trade items, traveled in advance of them, altering social, political, and religious institutions within tribes and diplomatic relationships beyond them. "The ways of life of most native peoples," Trigger concludes, "were considerably altered by changes produced by a European presence in North America long before the first detailed accounts of these groups were recorded."[145] Students of the de Soto expedition are arriving at a more tempered variety of the same conclusion.[146] Still, the entrada remains the nearest thing to moment-of-contact data that scholars will ever have to supplement the archaeological record, and its usefulness in that way has by no means been exhausted. Its potential as a source for determining changes in the aboriginal pattern of settlement, and through that of changes in relationships both within and beyond groups by employing careful linguistic analysis of the names mentioned and thorough study of the practices observed, is just beginning to be tapped.[147]

Given all this, it would be hard not to conclude that we are living within the most fascinating moment in the entire posthumous history of the de Soto expedition. A conclusion equally hard to avoid would be that it is when public interest seems lowest. Collectively, the work is an underwritten effort. It continues through grants; the results appear in subsidized journals. Efforts to bring it to a larger public—a radio drama,[148] a pair of film documentaries,[149] a popularized rehearsing of the scholarly work,[150] a series of public-welcome conferences such as those at the University of Arkansas in 1988 and 1990—are few, and even these must be subsidized. There is nothing to parallel the public demand that pushed Theodore Irving's pioneering biography through its repeated editions a century ago. To study the posthumous history of the de Soto expedition is to observe an almost revolutionary reconceptualization of how the past may be studied to the greater profit of the present. It is also to gaze once again upon one of the more discouraging ironies of our time: the growing isolation of our past— now more interesting, complex, multilayered, and accurate—from the larger audience that could so benefit from its presence.

Living in a Graveyard

Native Americans in Colonial Arkansas

WILLARD H. ROLLINGS

. . . upon the arrival of our men at the river [Mississippi River], more than six thousand Indian warriors showed themselves on the other side, well armed and with a large number of canoes in which to oppose their crossing.

—GARCILASO DE LA VEGA, THE INCA
MAY 1541

. . . we were sensibly afflicted to see this Acanscas [Quapaw] nation, once so numerous, entirely destroyed by war and sickness. It is not a month since they got over the smallpox which carried the greatest part of them. There was nothing to be seen in the village but graves.

—JEAN FRANCOIS BUISSON DE ST. COSME
JANUARY 1699

In the spring of 1541 when Europeans first arrived in the area known today as Arkansas, the region was densely populated with thousands of Indian people living around elaborate ceremonial centers set amid vast fields of corn. Within a relatively short time, because of disease and drought, these early Arkansans disappeared. They died in the thousands, and the land became a vast graveyard. The depopulation that followed de Soto's disastrous visit shaped the history of colonial Arkansas.[1]

Throughout the entire colonial period, Arkansas remained relatively empty of human beings. Only the Caddo, Quapaw, and Osage lived in the periphery of the area. Central Arkansas remained unoccupied. The dramatic depopulation of people created a decline in hunting, and colonial Arkansas became a region filled with vast numbers of wild animals.

The abundance of game attracted the Amerindian hunters to the interior, but their harvests made only limited demands on the resource, and the animal populations remained high. Living along some of the major western rivers—the Mississippi, the Arkansas, and the Red—the Indians of Arkansas were visited by increasing numbers of European traders in the seventeenth century. Once these colonials arrived with amazing new animals, powerful new weapons, novel metal tools, and new economic conceptualizations, the indigenous peoples, for a combination of social, economic, and political reasons, gradually became active commercial hunters.

All three tribes competed for the Arkansas game. The Quapaw were devastated by a series of seventeenth- and eighteenth-century epidemics and were unable to effectively challenge the others. Over time the Osage hunted deeper into Arkansas and drove the Caddo from the region; they then dominated the Ozark and Ouachita highlands and exploited the wildlife. By the late eighteenth century, the rich and empty lands of Arkansas became attractive to eastern tribes. Despite Osage resistance, as the colonial period came to an end, numerous eastern Indians were moving into the territory. After the United States acquired Arkansas (as part of the Louisiana Purchase in 1803), President Jefferson began urging this migration, and hundreds participated. The vacant lands were soon filled by eastern peoples—first Indians, then Euro-Americans. The colonial graveyard became a nineteenth-century boomtown.

In 1541 Arkansas was inhabited by thousands of Native American people. As Hernando de Soto and his men prepared to cross the Mississippi River in the spring of that year, they were confronted by several thousand warriors. Afterwards, the Spaniards spent the next two years traveling along the river valleys of northeastern and south central Arkansas. The explorers passed through large Indian towns and, in the surviving records of the entrada, described the people they saw. The accounts of the Gentleman from Elvas, Luys Hernández de Biedma, Rodrigo Rangel, and Garcilaso de la Vega all mention the large Native American communities. Even discounting the exaggerated numbers of Garcilaso, the other records substantiate his general impressions. The Gentleman of Elvas wrote:

> For two days the governor marched through the land of Casqui before arriving at the town where the cacique was, and most of the way continually through land of open field, very well populated with large towns, two or three of which were to be seen from one town.

The populated land was considerable, and it had many people and many maize fields.

Near the village flowed a river of Cayas and above and below it was densely populated.

While a league and a half-league distant were other very large towns where there was a quantity of maize, beans, walnuts and dried plums. This was the most populous region which had been seen in Florida and more abounding in maize, with the exception of Coça and Apalache.[2]

In Biedma's briefer account, he, too, mentioned the large populations: "We headed southwest to another province which is called Quigate. This was the largest town we found in Florida. . . . We had information that on this river upstream was a great province called Cayas. We went to it and found that it was all scattered populations. . . ."[3]

Rangel also observed that:

On the other bank of the river, up to seven thousand Indians gathered to defend the crossing, and with up to two hundred canoes, all with shields sewn together. . . . And the next day, Friday, they went to Quiguate, which is the largest town they saw in that land, next to the river of Casqui; and they found that afterwards that the river was well populated below. . . . They found the town populated, and in it they took many people and clothes and a great deal of food and much salt. . . . They passed through a small village [poblezuelo], and on Wednesday, the second of November, they arrived at Utiangue, which is a very well populated savannah of attractive appearance.[4]

While archaeologists and ethnohistorians still argue about de Soto's exact route, most agree that he traveled along the St. Francis, White, Arkansas, and Ouachita river valleys and that these were filled with Native Americans. As the Spaniards marched across Arkansas, they repeatedly encountered large Indian groups with elaborate ceremonial and civic centers surrounded by widespread farmlands. The various chroniclers of the entrada all described thriving indigenous communities stretched out along rich river valleys. Archaeologists have confirmed these accounts.

Just one hundred and thirty years later the Indian communities visited by the expedition were gone. After the departure of de Soto's men, Arkansas was not visited by Europeans again until the mid-seventeenth century, when French explorers arrived. Their descriptions of the region differ greatly from those of the sixteenth-century Spaniards in that no sizable Native American populations were recorded. The Casqui, Pacaha,

Colingua, Utiangue, Quigualtam, Tula, and Lacane people of de Soto's time had disappeared.[5]

The French did not come upon large, active ceremonial centers surrounded by thousands of farming Indians; the region was by then deserted and only thinly populated. When Father Marquette came to the mouth of the Arkansas River in 1673, he was not greeted by six thousand threatening warriors like those who had challenged de Soto; instead, he was met by friendly Quapaw living in four moderate-sized villages.

In 1682, Robert Cavelier Sieur de La Salle visited the Arkansas. He and his men also found it empty of the large sixteenth-century Indian communities described by de Soto's men. When Henri de Tonty sent men to establish the first European trading post in Arkansas in 1686, they constructed it near the mouth of the Arkansas River at the base of an abandoned sixteenth-century Mississippian ceremonial mound.[6] The French priest Jean François Buisson de St. Cosme reached the river in 1699, and found Quapaw villages dominated by the graves of the dead.

French traders were beyond Three Forks (where the Verdigris and Neosho Rivers join the Arkansas River) before they encountered the villages of the Wichita. It appears that for most of the seventeenth and eighteenth centuries, with the exception of the Quapaw near the mouth, the Arkansas River valley was unoccupied. The old villages were deserted and had fallen into ruin, and the elaborate ceremonial centers described by the Spanish had become overgrown and did not leave enough remains to warrant notice by any of the later explorers.

Arkansas had undergone an enormous population decline. Scholars today argue about its cause, but most support the idea of virgin-soil epidemics. Recent work, however, indicates that the depopulation might have been the result of long-term drought that struck the region from 1549 to 1577.[7] Whether it was caused by epidemic diseases or drought, or a combination of both, it is clear that by the mid-seventeenth century Arkansas was inhabited only along the periphery, and that most of the area was empty of human population. The large, thriving Mississippian communities were gone, and Arkansas retained only the smaller villages made up of the surviving natives and recent eastern immigrants .

Thus by the late seventeenth century only the Caddo, the Quapaw, and the Osage lived in the land that is now Arkansas. The Mississippian Caddos organized into the Kadohadacho Caddo along the big bend of the Red River and the Cahinnio Caddo along the upper Ouachita River valley.[8] Although some claim that the Quapaw may also have been Mississippian survivors, most scholars now believe that they were recent Dhegian

"Quapaw Warrior," Charles Banks Wilson's impression of what an eighteenth-century Quapaw might have looked like.

Courtesy of the artist.

emigrants who established several small communities near the mouth of the Arkansas and White Rivers.[9] The Osage were a people related to the Quapaw by language, culture, and shared traditions, and spent most of the year in their prairie villages north of the Ozark plateau. They lived and hunted in northwestern Arkansas in the Ozark and Ouachita Mountains during the fall and winter. These Native American groups were the only inhabitants of Arkansas for most of the seventeenth and eighteenth centuries and lived among the remains of the Mississippian culture.

Unfortunately, much more is known about the pre-Columbian people

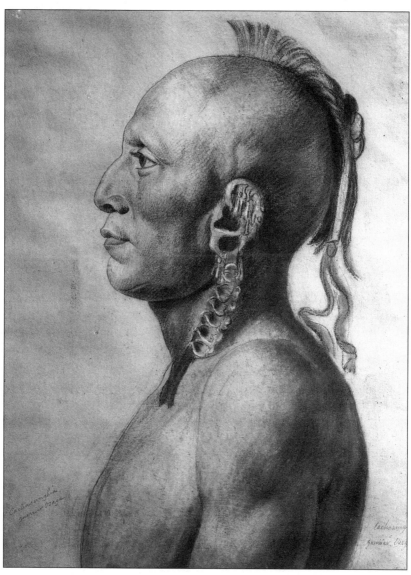

"Cashunghia, Gerrier Osage."

Crayon sketch inscribed by St. Memin.
Collection of the New-York Historical Society.

of the region than about the Caddo, Quapaw, and Osage. They have all suffered from scholarly neglect, perhaps as a result of their small populations. Their resistance to white settlement was limited, and they tended to avoid wars with Euro-Americans; thus historians who have focused on Indian-white relations have largely ignored them. Recent ethnohistorians who examine persistence and change within Native American societies and stress adaption have also overlooked Arkansas people and instead focused on other tribes.[10] The Caddo and Quapaw have been the subject of only limited historical research.

To understand the history of Native Americans in the colonial era, one must first understand the geography of Arkansas. There are two major physical divisions. In the north and west there are rugged highlands known as the Ozark and Ouachita Mountains. In the south and east the widespread Mississippi Alluvial and West Gulf Coastal Plains dominate. Eastern Arkansas contains wide expanses of flat land covered with bands of hardwood forests and open savannas. The western mountains are separated by the Arkansas River flowing southeast across the state. The White River drains the Ozarks and flows southeast into the Mississippi River near the mouth of the Arkansas. The Ouachita Mountains are drained by several tributaries of the Ouachita River, which flows south to the Saline in the alluvial plains. The Red River crosses the southwest corner of the area as it makes its great bend to the south. In the east the St. Francis River flows south through the lowlands before joining the Mississippi.

This geography directly shaped the living patterns of the Native Americans. By the eighteenth century, the Ozark and Ouachita Mountains were rarely the permanent home of any Arkansas Indians and remained largely unoccupied (they remain thinly populated even today). The terrain is rugged with forested ridges cut by deep wooded gorges. Although filled with deer, bear, and other wild game, the mountain soils would not support large-scale horticulture. Winters were colder and more severe than in the valleys and flat lands. Although the site of early hunting and gathering people, the mountains were only occupied when Caddo, Quapaw, and Osage men sought deer in the fall and winter. With the exception of these seasonal camps, the Native Americans of Arkansas lived primarily along the rivers of Arkansas and on the flat alluvial lowlands.

Arkansas rivers, fed by springs, creeks, and streams, formed sloughs, lakes, marshes, and wide expanses of grassy wetlands. Their valleys were excellent habitats for large populations of wild game. The wildlife attracted by the rich growth provided an abundant food supply for the Quapaw and Caddo. The seasonal flooding of the rivers covered the lowlands with fresh

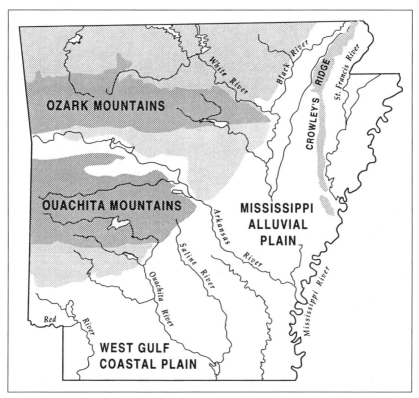

Physiographic Landforms of Arkansas.

topsoil, replenishing the land and maintaining the fertile soil. It was in this bountiful region that the Quapaw and Caddo chose to live. The Caddo spread out into kin-based farmsteads, while the Quapaw lived more compactly in small villages.

Gardening was the work of the women. They planted along the fertile river bottom lands, because these contained soil that was friable and easily tilled with the wood and bone tools available, and on the natural levees. Individual families worked the fields, so gardens varied according to each family's size and needs. In the spring they burned the debris from the previous year's harvest to clear the land for the next planting. This organic material was worked into the soil as fertilizer. Beans, planted every year, also helped replace the nitrogen removed by the corn. Plots were used as long as the land could support the crops. Despite repeated flooding, spring burning, and nitrogen fixing, the soil would gradually become less productive, and new sites were chosen in the same general area.

Corn was the most important crop the Amerindians cultivated. They also planted squash, pumpkins, and beans among the corn, because these grew well together and the vines prevented erosion. Their broad leaves created shade that helped conserve moisture in the soil and cut off sunlight to unwanted weeds. Planted among the corn and squash, beans vined around the corn stalks. Although by themselves not nutritiously complete, corn and beans combined brought together amino acids essential for a balanced and healthful diet. In good years Quapaw and Caddo gardens provided a large part of the yearly food supply.

It was, however, dangerous to rely on a single source of food. River floods sometimes came too early or too late and washed crops away. Insects or animals sometimes destroyed the plants. Thus the Native Americans of Arkansas had to maintain a diverse subsistence economy. Quapaw and Caddo people were skilled harvesters of wild plant life. Both possessed a rich knowledge of botanical information. They gathered walnuts, pecans, hickory nuts, paw paws, persimmons, and chinkapins. They also used the pine and oak trees from the forests, and the cottonwoods, walnuts, willow, hickory, bois d'arc, cypress, and pecan trees growing along the river valleys as material for housing and tools.

Caddo and Quapaw hunters supplemented their horticultural and gathering economies with meat from the abundance and variety of wild game available.[11] All the early accounts of Europeans in the region during this period are filled with descriptions of the vast wildlife population (once the Caddo, Quapaw, and Osage hunters became involved in the eighteenth-century trade with the Europeans, they traded tens of thousands of deer-skins every year).[12] While there were ample animals to supply the subsistence demands of the Quapaw and Caddo, Native American hunters possessed a keen understanding of animal behavior and regularly harvested game in both the river valleys and the Ouachita and Ozark forests to supplement their diet. The year began with a hunt, for the last days of winter were often hungry times since food stores were often depleted. They had a variety of animals to kill, including the bison, which were pursued in northeast Arkansas particularly.[13] In time, as Arkansas bison were destroyed, the Red River Caddo traveled west to hunt them on the south-central plains. Once they acquired horses in the late seventeenth century, the Caddo could hunt bison more effectively, and it remained an important element in their diet throughout the colonial period.[14] While the taking of game began in the winter, it continued into the summer when the Indians sought white-tailed deer, bear, elk, wolf, otter, turkey, quail, rabbit, raccoon, opossum, and muskrat.

Late summer and early fall was an especially prosperous time for the

Native Americans of Arkansas. Their valley villages were located beneath both the Mississippi and central bird migration flyways. The marshes, sloughs, and wetlands near the Quapaw and Caddo villages filled with water fowl as ducks and geese passed through. Wild turkeys, normally widely dispersed, gathered in large flocks in autumn and were easily harvested. Beaver also became active during this time. For much of the year, beaver remained in the water, moving about only at night, but in October and November they abandoned their nocturnal aquatic life and left their lodges to gather food for the coming winter. These daytime excursions were excellent opportunities for hunters to gather this animal, fat and sleek from the summer season.[15]

The white-tailed deer, which preferred to live along the edge of forests, were best hunted in the fall. While the forests provided cover and protection, they were too dark to support the growth of shrubs and other deer "browse"; but this could be found in the edge environments. The Quapaw and Caddo understood this and burned back the forests to create an edge environment and attract more deer.[16] The fall was the ideal time to hunt whitetails because it was then that the animals collected in large groups around the abundant oak forests, where they fed on the acorn crop. September through October marked the mating season. The deer deviated from their normally shy and reclusive behavior, and the bucks became belligerent and aggressive. Quapaw and Caddo hunters were keenly aware of this change in behavior, and their knowledge allowed them to harvest more effectively.[17]

During the winter months the Arkansas people also hunted the black bear. This creature did not truly hibernate, but from November to April was relatively inactive. Bears fed on the fall acorn crops in order to put on weight, and their pelts thickened for the coming cold. After the first snows of January and February, the Caddo and Quapaw located and killed the bears. The people enjoyed the fresh meat, and particularly enjoyed the oil rendered from the fat. Bear oil was used in cooking and was a popular addition to the Native American diet.[18]

Throughout the winter the Quapaw and Caddo continued to harvest turkey, raccoon, opossum, waterfowl, and other local animals. By March most of their stored food was gone, and it became more difficult to acquire meat—birds began their return north; beaver returned to their nocturnal patterns; white-tailed deer no longer concentrated in the oak forest and once again became shy and reclusive; and rabbits and other small mammals were thin from the winter. As soon as the danger of a killing frost passed, the women were quick to plant their spring crops, and their men, freed by the warmer weather, began hunting further from the village sites to begin the yearly cycle once again.

Life was good for the Caddo and Quapaw. The earlier depopulation had eased the pressures on game which, with only subsistence demands, thrived, thereby creating an abundance that provided ample food and material for clothing and tools. But these rich resources also attracted the attention of the Europeans, who saw the Arkansas and Red River valleys as eighteenth-century highways into the interior. In the seventeenth and eighteenth centuries, Europeans began arriving in the region and looking for precious minerals, routes to the Pacific and Spanish New Mexico, and eventually for the wildlife for food and trade.

Prompted by a combination of religious, economic, and political reasons, the French were the first to penetrate the region in the seventeenth century. Bringing Christianity to the native peoples was an important concern, and Catholic missionaries visited the Caddo and the Quapaw along the rivers. Traders sought new supplies of beaver pelts and other valuable animal resources. Finally, political concerns prompted French expansion to the west. They sought control of North America in order to exploit it economically and to deny its wealth and strategic location to European rivals. Soldiers went into the interior to claim territory for the French Crown. They could never claim real sovereignty from the Native American inhabitants, but by establishing alliances with the Caddo and the Quapaw, the French could exert some influence in the area and deny access to both the Spanish and the English.[19] Never numerically strong, they were forced to move carefully and prudently into the interior. There were simply too many Indians and too few Frenchmen to do otherwise.

In 1695, fur markets in France were glutted and western exploration was so costly that the government attempted to halt travel west of the Great Lakes. These efforts only slowed the movement; they did not stop it. French adventurers continued traveling down the Mississippi and up along the western rivers. They continued to move among the native peoples of the region, and in some cases introduced new and deadly illnesses. They also reintroduced old diseases to unprotected populations made up of individuals born between outbreaks. Sometime after Marquette's visit in 1673 (probably in 1698 as Father St. Cosme suggests), smallpox attacked the Quapaw. The Caddo also were victims as epidemics struck eastern Texas and the southern Mississippi Valley in 1686 and 1691, further reducing the already small aboriginal population of Arkansas.[20]

Imperialistic restraint was short-lived, and at the beginning of the eighteenth century, Louis XIV and his political advisors began encouraging exploration and settlement into the West.[21] Concerned about the growing power of both the British and Spanish, the French sought to deny the English access to the interior by establishing a series of outposts along the Mississippi Valley, linking the Great Lakes with the Gulf of Mexico. This strategy would also enable them to keep a close eye on the Spanish occupying the western part of North America.

Arkansas played an important role in this new policy. Henri de Tonty had already established (1686) a French presence in Arkansas with his trading house near the Quapaw villages. This outpost, commonly known as Arkansas Post, was an important Euro-American community throughout the colonial period. In 1699 French priests from the Seminary of Quebec founded the Mission of the Holy Family of Tamaroas, later known as Cahokia, on the east bank of the Mississippi just south and opposite of the mouth of the Missouri River. That same year Pierre Le Moyne, Sieur d' Iberville, established the first of a series of outposts along Mobile Bay and the mouth of the Mississippi River. In the fall of 1700, Jesuit priest Gabriel Marest created another mission just south of Cahokia on the west bank of the Mississippi. In 1703 they recrossed the river and moved south to the mouth of the Kaskaskia River. These outposts served as bases for further eighteenth-century French exploration and trade in the West.[22]

Despite this increased presence, the initial impact of the imperial changes was limited. At about the same time the French went to war with the English, and for the next eleven years the War of the Spanish Succession limited the advance into North America. While the conflict continued, there were few resources to spare for new colonial enterprises. The western posts languished, and the Gulf Coast settlements struggled to survive.[23]

With peace in 1713, the French once again revived their North American ambitions to hem in the English and keep a close eye on the colonies of their Spanish Bourbon relatives. They began to renew old alliances neglected during the war and establish new ones among the western tribes. The easiest method was through commerce. Honest trade engendered friendly relations with the Native American groups, and out of quasi-commercial relations came friendship, loyalty, and military support. Eighteenth-century French success was limited only by the paucity of trade goods, the skill of French diplomats, and the good will and goals of the Indian people.

Colonial enterprises were expensive, and the Crown decided to avoid some of the cost by leasing Louisiana (of which Arkansas was a part) to Antoine Crozat, a wealthy financial counselor to Louis XIV. Crozat formed an investment company to accumulate sufficient capital to develop and exploit the region. He encouraged expansion from the Mississippi River bases, and French trappers and traders went into the west. In 1713 Louis Jucherau de St. Denis was sent up the Red River to establish a trading post among the Caddo. He founded it among the Natchitoches Caddo. St. Denis also hoped to initiate commercial relations with the Spanish living nearby. After setting up the trading station, he traveled west and spent the winter among the Hasinai. That spring he went on to the Spanish settlements of northern Mexico and eventually all the way to Mexico City (where he was briefly jailed). The arrival of a French trader from Louisiana was unwelcome in Mexico and alarmed the Spanish, who countered by building a series of missions just west of the Red River Caddo among the Hasinai. By the early eighteenth century, both nations had a significant presence among the Red River Caddo of Arkansas. Despite St. Denis's energetic work, Crozat's company was never profitable, and in August 1717 he gave up his lease and returned the colony to the Crown.

Arkansas then came under the control of another French commercial venture, the Mississippi Company, a part of the Company of the West, directed by Scottish financier John Law. It spent enormous sums of money to explore and exploit the natural resources of Louisiana. One goal was to open trade routes to the Spanish colonies and exchange French goods for Mexican silver. Law also wanted to find mineral deposits and sent explorers west. Native Americans were an important element of these plans, for despite the general poor quality of southern skins and furs, animal pelts remained a profitable item. Law planned to establish company plantations along the Mississippi Valley to raise foodstuffs for the French Caribbean islands, and sought Indian slaves to work on them. He also sought to acquire horses and mules for the colony. Company agents went west into Arkansas to acquire both slaves and livestock from the natives of the region.

In 1719 Jean-Baptiste Bénard, Sieur de La Harpe, went up the Red River passing through Natchitoches and traveling beyond the big bend, where he met with the Upper Nasoni, Nanatsohos, Yatasis, and other members of the Kadohadacho Caddo. La Harpe established a post among them known as Fort Malouin (located near present-day Texarkana).[24] Eager to establish peace and trade with other Native American people, La Harpe left the Red River and traveled overland to the north. After three weeks he arrived at a large Tawakoni (Wichita) village filled with five thousand people. (While there has been much debate about the actual location of the town, most agree that it was probably on the Arkansas River just south of present-day Tulsa.) While La Harpe was there, a Chickasaw Indian came to trade with the Tawakoni, evidence of the ever-expanding European-based commercial network.[25]

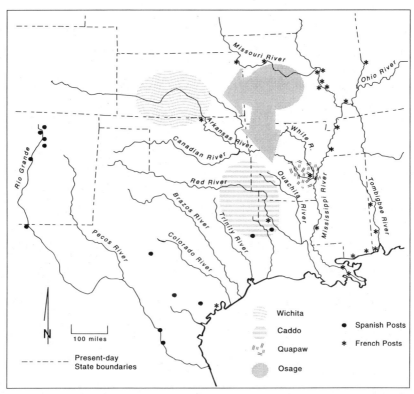

Eighteenth-century Settlements in the South-central United States.

That same year, 1719, the Mississippi Company also sent Claude-Charles Du Tisné across the Ozark Plateau and out to the Wichita villages just north of the village visited by La Harpe. These two French excursions prompted the Spanish to renew their efforts to establish peaceful relations with the plains people. In 1720 Pedro de Villasur was sent out to investigate their activity, and although his party was attacked and destroyed by the Pawnee, its presence convinced the French to respond with a new outpost among the Wichita on the Upper Arkansas.

Since La Harpe had already been among the Tawakoni, the company sent him up the Arkansas to establish a new post. He left New Orleans in December 1721, and in February arrived at the Quapaw villages at the Arkansas's mouth where he tried to secure food and an additional boat for his trip up the river. The Quapaw, although generally friendly with the French, were reluctant to help La Harpe go upstream to trade with their western rivals, so they refused to trade for a boat or food. La Harpe stole a pirogue from the Quapaw and headed upriver. Beset with unseasonably bad weather, including rain, snow, and hail, the party made slow progress. Boats overturned, food and supplies were lost, and after five weeks and little progress, La Harpe turned back. Although they had gone a short way up the Arkansas (clearly no further than present-day Morrilton in Conway County), La Harpe abandoned the company's plans for a new post among the Wichita.[26]

Despite their refusal to aid La Harpe, throughout the eighteenth century the Quapaw consistently maintained a peaceful relationship with the French colonialists. Fortunately for the Arkansas Indians, the political concerns of the French compelled them to pay for furs, despite the weak demand in Europe for deer, bear, raccoon, muskrat, and opossum skins, and the poor quality of those skins stored in the warm and humid South.[27] The Quapaw and Caddo also traded food with the French; corn, beans, squash, deer meat, and bear oil were all important items.[28] Livestock was needed for the colonies, and the Caddo, living near the Spanish source of horses, acquired enough of them in the eighteenth century to trade with the French. The Quapaw were too far removed from the horse frontier and apparently only had limited participation in this trade.

British traders and Native American agents for colonial plantations and the Charleston-based trading houses arrived in the region soon after the French. Seeking both furs and Indian slaves, they moved among the southeastern Indians, traveling along the southern river valleys. Encouraged by the British market, Chickasaw warriors raided the Mississippi Valley and captured Choctaw and Quapaw for the slave trade.[29]

The French were also involved, exacerbating the disorder and violence in the region. They persuaded the southern Indians to attack the eastern allies of the British and take captives for France's colonial plantations. They also wanted the Mississippi Valley people to take slaves from the western tribes, mainly from among the Caddoan-speaking Wichita or Pawnee living beyond the French trading frontier on the plains. The Quapaw and Caddo were encouraged to engage in this enterprise. However, the Quapaw were weakened by disease and raids from eastern tribes and seldom traveled far enough to capture western people, while the Caddo were usually reluctant to enslave their plains kin. Thus, although the Osage to the north actively engaged in the slave trade, the other Arkansas people were more likely victims rather than participating partners.

The Quapaw, however, sometimes fought alongside the French, and were especially willing to strike at Indian people who threatened their own well-being. The Chickasaws, attracted to the region by the abundant game and the small native populations, often hunted and took game in Quapaw lands, and challenged them for control of the Arkansas. Supplied with fire-arms, ammunition, and food, the Quapaw eagerly joined in the eighteenth-century colonial campaigns against the intruders. But the Arkansas Indians were not merely pawns in the European struggle; rather they took advan-tage of the French animosity against their adversaries to acquire arms and ammunition to fight common enemies.

Indeed, weapons made up an important part of the French trade with the Quapaws and the Caddos. They were more important, in fact, than metal tools or woolens, however much the Quapaw and Caddo welcomed these new goods (though they felt little need for them). Flintlock muskets were useful for hunting and, more important, for defense against enemy attacks. As more and more Europeans came into North America, they pushed Indian tribes west, and the violence created by the British slave trade threatened the Arkansas Indians. Aggressive and better-armed tribes began hunting Quapaw game and capturing their women and children for slave labor. French traders brought guns and ammunition; items that the Caddo and Quapaw, despite their considerable intellect and skill, could not produce.

Thus armed with muskets they could defend themselves and their terri-tory from raids by Illinois, Chickasaw, Choctaw, and other eastern peoples. They could kill more game to feed and clothe their families. The French, more concerned with denying land and influence to the English than with seizing it from the Quapaw and Caddo, were willing to allow this arms trade with their Indian allies to continue.

Unfortunately for the western Caddo and their kin, the Wichita, the Spanish maintained a very different policy regarding Indian people. These imperialists, who were more intent on acquiring territory and changing the Indian people into Christian peasants, were reluctant to trade weapons with people they were trying to conquer and convert. Thus the western Caddo were denied firearms and ammunition. At the same time, some eastern tribes, armed with guns, began concentrated attacks on both the Upper Arkansas Wichita and Red River Caddo, to secure slaves and horses for trade with the French.

The Osage, part-time Arkansas residents, maintained an active com-merce with French traders located near their villages at Fort Orleans and Fort Cavanaugh. However, they moved further south in the eighteenth century to cut off French trade with the Wichita and Caddo. In time, the Osage were able to effectively blockade the Arkansas and force the French to shift their route to the Red River through Natchitoches to reach the western Indians. They were successful in driving the Wichita from the

Arkansas Valley to the Upper Red River, where in the 1750s the Tawakoni established two walled villages, known incorrectly as the Spanish Fort (this outpost became an important French trading center for the southern Plains Indians).[30]

The Caddo also fell victim to Osage attacks. The raiders targeted settlements along the Red and Ouachita Rivers and were so devastating that by the mid-eighteenth century they were able to prevent the Caddo from hunting in the Ouachita and Ozark Mountains.

The Quapaw, who shared a common language, culture, and a sense of common ancestry with the Osage, were never the subjects of their devastating attacks. Instead, they continued to be plagued by epidemic disease. The Quapaw population declined in the eighteenth century until they could no longer support four villages and finally consolidated into three communities. Weakened also by warfare in the Mississippi Valley, the Quapaw were no threat to their northwestern relatives. They never challenged the Osage for territory, and because of the abundance of game, the Quapaws' limited demand was never cause for concern. The Osage kept peace because they wished to continue trading at Arkansas Post, located at one of the Quapaw villages.

Arkansas possessed a unique history in seventeenth- and eighteenth-century North America. Depopulated by the Europeans who introduced disease, much of the region was sparsely inhabited when large colonial populations arrived. For much of the eighteenth century, the center of Arkansas was empty of permanent Indian communities. Animal populations increased, and as European traders began exchanging for animal products, other Native Americans, encouraged by the absence of a significant Indian population, were attracted to the abundance of game.

In the eighteenth century increasing numbers of Indian people from outside the area were drawn to Arkansas, and the Caddo and Quapaw were unable to stop them. Warfare, disease, and economic and ecological deterioration in the east further stimulated this migration. Native American refugees from the Iroquois wars had poured into the western Ohio Valley in the late seventeenth century,[31] and attracted by the plentiful game and empty forests, various members of the native groups of that region began crossing into northeastern Arkansas to conduct their hunts. Miamis, Peorias, and Piankashaws crossed the Mississippi to hunt the river basin flatlands and the eastern portions of the Ozark Plateau. In the south Chickasaw and Choctaw raiders began hunting in the Ouachita and the southern Ozark Mountains.

Events on the European stage, meanwhile, were about to bring further changes to Arkansas's native populations. In 1756 the French went to war with the British and, despite the support of many Indian tribes, were defeated and forced to leave North America. In the Treaty of Paris (1763), the British acquired Canada and Illinois and gave Spain all French holdings west of the Mississippi River, including the Arkansas region. Although the cession occurred in 1763, Spanish officials failed to arrive in Arkansas until 1769, and for several years there was very little dramatic change. Indeed, the first orders to the commander of Louisiana contained a directive that the local commanders should speak with the Indians and assure them that little change had taken place, "in order that they might understand that no innovations being made in anything."[32]

There were to be changes, however, in that the Indians and their resources were to be exploited by the Spanish alone. Unlike the French system, the state closely supervised colonial activity, and economic exploitation was not to be directed by private investment companies. Indian trade was regulated by government officials and conducted within the Spanish mercantile framework. Spain licensed her traders and expected them to behave according to colonial law.

The traffic in slaves and livestock was forbidden, considered to be too disruptive in the Spanish colonies. Both engendered violence, and most of the horses and mules exchanged in Louisiana were stolen from Spanish colonies in Texas and New Mexico. Colonial officials imposed new restrictions on the firearms trade, allowing Indians only enough arms and ammunition to hunt but not to wage war.[33] Many of the restrictions were ignored in Arkansas, and since there was never a large Spanish presence at Arkansas Post, those intent on ignoring these laws could usually do so. The horse trade continued, and the commerce in deer skins grew.

By the late eighteenth century, British traders had moved to the Mississippi Valley and frequently crossed into Spanish Arkansas to do business with the Quapaw and Caddo. In 1776 Jean Blommart, a leading merchant in Pensacola, established a trading post across the Mississippi from the mouth of the White River. That same year another Englishman established a temporary station along the Arkansas River at El Cadron.[34] British and French merchants operating out of Canada continued to travel into Arkansas for the remainder of the colonial period.

Despite the new policies, Spanish trade restrictions were not uniformly or strictly enforced, and the market for slaves and livestock persisted. With authorities clamping down in St. Louis, Ste. Geneviève, and Natchitoches, the traders moved to where there was less Spanish control; Arkansas Post, which was isolated and poorly manned, became a gathering point for those who refused to obey the new regulations.[35] At Natchitoches, along the Red River, and the other Spanish posts in the region, Lt. Gov. Athanase de Mézières strictly enforced the laws. Consequently, those agents operating out of Natchitoches among the Hasinai and Kadohadacho were not allowed to barter for slaves or livestock, and their business in firearms was limited. Many could not abide these controls and were thus attracted to Arkansas Post.

The restrictions on firearms trade at Natchitoches and other posts in that area seriously eroded the position of the Red River Caddo, who fell victim to increased Osage aggression. The better-armed Osage took advantage of the Caddo weakness and continually raided their villages on the Red River and their camps in the Ouachitas. Spanish records from Natchitoches were filled with reports of these attacks: "Thus, all at once this district has become a pitiful theater of outrageous robberies and bloody encounters."[36] The economic opportunities were so great in the south that in the 1760s a group of Osage permanently left their northern prairie villages and moved to the Arkansas River valley (around present-day Muskogee). From these bases, the attacks on the Caddo and Wichita accelerated.

Osage raiders heading south sometimes detoured through the Ouachitas to clear the area of outside hunters. Other times they would skirt the western edge of the mountains until they reached the Red River, and then strike east and west among the widespread Caddo farmsteads. Horses were particularly valued, and in one month alone over 750 were stolen. Attacks were so severe in 1771 and 1772 that most of the Caddo abandoned the Red River and fled south.[37]

On several occasions de Mézières tried to gather the Caddo and the Wichita together to attack the Osage. He planned a fall campaign so that their villages and food could be destroyed before winter. The assaults never occurred, however, for de Mézières returned to France before they were carried out, and his replacement failed to act.[38] The Osage were able to pass unmolested through western Arkansas and attack the Caddo at will, and without any organized resistance, the Caddo continued to suffer from such aggression. In January 1774, the Spanish at Natchitoches reported:

> They [Osage] throw themselves by force on this district. They have tried to pillage the Quitsey (Kichais): they have dispersed them, as it were, by obliging them to take refuge in places hidden and unknown to their enemies. Every day they have parties among the Big and Little Caddo, which being continually tormented, will perhaps also decide to disperse.[39]

Epidemic disease struck the Red River Caddo again in 1777 and devastated an already weakened people. Most of them abandoned the area and moved south to the Sulfur and Trinity Rivers. Throughout the remainder of the eighteenth century, the Osage continued their hammering raids. They disrupted the winter hunt of 1780–81 and stole more horses in 1782–83. In November 1783 the Kichais left and moved south, leaving only the Big Caddo along the Red River.[40] Only in the nineteenth century, when stronger, better-armed tribes from the east moved in among the Caddo in the Red River region, were they able to resist the Osage.

Despite the growing pressures, the Quapaw avoided most conflict with their powerful northern kin, largely because both wanted peace. The Osage needed access to the traders who came to Arkansas Post, and the Quapaw, drastically reduced by European disease, were simply too weak to fight them. Occasional violence occurred when Osage warriors came upon Quapaw hunters. They would often destroy the Quapaw's furs, beat the hunters with bows, and drive them out of the area. These attacks were usually followed by the appearance of the Osage at the Quapaw villages bearing gifts and asking for peace.

Both tribes shared a cultural practice that allowed for the payment of gifts as compensation for death or injury. The Osage not only needed access to trade at Arkansas Post, but they also used the Quapaw as a buffer to blunt or slow the attacks of the Chickasaw and Choctaw. Without them, there would have been no tribe to absorb the blows of the southern Indians who had begun to appear in the region, nor to prevent other tribes from occupying the Lower Arkansas Valley.[41]

Illinois and eastern tribes—such as the Delaware and Shawnee—began crossing the Mississippi in the late eighteenth century in large numbers. Initially, they were temporary hunters, but with the available game and the lack of any real resistance in the area, they began establishing permanent villages in northeastern Arkansas. The Chickasaw and Choctaw also continued to cross the Mississippi into the region and traveled up the Arkansas River to challenge the Osage for hunting rights in the mountain forests.

The Spanish welcomed the Native Americans, for they believed that the eastern Indians would blunt the Osage attacks and serve as a buffer to the expanding Anglo-American frontier. In 1780 they encouraged several Illinois tribes to settle near the eastern edge of the Ozarks along the White and St. Francis Rivers. Other eastern tribes were also invited to Arkansas. In the spring of 1787, a group of Delaware arrived at Arkansas Post and asked permission to settle on the White River. In December 1788 some

"Femme Indienne des Iowas des Missouri."

Crayon sketch inscribed by St. Memin.
Collection of the New-York Historical Society.

"Indien Delaware."

Crayon sketch inscribed by St. Memin.
Collection of the New-York Historical Society.

Miami arrived and were soon followed by another band of Miami who settled along the Ouachita River.[42] In the early 1790s, Louis Lorimier, the Spanish agent at Cape Girardeau, established a sizable Shawnee and Delaware community just north of Arkansas.[43]

As word spread of the abundant game and available unoccupied land, other eastern tribes from as far away as the Carolinas began arriving in the territory. The Cherokee, living in the mountains of Tennessee, Georgia, North Carolina, and South Carolina, appeared along the Lower Arkansas as early as 1786. Small bands hunted in the region, and in 1796 ten Cherokee families, led by Ko-ora-too, moved to the St. Francis River. As conditions became crowded and inhospitable in the east, those Cherokees who wanted to continue their hunting lives joined this western band and later established other communities along the White River.[44]

The Indian immigration continued for the remaining years of the colonial period, and it increased in the nineteenth century after the Louisiana Purchase of 1803. As part of President Thomas Jefferson's plan to ease the pressure and violence on the eastern frontier, he proposed moving eastern tribes into Arkansas. Indeed, the desire to remove these Indians had been part of the motivation for territorial expansion.

Historians have often overlooked an important element of the unfortunate Removal Policy: the presence of the western Indians, who lived and hunted on the lands where the United States planned to move the eastern tribes. Before they could be uprooted, room had to be made for them in the West. With powerful Indian tribes occupying the regions north of the Ozark Plateau, Jefferson looked to newly acquired Arkansas as a potential home for the eastern Indians, as it still contained an abundance of game and remained relatively void of human habitation. With the Caddo driven out and only the Quapaw and Osage living along the periphery, the territory was seen as an ideal place to move the eastern tribes.

Jefferson and his successors worked to convince the Quapaw and Osage to give up their claims on Arkansas land and aggressively encouraged the eastern people to move there. Lured to its vacant forests and rich bottom lands, and pushed both by the Anglo-American settlers and unofficial administration policy, hundreds of eastern Indians moved to Arkansas well before the Removal Act of 1830 became official United States policy. Shawnee, Delaware, Choctaw, Chickasaw, and Cherokee flocked to the region, but these tribes would not be allowed to linger. The land was simply too valuable and too attractive to the Euro-Americans, and immigrant tribes were allowed only brief stays in Arkansas before they, too, were pushed west, thereby being denied the opportunities of the region.

Protohistoric Tunican Indians in Arkansas

MICHAEL P. HOFFMAN

By the fifteenth and sixteenth centuries, Native Americans of the Arkansas Mississippi alluvial valley had achieved the highest cultural level on the continent north of Mexico. Chiefdoms, which extended over hundreds of square miles, included thousands of kinsmen. Haughty, powerful chiefs controlled diverse resources and supervised their uses. Formalized warfare for the acquisition of territory was common. Large town centers contained temples, public buildings, and chiefs' houses elevated on large earthen mounds. A complex religion that focused on the sun, ancestor worship, warfare, and fertility permeated all aspects of society.[1]

When French contact with the native inhabitants of the region began in the last quarter of the seventeenth century, most of eastern Arkansas was uninhabited and the four villages of the Quapaw near the mouth of the Arkansas River represented the only significant ethnic group left. Many questions have been asked about the dramatic changes in eastern Arkansas Indian life between 1500 and 1700, but there have been few definitive answers. Disease, drought, warfare, and migration all have been invoked to explain the decline in population.[2]

One question relating to the period in eastern Arkansas concerns the ethnic identity of the Indians involved. What tribe or tribes were responsible for the great achievements there and what happened to them? Recent, sometimes controversial, research and interpretations by archaeologists indicate that Tunican peoples dominated the eastern half of Arkansas during the first part of the protohistoric period from A.D. 1500 to the middle of the sixteenth century.

The term "protohistoric period" is used by archaeologists specializing

61

in Native Americans of the Southeast to designate the span of two hundred years between A.D. 1500 and 1700, a time of mostly scanty European presence. In Arkansas, this includes the de Soto entrada of 1541–43, which ends the early protohistoric period; the protohistoric "dark ages" between 1543 and 1673 in which there are no European accounts of Arkansas Indians; and the late protohistoric period covering the twenty-seven years of French contact between 1673 and 1700.

Information about Indians of the protohistoric period comes from a variety of written, linguistic, ethnological, and archaeological sources that sometimes correspond and sometimes do not. The narratives of the de Soto expedition and the French accounts of late-seventeenth-century Indians along the Mississippi River supply the only contemporary written sources. Native traditions about habitation and migrations recorded later by whites provide additional accounts of varying accuracy. Linguistic study of native words recorded during European contacts with tribes helps to identify ethnic groups. Language affiliations of tribes also suggest earlier historical relations. Ethnologists familiar with comparative tribal customs contribute to protohistoric identifications and suggest earlier relationships based on similarities and differences. Bioarchaeologists who study skeletons recovered in archaeological projects make available information about biological distances of protohistoric populations and marriage practices which may correlate to ethnic groups. Finally, archaeology, excavation, and analysis and interpretation of cultural remains, provides a major source of information about Indians of the protohistoric period. The ideal method of establishing a tribal archaeological identity is the "direct historical approach," in which a historically well-documented tribal community is excavated in order to associate it with an archaeological complex. Then it is assumed that other sites with similar artifact complexes were occupied by the same or related ethnic groups. However, this approach has rarely been possible in Arkansas because of the perturbations of the protohistoric period—massive population decline, migrations, warfare, and tribal amalgamations and extinctions.

Tunican refers to a group of associated native languages of the Lower Mississippi River valley which are unrelated or perhaps very distantly related to other Native American language divisions. Most of the languages of the Tunican division and most of the Lower Mississippi Valley tribes who spoke them have been extinct since the late eighteenth century. Included are such groups as the Koroa (who were present in eastern Arkansas in the seventeenth century), the Yazoo, Tioux, and Grigra (who were so decimated by the French and Indian allies in their war with the Natchez that survivors were absorbed by neighboring non-Tunican tribes),[3] and the Tunica, who resided at the mouth of the Yazoo River in western Mississippi in 1699.[4] Only the latter survived. The word *tunica* means "people," and in several variations (*Tonika, Tanika, Tanikwa, Tanico*) it was a term that Europeans used generally for people who spoke the distinctive Tunican languages.[5]

A great deal of research has been done in this century on the language, lifestyles, and history of the Tunicas. At the turn of the century, John Swanton compiled early European accounts of them and performed limited ethnographic fieldwork on the group near Marksville, Louisiana.[6] Linguist Mary Haas compiled a Tunica dictionary and published works on their myths and religion in the 1940s and 1950s.[7] The principal recent scholar of the tribe is Jeffrey Brain, an archaeologist and ethnohistorian from the Peabody Museum at Harvard University, which has had a research program in the Lower Mississippi Valley since the 1930s. Over the last twenty years, Brain has been able to trace the tribe's archaeological and historical presence from its current location at Marksville on the Red River to areas near the mouth of the Red River in Louisiana and the mouth of the Yazoo River in western Mississippi, where the tribe had moved in 1699.[8] Particularly at the Trudeau site in Louisiana, which was occupied between 1731 and 1764, native manufactured ceramics and other artifacts provide a basis for the definition of an archaeological complex characteristic of the tribe that is useful for making comparisons to Arkansas materials.[9]

Brain has been unable to document the Tunica prior to 1699 through his own fieldwork nor can he document overwhelming evidence of ceramic continuity. Leaping past the "dark ages" of the protohistoric period, he identifies the Tunica with the western Mississippi de Soto–era entity of Quiz Quiz, which he locates on the Sunflower River drainage near Clarksdale in northwestern Mississippi.[10] This identification is based on a remark in the de Soto narratives that the *men* worked the fields at Quiz Quiz (unusual in the Southeast but characteristic of the later Tunica); on Tunica traditions that they once lived farther north near the Mississippi River; and on the fact that Choctaw and Chickasaw peoples referred to Mississippian culture sites near Clarksdale as "Tunica Oldfields." Brain concludes that Tunicans were present during the sixteenth century in eastern Arkansas as well.[11]

John Swanton and Arkansas historian Samuel D. Dickinson have long recognized a protohistoric Tunican presence in Arkansas,[12] but that theory has only recently been considered in depth. Marvin Jeter of the Arkansas Archaeological Survey has examined this possibility extensively, particularly for southeastern Arkansas and the Lower Arkansas River valley.[13] Robert Rankin, a linguist at the University of Kansas, has recently renewed

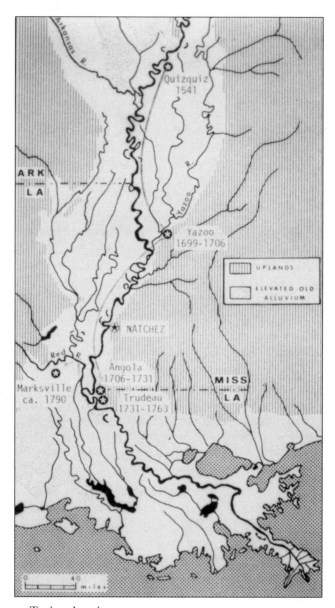

Tunican locations, 1541 to present.

Reproduced from Jeffrey P. Brain, "On the Tunica Trail,"
Department of Louisiana Archaeological Survey and Antiquities
Commission, Anthropological Study 1, (Baton Rouge, 1988).
Courtesy of the University of Arkansas Museum, Fayetteville.

1732 drawing of Tunican chief, Bride les Boeufs. Also shown are the wife and son of the Tunicas' great chief, Cahura Joligo, who was killed during a Natchez raid the previous spring.

Peabody Museum, Harvard University.

Swanton's argument that Pacaha and other towns visited by de Soto in northeastern Arkansas were Tunican.[14] Finally, the author is doing major research on the Tunicans and the Quapaw of eastern Arkansas.[15]

While most archaeologists have linked protohistoric remains in the Middle and Lower Arkansas River valley with the Quapaw, there is good evidence that until the mid-seventeenth century Tunicans were the dominant native population in the area.[16] The former, widely-accepted view is based primarily on the identification by James Ford of the Menard site near the mouth of the Arkansas River as the Quapaw village of Osotouy.[17] Ford carefully compared French descriptions with topographic features to reach his conclusions. He studied material that had previously been excavated from the site, did his own excavations, and found European trade goods there, a fact that seemed to cement the Osotouy identification. Ford concluded that the Mississippi and protohistoric-period materials from Menard were those of the Quapaw tribe as were similar materials found nearby. Philip Phillips[18] subsequently labeled the complex the "Quapaw phase." Other specialists recognized about two dozen additional sites in the area adjacent to the mouth of the Arkansas River to just above Little Rock. A somewhat similar archaeological unit along the Arkansas River between Little Rock and Ozark, the Carden Bottoms phase, also was determined to have been related to the Quapaw people.[19]

Recently, however, reservations have been raised about the identification of the "Quapaw phase" with that tribe.[20] One problem, popularly referred to as the "Quapaw Paradox," was that the ceramics of the phase revealed strong ties to native eastern Arkansas late-Mississippian cultures, while tribal traditions and linguistic and ethnological ties indicated strong recent Quapaw links with other Dhegiha Siouan tribes outside the Lower Mississippi Valley. The four villages on the Mississippi, or a short distance upstream from the mouth of the Arkansas River, described in the late seventeenth century by the French[21] correlated poorly to the many protohistoric sites distributed along the Arkansas River up to the vicinity of Little Rock. Also, the distinctive Quapaw long bark-covered house has not been evidenced in the excavations.[22]

Because of these inconsistencies, Arkansas archaeologists who work in the region have abandoned the term "Quapaw phase" in favor of the more neutral "Menard Complex." Many believe that intensive study of these remains will result in the division of the Menard Complex into several more precisely defined cultural units.[23]

Tunicans were certainly on the Lower Arkansas River in the protohistoric period. The Marquette map not only places Quapaw villages

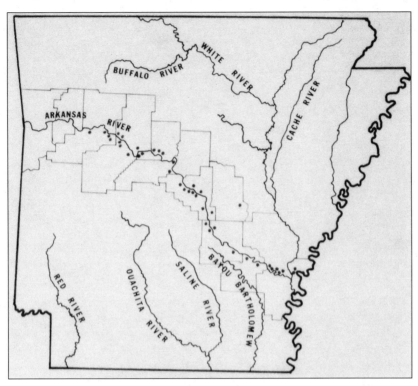

Protohistoric phases along the Arkansas River.
Courtesy of the University of Arkansas Museum, Fayetteville.

on both sides of the Mississippi River, but it indicates a series of non-Quapaw villages some distance up the Arkansas River.[24] Two of these, Tanika and Akoroa, are clearly Tunican. Linguist Robert Rankin relates a third, Papikaha, to the northeastern Arkansas Pacah of the de Soto era of the previous century which he also thinks was Tunican-speaking.[25] As Marvin Jeter has noted, later French sources make no mention of Tunicans on the Arkansas, but the La Salle expedition learned in 1682 of some Tunica and Koroa living at the mouth of the Yazoo River in Mississippi.[26] Quapaw tradition provides an explanation for these late seventeenth-century distributions. In the 1820s Paheka, the grandfather of the Quapaw principal chief, related the following to George Izard:

> The first red skins [Indians] whom we met with were settled some way below the Ny-Whoutteh-Junka [the Little Muddy River, now the St. Francis]; they were called Tonnika. We attacked and put them to flight.

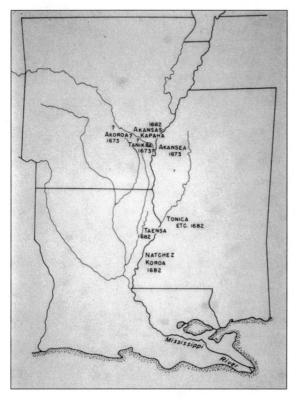

Approximate locations of Indian groups contacted or recorded by Jolliet and Marquette in 1673 and La Salle in 1682.

Reproduced from Marvin Jeter, "Tunicans West of the Mississippi," *The Protohistoric Period in the Mid-South, 1500–1700,* ed. David H. Dye and R. C. Brister (Jackson, Miss., 1986). Courtesy of the University of Arkansas Museum, Fayetteville.

Some time afterwards we entered this river, which we call Ny-Jitteh [Red River, now the Arkansas]. We soon discovered that there were other red skins in the country. Parties were sent out to look for them. They were found encamped in the Great Prairie [between the Post of Arkansas and the town of Little Rock]. We attacked them; they made a valiant resistance, but we beat them and drove them away. This nation called itself Intouka; the whites at that period gave them the name of Illinois. Then we were left entire masters of this country.[27]

A Quapaw informant told Izard that the grandfather of the principal chief was the leader in the migration to eastern Arkansas.[28] While it is impossible for that genealogical assertion to be correct chronologically, it does suggest fairly recent events.

If the Morse-Hudson route of the de Soto expedition in Arkansas[29] is accepted and "the River of the Cayas" is the Arkansas River, then there is good evidence that Tunicans were on the river in the 1540s. The chiefdom of Cayas-Tanico, which Hudson[30] locates at Carden Bottoms near

Dardanelle, is widely accepted as such.[31] Jeter, in developing a "maximum Tunican" scenario, includes other Arkansas River and Central Arkansas towns visited by the de Soto expedition.[32] The Carden Bottoms locality has yielded a sixteenth-century brass bell type called a "Clarksdale Bell," as well as other early brass artifacts and glass beads.[33]

Until very recently, archaeological investigations of protohistoric sites along the Arkansas River were thirty to fifty years old and reflected pre-modern techniques and perspectives.[34] Significant excavations at the Goldsmith Oliver Site 2 (3PU306) were necessitated, however, by the expansion of Adams Field airport at Little Rock in 1987. Marvin Jeter, the senior person responsible for the analysis and write-up of the site, reported that a successful broad scale, multidisciplinary analysis was conducted by specialists in bioarchaeology, historical artifacts identification, botany, and zoology.[35]

The excavation revealed evidence of both domestic and mortuary activities. Although no complete house outlines were formed, postholes and burned clay, called daub, point to the presence of wattle and daub dwellings.[36] The site apparently served as a residence for at least a few family units. Archaeologists found sixteen human burials with eighteen individuals, along with grave offerings that included European trade goods, pottery, and other artifacts of the Menard Complex very similar to those found at the Kinkead-Mainard site a few miles upstream.[37] Among the few trade items were seven glass beads that were dated to the first half of the seventeenth century.[38] A thorough bioarchaeological analysis of the skeletons at the site by Barbara Burnett revealed an unhealthy, biologically stressed population lacking adequate nutrition, with young women and children being particularly affected. Burnett attributes these problems "to the cumulative effects of cultural disintegration that impacted subsistence practices" rather than directly to epidemic disease introduced by European contact.[39] Floral analysis indicated that maize was the main plant food, and a study of faunal remains suggested that hunting large game such as deer and bison and the taking of large fish such as catfish and gar were important. The Goldsmith-Oliver 2 site provided solid evidence for an early seventeenth-century community affiliated culturally with others in the Lower Arkansas and adjacent Mississippi river valleys.

Ceramics from protohistoric sites provide additional evidence of Tunican presence along the Arkansas River. Some show similarities to those defined by Brain as characteristic of the Tunica in Mississippi and Louisiana, including widespread occurrence of his "Tunica mode," a horizontal row or rows of punctuations on the neck or rim of vessels, and pottery similar to the "Winterville Incised" type, a style that includes incised

Tunican-related pottery from the Kinkead-Mainard site.
Courtesy of the University of Arkansas Museum, Fayetteville.

guilloches, festoons, and concentric circles.[40] There also are pottery shapes
and design styles in protohistoric Arkansas River sites that are not part of
their ceramic complex. These reflect indigenous Arkansas River Tunican
trade with adjacent peoples like the Caddo of the Ouachita Mountains.[41]

Arguments against this presence along the Arkansas River could be
made by those who do not accept the Morse-Hudson route. While contemporary Arkansas archaeologists generally accept that route, there are ardent
proponents of variations of the model first proposed by John Swanton.[42]
In their view the River of the Cayas was the Ouachita River and Tanico
was near modern Hot Springs. Thus far no archaeological complexes have
been identified in this region that are similar to Brain's Tunica sites in
Mississippi and Louisiana. There are many known locations, but the late
ones are all of the Caddoan culture.

Northeastern Arkansas, the area of the Mississippi Alluvial Plain north
of the mouth of the Arkansas River, was heavily populated in late prehistoric and early protohistoric times, but was virtually abandoned by the latter
part of the seventeenth century. The de Soto narratives give impressive
descriptions of the grandeur of the complex Indian towns and polities in
northeastern Arkansas—such as Pacaha, Casqui, and Quiguate.[43]

Scholars still debate the ethnic affinities of these chiefdoms, particularly that of Pacaha. Linguist Robert Rankin, following Swanton, has developed a strong case that none of the towns or chiefdoms recorded in the de
Soto narratives reflect Siouan words and thus the Dhegiha Siouan Quapaw
were either missed by the expedition's meanderings in eastern Arkansas

or had not yet immigrated to the region.[44] Three Indian words that the Spanish recorded at Pacaha—*mochila, macanoche,* and *caloosa*—reflect Tunican phonology, phonetics, and semantics, not those of the Siouan-speaking Quapaw.[45] Dan and Phyllis Morse, who prefer to use Garcilaso's second-hand-account term *Capaha* for Pacaha (in order to make a phonetic connection with *Ogaxpa,* or "Quapaw"), suggest that the three words were those of Tunican interpreters and did not express the native tongue of Pacaha.[46]

The Morses have attempted in their investigations since 1969 to identify protohistoric sites in northeastern Arkansas with the towns of the de Soto narratives, and appear to have been largely successful.[47] Archaeological evidence to date indicates that structures in these protohistoric villages were constructed of wattle and daub as done by Tunicans, and not with pole and bark covering, a distinctive characteristic of the Quapaw.[48] Pottery from protohistoric northeastern Arkansas sites is generally similar to the sixteenth-century northwestern Mississippi areas that Brain has identified as representing the Tunican chiefdom of Quiz Quiz.[49] Thus, there is linguistic and archaeological evidence that there were Tunicans in sixteenth-century northeastern Arkansas. Based on these data, Jeter includes almost all of the de Soto–era towns in northeastern Arkansas in his "maximum Tunica" realm.[50]

Marvin Jeter has brought together information supporting the presence of Tunicans in southeastern Arkansas as well during the protohistoric period.[51] In the late part of the period, during early French contact, there are two references to Arkansas Tunicans. Joutel and other survivors of the Texas expedition of La Salle were told of a Tunican village on the Lower Ouachita River in Arkansas.[52] In 1690, Henri de Tonty twice visited Koroan villages near Bayou Bartholomew (located in extreme South Arkansas near the Louisiana state line).[53] Thus, according to French accounts, Tunicans were in Southeast Arkansas at least until 1690 and perhaps until a few years later.[54]

Documentary evidence for their presence in southeastern Arkansas during the early protohistoric period is much more equivocal. The Morse-Hudson route postulated for the de Soto expedition in the state places Tanico and Coligua on or near the Arkansas (River of the Cayas) and not along the Ouachita.[55] The other major alternative, the Swanton-Brain route, places Tanico and Coligua in the Ouachita River drainage of the Ouachita Mountains.[56] In this scenario, Tanico was at Hot Springs, a logical postulate on geographical grounds, since the community was associated with salt springs. Jeter presented this view in 1986, but by 1989 had changed his position and agreed that the Arkansas River was the River of the Cayas.[57]

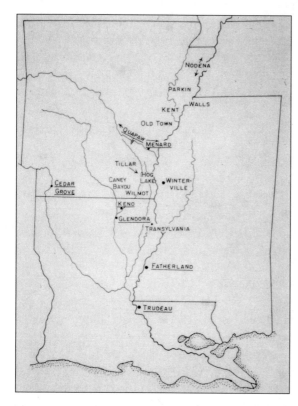

Late prehistoric, protohistoric, and early historic archaeological sites and phases. The underlined names indicate sites or phases which have produced evidence of the historic period (post-1700) occupation.

Jeter postulates that the Tiller and Hog Lake phases of Bayous Bartholomew and Macon in southeastern Arkansas represent Tunican peoples of the fifteenth to seventeenth centuries.[58] His argument is based in part on the fact that these tribes were observed in the area by Europeans during this period. There are also important ceramic similarities in pottery attributed by Brain to the Tunica at the mouth of the Yazoo River and at the Trudeau site near the mouth of the Red River in Louisiana. These similarities include the Tunica mode as well as distinctive varieties of Winterville Incised.[59] The Tiller and Hog Lake complexes are both based on mortuary data excavated primarily by early archaeologists working for the Smithsonian Institution or by later amateurs, and have not been precisely dated. The absence or near absence of European trade items probably places the complexes before 1650.

In summary, there is evidence from written accounts that Tunicans were in southeastern Arkansas during the latter part of the seventeenth century, but they had left the region by 1700 or shortly thereafter. The

Swanton-Brain version of de Soto's route places the group during the early protohistoric period near the Ouachita River in the mountains, an area thus far devoid of archaeological remains that resemble those attributed to Tunican peoples in other areas. The Morse-Hudson de Soto route in Arkansas includes only Caddoan-speaking people in the Ouachita Mountains, an interpretation that the archaeology confirms. The Tiller and Hog Lake complexes of Bayous Bartholomew and Macon of the 1500–1650 period show significant ceramic similarities with slightly later archaeological manifestations in western Mississippi and eastern Louisiana associated with the historic Tunica tribe.

This survey of the evidence for protohistoric-period Tunican presence in Arkansas indicates that these people were in the Mississippi and Arkansas Valleys between 1500 and 1543. Sometime in the last half of the sixteenth century or shortly thereafter, their population in northeastern Arkansas disappeared. Tunicans were responsible for known protohistoric remains along the Arkansas River and still had several communities upstream from its mouth in 1673. Later seventeenth-century French accounts do not mention these Indians on the Arkansas River, so it can be presumed that they had disappeared during the last quarter of that century. Two French accounts attest to the presence of Tunicans along Bayou Bartholomew and Bayou Macon in Southeast Arkansas, but the group was gone by 1700. The last quarter of the seventeenth century found the tribe located at the mouth of the Yazoo River in Mississippi, presumably having attracted Tunicans from Arkansas. The Koroa of Northeast Louisiana and adjacent Arkansas were associating themselves with the Natchez of Mississippi at the same time.[60]

There were probably several reasons for these Tunican movements. In northeastern Arkansas the dislocations of the de Soto entrada must have been significant. While epidemic disease has been linked with population decline in the late sixteenth century, this has not been confirmed by bioarchaeological analysis (although there is some doubt that late sixteenth-century populations have actually been examined).[61] On the basis of tree ring information, Burnett and Murray speculate that sixteenth-century drought stimulated the abandonment of northeastern Arkansas,[62] but this theory has yet to be seriously analyzed. Another possibility for the Tunican abandonment of northeastern (and later all of eastern Arkansas) is displacement by the Quapaw. According to Quapaw tribal traditions, they moved from the north downstream into Arkansas, fighting and displacing Tunicans as they went. This pressure on northeastern Arkansas tribes may have begun in the late sixteenth century and continued throughout the region. There was still warfare even after the Tunicans left Arkansas. In 1702 Koroas killed

Father Nicolas Foucault, who was a missionary to the Quapaws, and in retaliation the Quapaws nearly wiped them out.[63]

This incursion theory of the abandonment of Arkansas by Tunicans cannot as yet be demonstrated archaeologically since no known complex is currently widely accepted as representing the Quapaw tribe. Brain has recently discussed this problem and postulates that a protohistoric stone tool complex called the Oliver Complex (after a site in Mississippi), consisting of small snub-nose end scrapers, leaf-shaped arrow points called Nodena points, stone pipe drills, and large triangular knives, may represent the Quapaw archaeologically.[64] These stone tools, not present in earlier deposits, may indicate the presence of Quapaw men who drove off Tunican males and married their women (thus creating ceramic continuity and stone tool discontinuity).[65] Brain argues that this combination was first evidenced in northeastern Arkansas in the sixteenth century and then spread southward with the advance of the Quapaw.

Jeter considers Brain's scenario unlikely because the Nodena points occur in northeastern Arkansas archaeological contexts in the fourteenth century, and the knives may simply be preforms for Nodena points.[66] The snub-nose scrapers are very late and may be associated with hide dressing activities of the European-stimulated deerskin trade that involved several ethnic groups rather than being distinctive of Quapaws. If intermarriage had taken place on a large scale, Tunican words should have been collected in Quapaw vocabularies; they were not. If Brain's Oliver Complex–Quapaw identification is incorrect, the perplexing problem of archaeological identity remains. It probably will not be solved until eighteenth-century Quapaw sites are found and excavated, and scientists are able to work back in time from a clear base line.

Jeter's "maximum Tunican"[67] interpretation is not proved, nor even generally accepted. A major difficulty with the hypothesis is that there is considerable archaeological variation in the protohistoric period materials from the large area that he regards as representing Tunican peoples. All of these materials are generally of late Mississippian culture, which in ceramics means shell-tempered vessels of a variety of shapes, including bottles, jars, and bowls decorated with incised, punctuated appliqué, and occasionally engraved and painted designs. Beyond that, however, the ceramics of sixteenth-century northeastern Arkansas are not closely similar to contemporary pottery along the Arkansas River valley, northwestern Mississippi, southeastern Arkansas, or northeastern Louisiana, all of which are considered to be in the "maximum Tunican" area. The extent to which ceramic similarity should reflect ethnic or linguistic homogeneity is unknown, but there is considerable variation in the "maximum Tunican" region. A nearby tradition firmly associated with a language group is that of the Caddo, which is represented by a distinctive less-varied ceramic complex and covers an area of Southwest Arkansas and adjacent parts of Texas, Louisiana, and Oklahoma in the 900–1700 period. However, there has been much debate recently about whether generally similar late prehistoric archaeological remains of the southwestern Ozarks and adjacent Arkansas River valley also represent materials ancestral to speakers of the grater Caddoan language family.[68]

Bioarchaeologists can lend an independent perspective on the question of whether peoples were related in the "maximum Tunican" area through an examination of nonmetric skeletal traits, from which they can postulate genetic distance. Two such studies have been attempted comparing Arkansas River Menard Complex protohistoric human remains with remains from northeastern Arkansas and the Caddo area of southwestern Arkansas.[69] The results are difficult to interpret. Menard Complex traits from sites in the Arkansas River valley are generally more similar to each other than they are to those of the other locations. More comparative studies are necessary, however, for the data to be meaningful.

The Tunican saga can be perceived as a tragedy both in Arkansas and later in Mississippi and Louisiana. By the seventeenth century European contact had brought disease, cultural disintegration, biological stress, extinctions, and amalgamations to the once populous, culturally dominant chiefdoms. The fewer than three hundred contemporary Tunican survivors are extensively intermarried with non-Indians, often economically disadvantaged, and have lost their language.[70]

Not all of Tunican history is tragedy, however. They have survived as an ethnic group while many Lower Mississippi River tribes have not. In spite of declining numbers the tribe was a powerful ally of the French in the seventeenth and eighteenth centuries and important in the salt, horse, and European goods trade.[71] There has been a revival of Tunica ethnicity, and the tribe won a long battle for recognition by the federal government in 1981.[72] In a display of solidarity they won another long struggle that involved the tribe, a pot hunter, professional archaeologists, and the state of Louisiana in a dispute over ownership of the "Tunica treasure," a hoard of grave goods from the Trudeau site.[73] The "treasure" as well as other artifacts are now proudly exhibited in a museum, part of a modern tribal complex funded by the federal government. Traditional crafts and ceremonies are also being revived. Tunican history will continue.

Rituals of Encounter:

Interpreting Native American Views of European Explorers

GEORGE SABO III

Native Americans often welcomed European explorers into their villages with elaborate greeting ceremonies. These ceremonies reflect the Native American view of Europeans and the processes through which they were incorporated into indigenous social systems. We are fortunate that late seventeenth-century Frenchmen participating in La Salle's famous exploration and settlement ventures left detailed descriptions of greeting ceremonies they participated in when they encountered two native Arkansas tribes—Quapaws and Caddos.[1] When considered from the viewpoint of comparative anthropology, these ceremonies provide valuable insights concerning the diverse cultural perspectives Native Americans brought to their encounters with Europeans.

Following the initial French exploration by Jolliet and Marquette of the Mississippi River to its confluence with the Arkansas in 1673, René-Robert Cavelier, Sieur de La Salle, was granted in 1677 a trading concession in the lands "through which a way may be found to Mexico."[2] Over the next few years La Salle succeeded in establishing bases in Illinois country for his trading and exploration ventures, from which he commenced his famous voyage down the Mississippi that reached its mouth on April 7, 1682.

Our interest in this voyage begins about a month before the explorers reached the Gulf Coast. On March 12, La Salle's canoes, carrying approximately forty Frenchmen and their Illinois guides, passed through a dense fog as they came upon the Quapaw village of Kappa, located on the west bank of the Mississippi River above the mouth of the Arkansas.[3] When they heard what sounded like the chanting of war songs, the apprehensive

Frenchmen struck for the opposite shore where, upon landing, they began to fell trees for the construction of a protective barricade. The Quapaws quickly sent out observers in a canoe, but soon mutual fear gave way to friendly interaction as the two groups exchanged calumets of peace and the explorers were invited into the village.[4]

Quapaw Indians were agriculturists and hunters who occupied four large villages in the vicinity of the Arkansas and Mississippi Rivers' confluence at the time of French contact. Villages consisted of multifamily, bark-covered longhouses surrounding an open plaza where public gatherings and ceremonies were held. Agricultural fields were located nearby. The residents were organized by patrilineal descent into twenty-one named clans, each with a guardian spirit—typically an animal or some element of nature—which conferred rights to perform specific rituals for the benefit of the entire community. The clans were divided into two intermarrying divisions, or moieties, called the Sky People and the Earth People. Longhouses occupied by members of these divisions were arranged on opposite sides of the village. This spatial arrangement, along with clan performance of rituals which sustained the entire web of relationships connecting human and spiritual communities, reflected the Quapaw ideal of the tribe as a unified whole that was greater than the sum of its constituent parts.

The Quapaws fed the Frenchmen on their arrival in Kappa, constructed cabins for their use, and on the following day honored La Salle and his men with a formal and highly ceremonious reception. They began with a calumet dance. Nicolas de La Salle,[5] a member of the expedition but no relation to its leader, provided a detailed description of the ceremony:

> In order to dance the calumet they all come into the place, especially the warriors, and the chiefs set poles all about . . . and upon them display what they intend to give. They brought two calumets adorned with plumage of all colors, and red stones full of tobacco. . . . These were given to the chiefs, who were in the middle of the place. These chiefs and the warriors have gourds full of pebbles and two drums, which are earthen pots covered with dressed skin. The first began a song accompanied by the chime of their gourds. These having ended, others struck up the same thing; then those who have done brave deeds go to a post set in the midst of the place and smite it with their tomahawks. And, after relating their gallant achievements, they gave presents to M. de La Salle, for whom they made the festival. . . .
>
> Meanwhile the chiefs are smoking the calumet and are having it carried to everyone in succession to smoke. M. de La Salle received fifty or sixty oxhides. The Frenchmen, with the exception of M. de La Salle,

also struck the post, relating their valorous deeds, and made gifts from that which M. de La Salle had given them for the purpose.[6]

This ceremony was followed by a feast and additional exchanges of gifts. The Frenchmen learned of three other Quapaw villages located nearby. La Salle made it known that he represented Louis XIV the king of the great French nation. On the following day, March 14, he "took possession" of the land with appropriate ceremony: Father Zénobe Membré, the Franciscan priest who served as chaplain, sang *"O crux, ave, spes unica"*; the Frenchmen moved in a procession that went three times around the open square of the village; they erected a cross and a wooden monument carrying the royal coat of arms and an inscription; La Salle read a proclamation; and, at appropriate points during the proceeding, his men shouted *"Vive le Roy!"* and discharged volleys of musket fire.[7]

La Salle's entourage left Kappa four days later, accompanied by two Quapaw guides. Continuing down the Mississippi, they passed by a second village, Tongigua, whose occupants were away hunting. Ascending the Arkansas River, they stopped at a third Quapaw village, Tourima, where they spent the night. The guides remained with the Frenchmen until they reached the villages of their allies, the Taensas Indians, a week later.[8] Following a successful descent to the mouth of the Mississippi, La Salle and his companions returned to the Quapaw villages. This time they were treated to feasts of dog meat—a special honor among the Quapaws reserved for those with warrior status. The Frenchmen also noticed that the cross they had planted earlier at Kappa was now surrounded by a circle of stakes.[9]

The documents produced in connection with La Salle's encounter with the Quapaws furnish a valuable record of ritual performances with distinctive symbolic significance. The primary elements of their greeting ceremonies—the use of the calumet, the pole striking ceremony, feasts, and gift exchanges—have consistent sets of meaning among Dhegiha-speaking Siouan tribes in which the Quapaws are included.[10]

French explorers and Native Americans attached different meanings to the use of the calumet. For the French, sharing the calumet was a ritual that served to create bonds of friendship between groups in order to facilitate safe passage, trade, mutual defense, or other forms of alliance.[11] The conceptual underpinnings of this view involved an assumption widely held among early modern Europeans that adversarial relations existed naturally between groups with contesting claims to property rights.[12] From this it may be suggested that French explorers participated in the calumet ritual primarily to mitigate hostilities they assumed the Indians naturally would be inclined to hold against them. In other words, for them the calumet ceremony was a useful element of frontier diplomacy, based on principles of political and economic interaction held by Europeans during the colonial era.

For the Quapaws, the calumet ceremony incorporated some altogether different concepts. In order to interact with outsiders (whether native or European), it was necessary to first confer upon them positions or statuses that existed within the Quapaws' own social system. They determined the appropriate status to assign largely from the kinds of interaction that took place with foreigners. Quapaw social organization was based on relationships of mutual obligation among groups of individuals sharing kinship ties reckoned through the male line. They regarded these lineages as possessing generally equal status. Political decision making, moreover, was placed in the hands of groups of leaders representing clans and moieties. Therefore, order and unity within the tribe was organized according to a principle of complementary opposition in which separate but equal descent lines were linked by the rule of reciprocity. The calumet ceremony served to extend this principle to relations with outsiders through the creation of "fictive" or ancillary kinship relations. Thus, in contrast to European assumptions concerning a natural human order based on adversarialism, the Quapaws brought the institution of kinship and associated concepts of communal order and unity to their first encounters with the French.[13]

The use of two calumets in the Quapaws' ceremonial reception of La Salle and the pole striking ceremony in which his men were invited to participate also represented the concepts of order and unity. Village populations consisted of several patrilineal clans that were combined into two larger divisions, or moieties. A common element of Dhegiha symbolism was to use two calumets to represent the interdependent relationship of the two tribal divisions: one side (the Earth People) maintained custody of the pipes while the other side (the Sky People) possessed the right to fill and light the pipe for ceremonial use. Political and ritual ties between clans and moieties, symbolizing the theme of complementary opposition, served to create a cohesive social entity—the tribe.[14] The use of two calumets thus signified the participation of the clans of both moieties, and hence the unity of the entire tribe, in the creation of an alliance with the French.

The pole-striking ceremony recorded in the account of Nicolas de La Salle represents another ritual shared among Dhegiha tribes, the best known example of which is the Omaha *He'dewachi* ceremony. Although the featured performance of warriors in striking the Sacred Pole would seem to suggest that this ceremony was intended specifically to honor their exploits, this ritual in fact celebrated the mutual dependence among those who performed heroic exploits and the other members of the tribe whose

supportive roles made possible the successes of the warriors. In their author-
itative ethnography of the Omaha tribe, Alice C. Fletcher and Frances La
Flesche state that this ceremony "was a dramatic teaching of the vital force
in union not only for defense but for the maintenance of internal peace and
order."[15] The encouragement the Frenchmen accompanying La Salle
received to participate in this ceremony points again to the fundamental
importance that Quapaws attached to the concepts of order and unity in
their interactions with foreigners, including Europeans. In regard to this
latter point, they may well have perceived the placement of the cross in the
village of Kappa as a French version of the Sacred Pole—the centerpiece
and predominant material symbol of the pole-striking ceremony. If true,
then the fact that this cross subsequently occupied the central point of a
sacred space delineated by a circle of stakes would further underscore the
fundamentally religious outlook that the Quapaws brought to all important
events that transpired in their world, including the arrival of the Europeans.

The feasting and gift giving that followed the calumet and pole-striking
ceremonies symbolically represented the initiation of formal reciprocal relations between the allied groups. Thereafter, generosity, cooperation, and
concern for mutual welfare would be expected components of any interactions between the two groups.[16]

In summary, the symbolic connotations ascribed to the primary
elements of Quapaw greeting ceremonies performed for La Salle and his
associates in 1682 represent important Dhegiha themes concerning tribal
order and unity. Complementary opposition among separate but equal
groups linked by the rule of reciprocity is the dominant theme represented.
It operated as an "ultimate sacred principle"[17] that served to guide social
interaction within a cultural system in which reciprocal relations between
major tribal divisions (lineages, clans, and moieties) gave rise to a unified
whole that was considered to be greater than the sum of its constituent
parts. By extending these principles to interaction with outsiders, the
Quapaws were in effect attempting to confer a similar sense of inviolable
order and unity upon their alliance with the French.

After his successful voyage down the Mississippi, La Salle returned to
France the following year where he enlisted royal support for his plan to
approach the Mississippi by sea. The Crown was especially interested in La
Salle's proposal to establish a colony a safe distance up the river from which
forays could be undertaken toward Spanish Mexico and its rich mines and
shipping lanes.[18]

Sailing from France on August 1, 1684, La Salle bypassed the mouth of
the Mississippi, whether intentionally or by mistake, and landed the

following February a considerable distance to the west in Matagorda Bay along the south coast of Texas. Here he established the settlement of Fort St. Louis, populated by approximately 130 men, women, and children. Conditions at the isolated settlement became so precarious by the spring of 1686 that La Salle decided to lead a group of twenty of his most able and trustworthy companions across land in search of a route to "his river,"[19] which they could then ascend to reach supply posts in the Illinois territory. Pushing as far as the Caddo Indian region of eastern Texas, La Salle became ill and was forced to return to the coast. He and eight of his company arrived back at Fort St. Louis in August, the others having either deserted or died along the way. On January 12, 1687, La Salle set out again, this time accompanied by seventeen men. On this journey La Salle was murdered by two of his more disenchanted companions before the expedition reached the Caddo villages. Animosities continued to develop as the party pressed on, and a short time after the travelers entered the settlements, La Salle's assassins themselves were murdered. Some of the surviving Frenchmen chose then to remain with the Caddos, but a party of six, including Henri Joutel, Father Anastasius Douay, and La Salle's brother Jean Cavelier, who also was a priest, pushed on through the Caddo region in what is now eastern Texas and southwestern Arkansas and eventually arrived at Arkansas Post, which Henri de Tonty had established among the Quapaws the previous year. Joutel and his companions were ceremoniously received in a number of Caddo villages on their journey.[20]

The seventeenth-century Caddo Indians were agriculturists who lived in dispersed villages—some stretching for miles along major waterways—consisting of several individual farmsteads each surrounded by crop fields and wood lots. A ceremonial area with a temple and the residence of the village leader, or *caddi*, was centrally located within each settlement. Most Caddo communities in the present states of Texas, Oklahoma, Arkansas, and Louisiana, were organized into one of three large confederacies, known as the Hasinai, Kadohadacho, and Natchitoches.[21] The Frenchmen passed first through lands of the Hasinai confederacy. Upon their arrival in these villages, they were taken to assembly houses and questioned by the elders. If word of the travelers' pending arrival was received in time, Joutel and his companions would be met along the road by a procession of elders dressed in formal garments and sometimes flanked by warriors and youths.[22] When they reached the lands belonging to the Kadohadacho confederacy, whose villages were strung along the Red River in extreme eastern Texas and southwestern Arkansas, greeting rituals began to take on a more elaborate character.

As they approached the first Kadohadacho village, the Frenchmen sent ahead a guide to announce their presence, and a welcoming party soon arrived. Among this group was the village headman, mounted on a "handsome gray mare."[23] He led the explorers to the bank of a river where they were told to wait. The headman went back to the village and then returned with a group of elders who wished to carry the Frenchmen the remaining distance (about a quarter of a league) into town. The travelers complied, somewhat reluctantly, after their guides informed them that this was the custom of the country. Jean Cavelier, identified as the leader of the French group, was the first to mount his carrier.

The Caddos took the travelers to the headman's residence, where more than two hundred villagers awaited. Next they explained that visitors were customarily washed upon their arrival, and one of the elders, holding a dish of pure water, cleansed each of the Frenchmen's foreheads. They were then seated on small wood-and-cane platforms that stood about four feet above the ground. Here they were joined by four village leaders who made speeches the travelers were unable to comprehend. Following these proceedings, the Frenchmen distributed gifts of hatchets, knives, glass beads, and needles, and informed their hosts of the destination they hoped to reach and of their wish to trade additional goods for provisions and guides.[24]

After spending a week in the Kadohadacho village, Joutel and his companions set out in a northeasterly direction. A few days later, while stopped to eat along a riverbank, they were met by an Indian who said that he had been sent by the elders of his village. He motioned the Frenchmen to follow him, and soon they were joined by several more Indians who first caressed the travelers and then escorted them into their village.[25] This was a Cahinnio Caddo community located along the Ouachita River in present southwestern Arkansas.[26] The Caddos took the explorers to the headman's house and gave them food, after which the elders who had assembled there also were fed. A crowd of women gathered around to observe the visitors. On the following day, the Caddos gave them gifts of skins and bows in return for the presents they had earlier received from their guests. Later that evening, the Frenchmen witnessed a ceremony the likes of which they had not previously seen.

In this ceremony a company of elders, attended by young men and women, came to the house in which the Frenchmen were lodged bearing a calumet and singing loudly. Entering the house, the group continued to sing and then took Jean Cavelier by the arms, led him out to a specially prepared place, and put great handfuls of grass under his feet. They washed Cavelier's face with pure water from an earthen dish and then seated him on a skin.

The elders took their places around the young priest and the leading elder stuck two forked sticks into the ground across which another stick was laid—all three sticks painted red. They placed two dressed skins—one of buffalo and one of deer—over the sticks and on these laid a calumet. The singing resumed to the accompaniment of hollow gourds filled with gravel. One of the Indians took hold of Cavelier from behind and began to rock him from side to side in time with the music.

The leading elder then brought two young girls to Cavelier, one carrying a necklace or collar band and the other an otter skin. These items were placed on the forked sticks alongside the calumet. The young girls then sat down on either side of Cavelier, facing each other with their legs extended before them. The leading elder placed Cavelier's legs across those of the girls. At the same time, another elder fastened a feather into the hair on the back of the Frenchman's head. All the while the singing continued.

Cavelier eventually became weary at the length of the proceedings and embarrassed about his position astride the two girls. He made signs to his companions to explain to the leading elder that he was not feeling well. This done, two of the Indians took Cavelier back to his house. However, the villagers remained outside of the house throughout the night, continuing their singing, and in the morning retrieved Cavelier in order to continue the ceremony. The leading elder took the calumet and filled it with tobacco, lit it, and held it out to Cavelier, retreating and advancing several times before finally placing it in the priest's hands. Cavelier pretended to smoke and then passed the calumet back. The rest of the Frenchmen took it in turn, followed by the Indians. After all had smoked, the calumet and the painted sticks were wrapped in a skin case and presented to Cavelier with the assurance that he could travel freely among all of the tribes who were the Cahinnios' allies. Joutel made it a point to observe in his narrative that this was the first time the Frenchmen had encountered the use of the calumet on their journey.[27]

The key elements of Caddo greeting ceremonies as witnessed by Joutel and his companions are: the processions of elders and their subordinates out of the villages to meet the Frenchmen, the carrying of Cavelier and his companions into the Kadohadacho village, the cleansing of the visitors upon their arrival in several Caddo villages, the placement of the Frenchmen in positions of honor either on elevated platforms or in the center of a congregation of elders and witnesses, and the performance of the calumet ceremony for Cavelier in the Cahinnio village. These elements of ritual performance indicate that the Caddos, like the Quapaws, considered it necessary to incorporate Europeans into their own social system as a prerequisite for subsequent interaction. The nature of Caddoan greeting ceremonies, however, reflects a social organization based on different principles than those of the Quapaws.

Caddo social organization was rigidly hierarchical, consisting of at least three major classes. These classes included village leaders, subordinate civil officers and other religious specialists, and commoners. The position of *caddi* was inherited. A fourth social class was represented in the position of the *xinesi*—the highest civil and religious authority at the level of the confederacy. Together the *xinesi* and *caddices* constituted a theocracy of leaders whose elite and sacred status provided them the exclusive right and responsibility to interact with the Supreme Being, *Ayo-Caddi-Aymay*, on behalf of their people.[28]

Elite social statuses among the Caddo were demarcated both by physical separation from nonelites, and by the assumption of a sanctified pose by the elites prior to engaging in sacred rituals they alone were authorized to perform. The leaders assumed their sanctified pose through performance of specific purification rites that typically included washing or bathing and the smoking of tobacco. During the performance of sacred rituals, elites usually were enclosed within the village temple, or, when public ceremonies were being performed, seated upon raised platforms erected in the center of the ceremonial grounds. Elevation was associated specifically with sanctity and high status, especially in the context of offering petitions or thanks to the Supreme Being. For example, Caddo families placed blessed food offerings on elevated platforms in their houses when they observed first fruits ceremonies in thanksgiving to *Ayo-Caddi-Aymay*.[29]

The hierarchical organization of Caddo society was symbolically represented when elders, flanked by their subordinates or mounted on horses, greeted the Frenchmen as they approached the villages. The carrying of the Frenchmen into the Kadohadacho village symbolized their incorporation within this system as elites, and the cleansing rituals to which they were subjected, as well as their subsequent placement in elevated or central positions of honor, further illustrates their figurative transformation into the sanctified pose required for interaction with high-status Caddos. These Indians structured their alliances with other groups through elite individuals whose sanctified status gave them the authority to act on behalf of their respective communities.

The calumet ceremony performed for Jean Cavelier in the Cahinnio village, in which the leading elder presented it as a gift to the French priest, represents one of the more elaborate expressions of the hierarchical nature of Caddo society and the practice of cementing alliances via ritually created ties between elite leaders of the newly allied groups. The portion of that ceremony in which Cavelier's extended legs were laid across those of the two young girls perhaps was meant to represent the "rebirth" of the French priest with status equivalent to that of a Caddo leader. In any case, this portion of the ceremony served to create within the French contingent a system of hierarchical ranking like that which ordered the social structure of the Caddo community. The figurative transformation of Cavelier's status made possible the subsequent stages of the ceremony, in which the two recognized leaders—Cavelier and the *caddi*—smoked the calumet to cement the alliance between their respective groups, followed by the presentation of the pipe to Cavelier to guarantee safe passage through the lands of the Caddos' other allies.

After their journey through the Caddo region, the weary travelers finally arrived at Arkansas Post on July 24, 1687. Jean Couture, one of the Frenchmen stationed there, welcomed Joutel and his companions and introduced them to the Quapaws. The Quapaws greeted the group with ceremonies that provided a sharp contrast to those that they had so recently experienced among the Caddos. The day after the Frenchmen arrived, the Quapaws performed a calumet ceremony for Jean Cavelier. To his relief, this time no young girls sat alongside him, nor was he held and rocked in time with the singing. The Indians set up the Sacred Post on the following day, and invited the Frenchmen to participate in the striking ceremony just as La Salle's men had been offered five years earlier. On this occasion, however, the Frenchmen put the Quapaws off, not wanting to accumulate any more skins that might prove burdensome during their planned ascent of the Mississippi.[30]

The Sacred Pole ceremony represents an important difference between Quapaw and Caddo encounters with Europeans. The Quapaw emphasis on group participation illustrates the principle of complementary opposition that creates a reciprocal relationship among groups perceived as being separate but equal. The Caddos, on the other hand, secured alliances through ritual ties established between the elite leaders of allied groups, where each group was perceived as consisting of hierarchically ranked classes of individuals. This difference in basic principles underlying Quapaw and Caddo approaches to the encounter with Europeans is illustrated in Figures 1 and 2. Figure 1 illustrates village organization, in which the Quapaw arrangement of Sky People and Earth People clans forming two "separate but equal" village sides contrasts with the organization of dispersed Caddo communities where a definite "center of power" is represented by the *caddi's* residence and temple. Figure 2 illustrates schematic

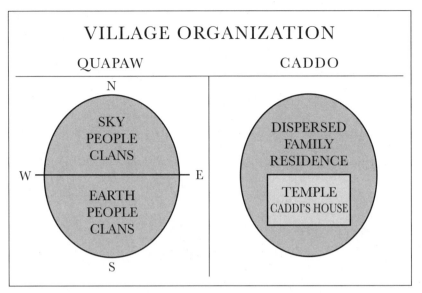

Figure 1.
Schematic diagram of Quapaw and Caddo village organization.

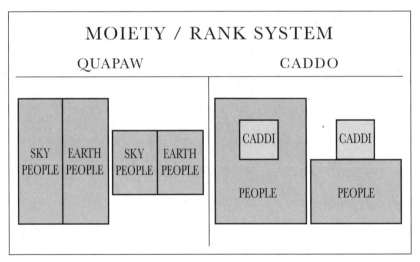

Figure 2.
Schematic diagram of Quapaw moiety system and Caddo rank system.

models of the Quapaw moiety system and the Caddo rank system. The moiety system is depicted as a square divided into two equal halves, which, when turned on its side, represents the complementary, reciprocal relationship connecting them. The Caddo rank system, on the other hand, is depicted as a square with a centralized locus of power represented by the office of the *caddi*. Turned on its side, this figure emphases the vertical, hierarchical relationship among categories of people that the ranking system sustains.

Quapaws and Caddos performed greeting ceremonies in their encounters with La Salle and his associates not merely for purposes of celebration or entertainment, but as "epitomizing events"[31] that conferred upon Europeans positions and statuses within indigenous social systems. By means of such incorporation, Quapaws and Caddos were able to extend to their relations with Europeans those basic principles and themes that ordered and gave shape to their own distinctive societies. But as the foregoing comparison shows, Native Americans did not comprehend Europeans in precisely the same ways: their perceptions were in fact the product of individual cultural patterns. Groups like the Quapaws and Caddos thus responded to Europeans each according to their own unique cultural perspective.

Almost "Illinark"

The French Presence in Northeast Arkansas

GEORGE E. LANKFORD

The realm between New Orleans and Fort de Chartres was shaped like a dumbbell, with population numbers and urban centers concentrated at the two ends. The midpoint on the system was venerable Arkansas Post, which stood near the junction of the Mississippi River with others draining a vast area to the west and northwest. That area has been well studied, but the loss of many of the records of the Post has left knowledge of the colonial development of Arkansas less complete than it should be.[1]

In the late eighteenth century, when French Louisiana became Spanish Louisiana, there were two waves of immigration into the realm west of the Mississippi, the first one the result of the cession of the east bank to the British in 1763 and the second the consequence of the American takeover in the 1780s. The second is known to have brought some new blood to Arkansas Post, but it has not been recognized that it also brought the potential of a significant development in Northeast Arkansas at the foothills of the Ozarks. The evidence of French presence in that area is scant, for the footprints those settlers left are mostly found in the deed records of the early American period, and their presence was short-lived.

Nonetheless, those footprints are there and can be discerned. There is enough evidence to indicate that in the last decade of the Spanish dominion there was a movement into northern Arkansas which could have led to a new population center, an "Illinark," to suggest an inelegant neologism. It may be easier to examine the evidence for this movement by looking at the lives of two different French families, one is an example of the settlers during the French period and the other exemplifies the settlers of the Spanish era.

JOSEPH FRANCOEUR

As Morris Arnold has made clear, through most of the eighteenth century, the military post at the Arkansas, with its accompanying merchants and few farmers, was a small affair. With population at low figures, sometimes incredibly so, and the very walls seemingly always in need of repair from decay and flooding, Arkansas Post was apparently on the verge of destruction for most of its colonial life. It existed for three major reasons: it was a necessary rest stop between the larger colonial populations in Louisiana and Illinois; it provided some military control over the Central Mississippi Valley, thanks to the Quapaw warriors; and it was a necessary entrepôt for the fur trade on the Arkansas and White Rivers. Its role as economic center for the region created an unusual population picture, for the small post usually had the smaller portion of inhabitants; the vast hinterland of valleys and hills held the hunters and their families, who probably outnumbered the Post population in most years.

What makes it difficult to ascertain the demographic relation of Arkansas Post to the scattered entrepreneurs of the fur trade is the fact that the authorities rarely knew for certain who was out there. Several observers through the eighteenth century made it clear that the hunters had created their own forms of government apart from the official structures represented at Arkansas Post. Many of them could think of the Post as the location of creditors whom they could not pay, and they found it advisable to avoid going in for visits. Then, too, the roller-coaster political events—from Osage and Chickasaw depredations to international wars involving the English and Anglo-Americans—called hunters to other parts, and they had no reason to notify the Post of their whereabouts or intentions.

> All persons hunting on the rivers were supposed to return every year as passports were not issued for longer periods. But there were large numbers of hunters who lived for twenty years or more in their camps without ever reporting to the Post. They constituted a large proportion, indeed sometimes a majority, of the European population in Arkansas during the French period.[2]

In the material gathered and published by Arnold and other researchers, few bits of information about the life of hunters surface, but the picture they give of the life of the hunters is more suggestive than carefully drawn.

One figure whose name emerges from the bureaucratic records is Joseph Francoeur. It may be a *dit* name; if so, his "real" name is not given in the published documents.[3] "Joseph" is known only from his daughter's marriage record, as is the fact that his wife was Marie Aimé. His sons had occasion to write several letters to the Spanish authorities in 1770, and they claimed to have lived on the White River for a quarter of a century. That puts them there in 1745, but that may indicate their births rather than the Francoeur occupation of the White, for their father was hunting in Arkansas at least two years earlier than that. In 1743 Anne Catherine Chenalenne, widow of Jean François Lepine, asked for an inventory of his estate so she could give to her daughter Marianne and son-in-law Guillaume Bienvenue, who had lost everything in an attack by the Chickasaw, their share. The inventory was done by Sieurs Louis Giscard *dit* Benoist and Charles Grosillion *dit* Tourangeau for the widow and Sieurs Jean LaFleur *dit* Emmanuelle and Pierre Imbau *dit* Lajeunesse for the children. In addition to "an old house with all the small buildings fit to shelter the cattle, consisting of three small buildings" close to the fort at Arkansas Post, sixteen hundred pounds of tobacco, three black slaves, and "an old crippled Indian woman," the estate contained notes of debts owed Lepine by six hunters, one of whom was "Francoeur." His note, dated March 18, 1743, recorded a debt of two hundred livres.[4]

While Francoeur may have moved around in Arkansas for a few years, he settled down at one place on the White River, probably by 1745. Arnold identifies the location by the current name of "Francure Township" in White County, and it is a reasonable guess that the Francoeurs lived in the vicinity of the present Georgetown.[5] His wife Marie was listed in the 1770 Arkansas Post census with their nine grown children: Jean, François, François (sic), Agnès, Jeanne, Marie, Angelique, Suzanne, and Anne.[6] It is unfortunate that there is never a mention of the sort of house he built for his growing family during the 1750s and 1760s, for it would be instructive to know what sort of architectural tradition was maintained by a French *coureur de bois* in Arkansas. The range of possibilities runs from Native American structures to French log construction, but neither documents nor archaeology have specified the house considered proper by someone like Francoeur.

He apparently did well in the fur trade, at least at first, for by 1749 he was already listed in the census as a "bourgeois," an employer of other men in the trade. "The 1749 census . . . lists a habitant population of only thirty-one, including the commandant and his wife. But there were forty hunters on the Arkansas River whose passports had expired, and nine on the White and St. Francis rivers."[7] The nine illegal hunters in the north broke down like this: "*Bourgeois:* Francoeur, *Engagés:* 4 [on White River]; *Bourgeois:* Tourangeaux, *Engagés:* 3 [on St. Francis River]."[8] Francoeur and his four subordinates thus were identified as the only Europeans known officially to live on the White River in 1749. The Tourangeaux on the St. Francis was presumably one of those responsible for the Lepine inventory in 1743 at Arkansas Post.

Within the next two decades, Francoeur died. The 1768 census of Arkansas Post included "The Widow Francoeur, 3 boys, six girls and 2 negro men."[9] The three Francoeur sons apparently were continuing in the family business ("good old hunters," they called themselves),[10] for they were revealed only two years later as being involved in an altercation with one of their creditors, a merchant named Tounoir at Arkansas Post. One (or all) of the Francoeurs had borrowed from him, probably the standard outfitting loan made by the Post merchants to hunters, with the debt to be repaid at the end of the season. For whatever reason, the Francoeurs produced bear oil, but no hides or furs. While the sequence is not clear, it is probable that the Francoeurs were forced to deal with Tounoir at Arkansas Post because of a flare-up of the persistent danger of raids by the Osage.

> In May of 1770, seven separate war parties of Osages ransacked many of the hunting camps along the Arkansas. . . . A few days later a number of hunters sent word that they were returning to the fort with their families, and some in fact soon began trickling in. The Francoeur brothers, for instance, arrived from the White River in June of 1770 with women and children; the children did not even have shirts. The Francoeurs had lived on the river for twenty-five years, had taken up with Indian women, and had had a large number of children by them.[11]

Tounoir must have determined that the only possession the Francoeurs had which could satisfy the debt was the store of bear oil which they had brought with them to the Post. He seized it, and he might well have kept it, but one of the Francoeur *engagés* took exception to his action and complained to the commandant. Arnold tells the story in detail:

> In 1770 a merchant named Tounoir took a great deal of bear oil from the boat of a hunter named Francoeur to satisfy a debt. Lambert, an *engagé* of Francoeur, petitioned the commandant in writing to order Tounoir to replace the oil; Francoeur owed him wages, he said, and he claimed preference to Tounoir because his claim was "due for hard work." Captain Demasellière, the commandant, thereupon ordered Tounoir to return the oil. When Tounoir refused, the commandant was obliged to send his sergeant to execute his order. At this point, Francoeur asked to have set off a debt of 944 *pesos* that Tounoir owed him; the note evidencing this debt, unfortunately, was in New Orleans in the hands of de Clouet, the former commandant. Demasellière wrote to the governor to ask that he order this note paid since Francoeur had nothing but his gun. The commandant

then ordered Tounoir to pay court costs—that is, the sergeant's fee for taking the oil back; when Tounoir refused, Demasellière had him jailed. A short time thereafter the commandant ordered Tounoir to leave the post, but before doing so, Tounoir got Francoeur to sign some sort of "certificate," probably a release of Tounoir's note; and, to insult the commandant and literally as a parting shot, as he was leaving at high noon, Tounoir and his company fired off a volley of thirty rounds. Francoeur thereafter signed an affidavit that he executed the release to Tounoir when he "was drunk and thus it is of no value."[12]

Other than the simple justice of the situation, there is a hint of another reason why Demasellière was not sympathetic to Tounoir. The merchant had ignored the commandant's orders not to resupply the hunters, because Demasellière wanted to force them to come in to Arkansas Post for licensing and other official controls. Shortly after the Tounoir-Francoeur contretemps he expressed his irritation that, while some hunters had come in, "others supplied by Tounoir, against my orders, have remained [along the White River]."[13]

The incident reveals several interesting facts about the Francoeurs. For one thing, they were all still together, but the marriage of some of the sons, if not the daughters, surely indicates that the old Francoeur household on the White River had expanded into a compound. The wives of the sons were identified as "Indians," and there were many children who dressed in native fashion (shirtless in the June heat). While the women's tribal affiliation was not indicated, these marriages suggest that the Francoeurs should be seen as part of the "Indian countrymen" phenomenon which was so important in the changing political and cultural structures of Native Americans across the Southeast. At the same time, the fact that they did not live in native villages, whether Quapaw, Osage, Caddo, or some other tribe, indicates that the Francoeurs were not filling quite the same role as the European traders further east, such as Colbert and McGillivray.

That lack of correspondence is borne out by the poverty of the Francoeurs. The commandant was sympathetic to the indebted hunter because he "had nothing but his gun." By contrast, the "Indian countrymen" to the east were for the most part quite successful and prosperous, providing new generations of mestizo leaders for the Native Americans.

What happened to the Francoeurs is not recorded in the documents. At least one of the girls, Agnès, daughter of Joseph Francoeur, went to Sainte Geneviève, where she married Jean Jaulin *dit* LaRochelle. In 1772 their son François was baptized, and six years later the baptism of their son Jean Baptiste was recorded; in 1786 came the baptism of their daughter

Jeanne.[14] Jean Jaulin died sometime before 1800, because in that year the widowed Agnès married Antoine Curain at Sainte Geneviève.[15] A decade later her daughter Jeanne married Christophe Piot there.[16]

In the 1770s Jeanne Francoeur married Pierre Pertuis, and both of them died before their son Louis was married at Arkansas Post in 1793.[17] One of the Francoeur sons, Jean, was listed in the Spanish militia there. The 1780 list for the militia company at Fort Carlos III included "Juan Batista Frincart," which is probably the hispanicized version of Jean Baptiste Francoeur, and he must have been a hunter, as no farm produce was listed.[18] The 1794 and 1796 censuses of Arkansas Post included François and Marie Francoeur (Francisco and Maria).[19] François must have died within the next year, because the 1798 census included only the Widow Francoeur.[20]

The family was not listed in the later censuses for the Illinois or Arkansas areas. There is one hint of a continued presence of the Francoeurs into the American period. The 1844 Government Land Office survey map for the Georgetown (White County) area shows the boundaries of a Spanish Land Grant labeled "Claim No. 2416 Francis Francure." The White County deed book ("A") dutifully picked up the metes and bounds of the tract, simply referring to it as "Private Survey No. 2416. Surveyed for Francis Francure who claimed in his own right 1600 arpens. . . ." Beyond this indication of a François Francoeur's late occupation of the site, there is no further evidence of French presence in that area of the White River. The Francoeurs were not listed in the later censuses for the Illinois or Arkansas areas, and later nineteenth-century references to "Negro Hill" and Georgetown (platted in 1908) ignore the earlier French establishment, suggesting that the Francoeur descendants had found other paths and other places, and that their presence in North Arkansas, after almost a century, was at an end.

ANTOINE JANIS

In 1781, as the Francoeur story was moving from the Ozarks country to the towns, the Janis story in northern Arkansas was being extended from the towns to the Ozarks. Antoine Janis was listed as one of the hunters on the White.[21] After a few years' absence, he was again listed, with his family of a wife and six children. He was named as "Antonio Janis" in the Arkansas Post censuses of 1794, 1796, and 1798.[22] His name recurs many times in the American deed records as the land ownership of Spanish grants was adjudicated after the Louisiana Purchase (discussed below). If the historical connections can be made and rightly interpreted, he and his family will constitute an instructive case of the French extension into Arkansas from the Illinois.

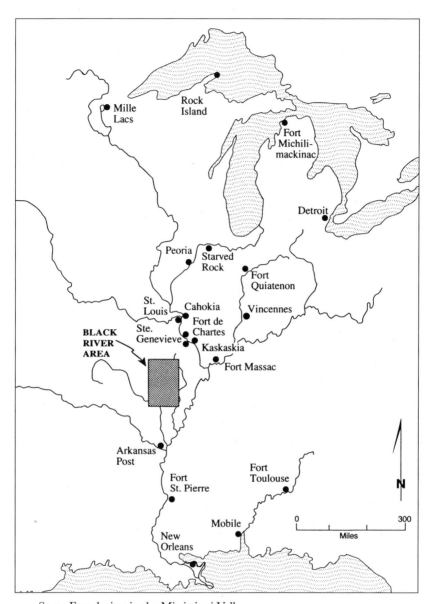

Some French sites in the Mississippi Valley.

Adapted from *French Colonial Archaeology*, ed. John A. Walthall
(Urbana: University of Illinois Press, 1991.)

Antoine Janis did not just appear from nowhere in the records of Arkansas Post. He was almost certainly a member of the well known Janis family who had for decades lived in Kaskaskia and Sainte Geneviève.[23] If his antecedents can be established, it will permit a much fuller picture of the dynamics of the settlement of the North Arkansas area in the late Spanish period.

Who were his parents, and where was he from? He is the right age to be the son of Nicholas Janis, patriarch of the family, but the son of Nicholas named Antoine was romantically involved with a slave named Mary Louise in Ste. Geneviève from 1792 to 1796, then into the 1800s in St. Charles, where he was a landowner with periodic appearances in the public records.[24]

He could be the son of one of the other sons of Nicholas. In 1781 a document protesting the behavior of the American army in Kaskaskia was signed by the Janis men: Nicholas, his sons Jean Baptiste, François, Antoine, and an unknown "Antoine Jr."[25] Antoine Jr. did not appear in the Kaskaskia census of 1787,[26] and he apparently never appears again in the Illinois records. Who was this Antoine Jr.? Jean Baptiste himself was only twenty-two, so he could not have been his father. His son, Jean Baptiste *fils*, for instance, was not born until 1784. Moreover, he did have a son named Antoine, who died young in 1805.[27] François was born in 1761, which means that he was only twenty in 1781 and thus could not have had an adult son named Antoine. It is more likely that he fathered the later Antoine, who married Félicité Bogy in 1826 and died in Sainte Geneviève in 1861.[28] The same is surely true of Nicholas's son Antoine, whose scandalous exploits and illegitimate children were still a decade in the future. Still, it is possible, if we grant him a birth around 1752 (a year after his father's marriage), an early marriage, circa 1769, and a precocious Antoine *fils* who would be permitted to sign a political document at age eleven.

The remaining alternative is the other son, Nicholas, about whom little is known. His existence was asserted by Arkansas historian W. E. McLeod.[29] The records, however, both of Kaskaskia and Sainte Geneviève, are silent about him. If for some unknown reason he chose to be called Antoine instead of Nicholas, then he would be a perfect choice for the Antoine Janis of Arkansas. Is it possible that two brothers could be named Antoine? It seems so. Given the tradition of receiving a saint's name (by birth date) and the perpetuation of given names in the same family, it is likely that in a large Catholic family there will be a duplication of names. Moreover, while *fils* is usually used for a generational shift, it is clear that it did not necessarily indicate a father-son relationship. An Antoine *fils* might well be the nephew of an Antoine (this holds true for many Anglo-American families of the same period—"Junior" often just distinguishes the younger from the older). The term *fils* could thus also indicate the smaller or younger person of the same name in a family, without signifying a generational shift. In this case, then, a "Nicholas Antoine" could be the brother of Antoine and could choose to go by "Antoine" rather than his father's name of Nicholas. As if to bear out this possibility, the Lawrence County deed records contain an astounding parenthetical remark. In 1817 the Arkansas Antoine's son Nicholas sold his right to his father's land claim; the deed referred to "Nicholas Janis (by nickname known as Antoine Janis)."[30] If this deed testimony be accepted, then Antoine's own son was named Nicholas, but called Antoine. If that were a repetition of the previous generation, then the Arkansas Antoine would himself be a Nicholas, and the mystery of his antecedents would be solved.

In any case, the Antoine Janis *fils* in Kaskaskia in 1781 is in the context of the Nicholas Janis family, and he never again appeared in the Illinois records. It is a handsome fit, however, to see him as the Antoine Janis who appeared for the first time in the Arkansas records as a hunter with a young family in 1789. His wife was named Angelique, and his children in the 1794 and 1796 Arkansas Post censuses were listed by name in Spanish: Antonio, Juan Batista, Francisco, José, Felipe, Maria, and Elena. The youngest, Miguel, apparently was born after 1796 because he was named for the first time in the 1798 census.[31] Before the story of this family in Arkansas is examined, however, it will be useful to look briefly at their earlier history. With the putative identification of Antoine as the son of Nicholas, it is possible to supply some of the historical background for this pioneer Janis in Arkansas.

Nicholas Janis was an important man both in French Illinois and in his family, as his consistent signature suggests; it is always just "Janis," without further specification. It has been claimed that he was the son of François Janis and Simon Brosseau of Champagne, France,[32] but that assertion is contradicted by other genealogical information. Tanguay's listing specifies a Nicholas born to the couple from Champagne who then went to Canada, but their Nicholas in turn is revealed as having a wife and family in Detroit spanning the years from 1745 to 1761, a period when Kaskaskia's Nicholas was already in Illinois first as a bachelor, then as a newlywed in 1751.[33] Without that connection, all that can be said is that Nicholas Janis appeared as a young man in Kaskaskia and Sainte Geneviève around the middle of the century. His first appearances in the records were in 1751, when he sold a house and land in Kaskaskia for four hundred livres, suggesting he had already been there long enough to purchase or build that property. That same year he married Marie Louise Taumur, daughter of Jean Baptiste Taumur *dit* La Source and Marie François Rivard, who had long been members of the Kaskaskia community.[34] Ekberg thinks that he first settled in the fledgling village of Sainte Geneviève for a few years, before selling his property there and moving to the older Kaskaskia.[35] What is clear is that he quickly became one of the pillars of French Illinois, established at that principal village on the east side of the Mississippi River.

He had six known children, and it was hypothesized that there was a seventh. They were Jean Baptiste (1759–1836), François (1761–1832), Antoine, Catherine, Félicité (ca. 1751–1837), and Françoise. Their marriages read almost like a survey of significant families of French Illinois: Jean Baptiste married Reine Julia Barbau; François married Pélagie Bienvenu; Catherine married Etienne Bolduc; Félicité married Vital St. Gem Bauvais; and Françoise married a Durocher. Jean Baptiste and François moved to nearby Prairie du Rocher, and all of the Janis families participated in the fur trade and farming, the characteristic occupations of the Illinois colony. They apparently grew prosperous at their endeavors, for when the French and Indian War came to an end in 1763, they became part of the British Empire rather than fleeing to another area of the world remaining under French domination. They were well aware of the fact that Arkansas Post, Ste. Geneviève, and the young St. Louis had become Spanish, but they seemed content to be British in Kaskaskia. C. W. Alvord described them this way: "Among the gentry, which was a rather elastic term, were also many well-to-do men, who had risen to prominence in the Illinois or else possessed some patrimony, before migrating to the West, which they increased by trade. . . . These members of the gentry lived far more elegantly than the American backwoodsman and were their superiors in culture. Their houses were commodious and their life was made easy for themselves and families by a large retinue of slaves."[36] A hint of the quality of life in Kaskaskia comes as a historical detail: when Nicholas Janis's daughter Félicité married Vital Bauvais in 1776, one of the gowns in her wedding trousseau was made from material which had come from France that same year.[37]

Life in British Illinois was not without its problems, though, and when George Rogers Clark arrived to conquer the Illinois on behalf of the new United States in 1778, he found that no battle was necessary, for the Kaskaskia French received them with enthusiasm and embraced the end of English control. They fed Clark's army and even provided volunteers for the winter march to capture Vincennes, a brief campaign whose victory made a hero of young Jean Baptiste Janis.[38]

Nicholas Janis had been a captain of the militia at Kaskaskia under the British, in 1777, and he apparently continued that role after the arrival of the Americans.[39] Moreover, in 1779 he was appointed a judge, a seat he kept for several years.[40] The happy relations between the citizens of the Illinois and their liberators turned sour, however. The Americans were poorly supplied, and the generosity of the French was repaid with Continental currency which proved to be almost worthless.[41] Alvord summarized succinctly what happened in those important years when the positive attitudes of the French toward the Americans turned to hostility.

> Since Clark with his half-naked Virginians had surprised them on that July night in 1778, the people of Illinois had passed through many phases of feeling towards the Americans. They had at first rejoiced that at last the liberty which had been the subject of their dreams was to be enjoyed. There followed a few months of peace under Clark's mild rule, when the French actually stripped themselves of their property to supply the troops with necessities and to further the cause which they had adopted. Then the anxious days came when the vandalism of the troops and the doubt about the payment for their goods made them less jubilant. They received Todd with his civil government as a prophet of a new era. Todd had failed and had handed them over to the military, and Montgomery had succeeded in so thoroughly cowing them, that their power of opposition was weak.[42]

The following years, marked by the attempts of several Americans to wield autocratic power in Illinois, were experienced as periods of anarchy punctuated by times of tyranny. Janis, as one of the justices of the court, found himself to be one of the political leaders of Kaskaskia struggling to maintain order and to find the right path for the French in the tensions of conflicting claims of American representatives. It was in the face of increasing demands for food and the forced quartering of troops in private homes that the French resorted to official protests, threats to appeal to Virginia, and finally the actual sending of the protest of 1781 mentioned above, which bears the signatures of most of the leading men of Kaskaskia.[43] This series of events over the years set the stage for a radical change in French Illinois. The document of 1781 said it very clearly: "All these acts of tyranny are the causes that our best inhabitants have withdrawn to the Spanish government, and others, who were expecting your justice, prefer Spanish laws to the tyranny and despotism which they have suffered at the hand of your people."[44] The great departure to the west bank of the Mississippi had only just begun.

When the change of government had failed to satisfy the French and the presence of the soldiers had led to disorder and tyranny, there began a steady stream of emigration to the Spanish bank, which ended in almost depopulating some of the villages of the American Bottom. Among the emigrants were the most important and progressive of the French inhabitants.[45]

. . .

The period of the greatest emigration occurred between the years 1787 and 1790, when anarchy reached its climax in Kaskaskia, and the Spaniards were holding out the greatest inducements to settlers on the western bank of the river. There has been preserved a list of the male inhabitants in Kaskaskia for the year 1790, in which the heads of families are enumerated. The number is 44. This is a decrease of over 77 per cent in the French population of the village since 1783. This list is interesting on account of the names which are missing. Almost all the men who had been leaders of the French people throughout the period of the county of Illinois were no longer residents of Kaskaskia. We look in vain for the names of Cerré, Vitale, J. Bte., and Antoine Bauvais, Corset, Lasource, the elder Charlevilles, Morin, De Monbreun, Langlois, Levasseur, Lafont, Carbonneaux. They have crossed the river to seek peace and safety under the flag of Spain.[46]

Carl J. Ekberg suggests that another motive for migration was the rumor that the Northwest Ordinance of 1787 would require them to release their slaves, which they conceived to mean economic ruin. While his neighbors crossed the river, Nicholas Janis held out in Kaskaskia through these years; the Janis family left in groups for Spanish territory in the late 1780s, but Nicholas did not leave until the end of the decade. Jean Baptiste and François and their families went from Prairie du Rocher to Sainte Geneviève (François first to the Saline south of the city, then into Sainte Geneviève). Antoine went to St. Charles, and the other Antoine went to the Black River, south toward Arkansas Post. It appears that Nicholas the patriarch did not move to Sainte Geneviève until 1790 or 1791.[47] It may be that he was waiting for the new town of Sainte Geneviève to stabilize, for another major impetus to settlement there was the total destruction of the original Sainte Geneviève on the low river bottom by flood in 1785, "L'Année des Grandes Eaux." The decision was made to relocate the town itself on the higher bluffs, and the immigrants from across the river came steadily to help settle the new Sainte Geneviève.

The personal wealth which the French lavished upon the visiting army was ultimately never repaid, and they came to consider their American experience a very expensive lesson. Janis and his fellow enthusiasts for the American cause found after the decade of the 1780s that they lost a great deal of wealth—the goods and food they had bestowed upon the American army, as well as goods lost to the depredations of the encroaching American civilians during the anarchy. With their departure to Spanish territory they abandoned years of investment in Kaskaskia and the other villages of Illinois. Nor were they ever to recoup their losses, even when the United States government tried to indemnify them years later.

> Those who had given freely of their goods for the support of the American cause were never to receive full recompense for their services. Most of the bills which were presented were finally paid by Virginia, but not until they had passed into the hands of speculators such as Bentley and Dodge, who had given to the original holders very small percentage of the face value of the claims. Later the United States attempted to compensate the French people for the losses they had suffered by granting them concessions of land; but the delays were so long, their needs so pressing, and their foresight so poor that the men to whom the grants were made sold them for a song to land-jobbers and speculators, long before the difficult land question of Illinois was finally settled a generation after the occurrence of the events for which the French and others had ruined themselves.[48]

The major beneficiary of this upheaval was the Spanish government. As historians have consistently made clear, the primary purpose of the Louisiana borderland in Spanish eyes was to stand as a buffer zone protecting New Spain from Anglo-American encroachment. The Spanish had been wooing the French of Illinois for decades, offering land and governmental support to their coreligionists. Alvord suggests that they had also moved to darker persuasions, such as encouraging Native American raids and offering no help to the French in their time of troubles, other than a promise of welcome on the west bank. The times conspired to grant the Spanish their wishes, and Spanish Illinois grew rapidly. The towns of St. Charles, St. Louis, and Ste. Geneviève soon became more than villages, and the French found themselves prospering as subjects of His Most Catholic Majesty.

The sparsely inhabited region to the south also benefited. Antoine Janis was not the only refugee from the Illinois who headed away from the towns toward the fur trading frontier of the southern Ozarks. Several bachelors and men with young families moved south into the area under the political control of Arkansas Post, and some of the names which appear on the census rolls of that district in the 1790s were last seen on the Kaskaskia census of 1787. Some, like Joseph Baugi (Bogy), went to the village at the

Post, but several went to the riverine locations where they would be close to the fur trade routes.

Antoine Janis was one of the latter. As noted earlier, he was not on the 1787 census in Kaskaskia, probably because he was already in the Ozarks. In 1789 Jean Dianne, a merchant at Arkansas Post, petitioned the commandant for help in collecting debts from many hunters on the Arkansas and White Rivers to whom he had extended credit. He named sixteen on the White, and Antoine Janis was one of them.[49] The debt was incurred at least a year earlier, perhaps even before that since hunters tended to stay away from the Post until they were able to pay their obligations (as noted in the case of the Francoeurs). He was not in hiding, however, because he was living somewhere with his growing family. They were not listed in the 1791 and 1793 censuses of Arkansas Post, but he and his family were named in the 1794 enumeration. His wife was Angelique (father's name not given), and the children were Antoine, Baptiste, François, Joseph, Philippe, Marie, and Hélène.[50] No agricultural produce is listed, which indicates that whatever they grew in their home garden was for their own use and not reported to the Post.

The 1796 Arkansas Post census is close to identical. Only Marie is missing, but that absence only lasted two years at most. Since Pierre LeMieux *fils* was later to claim an interest in Antoine Janis's land because he was an heir of Pierre (François?) who married a Janis daughter,[51] it seems likely that Marie was listed in the 1796 census with her new husband, François LeMieux.[52] François LeMieux was also listed in the 1787 census of Kaskaskia, where his father Claude had even been elected a justice at one time.[53] If François and Pierre were brothers, their relationship in the documents would seem reasonable. The Janis listing in the 1798 census presents a minor mystery, for seven of Antoine's children are listed again, but the names are not quite the same. In addition to Antoine and Angelique, there are Antoine, François, Joseph, Alex, Michel, Hélène, and Marie. Jean Baptiste and Philippe of four years earlier are missing, but they have been replaced by Alex and Michel. Marie has returned and is called Janis, and François LeMieux has disappeared, possibly deceased. Instead, there is now a separate listing for Pierre LeMieux, his wife Victoire, and his daughter Victoire.[54]

The Arkansas Post records cease at that point, but the Janis family reappears fifteen years later in deed records. In 1801 five plots on "Black River fork of White River," New Madrid district, were granted by Henri Peyroux (commandant at New Madrid) to John Latham, who rented or sold them to Etienne St. Marie *fils*, who "inhabited and cultivated" them over the next two years. At some point, perhaps in 1803, the Janis family acquired the grants. When the U.S. Commission was established to adjudicate land claims, the five grants were claimed as follows:

1000 arpens   Antoine Janis
 750 arpens   Nicholas Janis
 750 arpens   François Janis
 750 arpens   Jean Baptiste Janis
 750 arpens   Joseph Guignolet[55]

Later deeds reveal that these members of the Janis family are the Arkansas Antoine and three sons, with a friend. The details of the two titles from the Deed Record Books of Lawrence County, Missouri Territory, in 1817 are very helpful in clarifying what happened.

Sept. 23, 1817

Nicholas (X) Janis (by nickname known as Antoine Janis) to William Russell of the Town and County of St. Louis, Missouri Territory, for $150, his right in 640 A on Black River being the settlement of said Nicholas Janis; & said Janis' right in 640 A on Black River, being the settlement of Anthony Janis, dec'd, Father of Nicholas Janis; & the right of Nicholas Janis in 640 A on Black River, being the settlement of Francis Janis, dec'd., who was a brother of Nicholas Janis.[56]

The "640 A" stands for 640 arpents, the French and Spanish land measure which was just slightly less than an acre. The illiterate grantor was the Nicholas "Antoine" Janis referred to earlier. He affirmed that he was the claimant of one 640-arpents grant, that his deceased brother François claimed another, and that their deceased father Antoine claimed a third, all on the Black River. A deed drawn up a week later clarifies the family structure still further.

1817 October 4

Jean Baptiste (X) Janis (commonly called Jo Janis): Michael (X) Janis, Maryann (X) Janis, Meno (X) Janis, now the wife of Jerman Charboneaux; Angelique (X) Janis, now the wife of Charles Curotte; & Louise (X) Janis, now the wife of John LaBass (whose proper name is John Fayce) ["Fayas," of whom more later], who are the children and heirs of Anthony Janis, deceased; and the said John Batiste Janis and Michael Janis are brothers of Francis Janis, dec'd; and the said Louise, Angelic, Meno and Maryann Janis are sisters of said Francis Janis, dec'd. Wherefore, for $200, the said John Batiste (X) Janis, Michael (X) Janis, Maryann (X) Janis, John (X) LaBass, Louise (X) LaBass (alias Janis), Jerman (X) Charboneaux, Meno

(X) Charboneaux (alias Janis), Charles Curotte & Angelic (X) Curotte alias Janis) sell to William Russell of the Town & County of St. Louis, Missouri Territory, their interest in the following lands, to wit: 640 A on Black River, the settlement of Anthony Janis, dec'd; 640 A on Black River, the settlement of Anthony Janis, dec'd; 640 A on Black River, the settlement of Francis Janis, dec'd.[57]

The Spanish grants under consideration are thus the same ones granted by Peyroux in 1801, and the Janis owners are the same family listed in the Arkansas Post censuses of 1796 and 1798.

1796	1798	1801	1817
Antoine		grant	deceased
Angelique			
Antoine (Nicholas)		grant	Antoine (separate deed)
Jean Baptiste	missing	grant	"Jo"
François		grant	deceased
Joseph			missing (separate grant)
Philippe	missing		missing
Alex			missing
Michel			Michel
Hélène			=Meno? m.Jerman Charboneaux
Marie			Marie Anne [Widow LeMieux?]
Angelique	not born?		m.Charles Curotte
Louise	not born?		m.Jean LaBass *dit* Fayas

From this comparison it appears that Philippe and Alex were either dead or had left home early, before the men became involved in Spanish land grants. Joseph seems to have had no stake in his father's or brother's grants, but he had his own, a venture undertaken with his brother-in-law Jean Fayas (discussed below). Marie Anne was still unmarried, but her sisters Meno, Angelique and Louise were married to Charboneaux (who had been listed as a bachelor in the 1794, 1796, and 1798 Arkansas Post censuses), Curotte, and Fayas. A later deed, in 1818, revealed that Pierre LeMieux, who had yet another Spanish claim, was also an heir of Antoine Janis.

In 1808, after Spanish Louisiana became part of the United States and the Board of Land Commissioners was established to determine which of the Spanish land grants should be honored, Joseph Legrand testified before the Commission on the Janis grants. He said that Antoine's one thousand arpent grant was inhabited by Janis, "a wife and six children," and cultivated from 1801 until the present, and that about thirty arpents were in cultivation in 1808. He affirmed that Nicolas and François only had five or six arpents currently in cultivation, Jean Baptiste had eight or nine, and Joseph Guignolet, who had lived there in 1803 with a wife and child, had fifteen or sixteen in cultivation. The Board, however, refused to confirm the five claims at that sitting.[58] In the ten years after that early hearing the claimants made many sales of their grants, on the chance that they would ultimately be approved. Jean Baptiste sold his claim in 1814.[59] In a September 1816 deed Antoine Janis sold what he asserted was his "only claim" on the Black River.[60] A year later he and his son François were both dead of unknown causes, for Nicholas and his siblings began selling their interest in the rights to their grants.[61] In 1818 the U.S. indemnification commission, tasked with trying to weed out the fraudulent land claims from the legitimate in the wake of the New Madrid earthquake of 1811–12, heard testimony that the plots owned by Antoine, François, and Nicholas had been "materially injured by the earthquakes," an indication that New Madrid validation was also being sought.[62]

Ultimately, only the grant of Jean Baptiste appears to have been approved. That one is known to have been located at Lauratown on the Black River, and it was plotted as a Spanish grant on the U.S. survey maps. It is likely that the others, those of Antoine, Nicholas, and François, were nearby, but the documentary descriptions do not permit identification of the locations.

Even their brother Michel had a grant, probably close at hand, for he, too, sold his rights in 1820.[63] So, too, did Meno's husband, Jerman (Germain?) Charboneaux.[64] Angelique Janis's husband, Charles Curotte, had a grant on which they presumably were living in the last days of the Spanish period.[65] Antoine's grandson Pierre LeMieux also had a grant, and its location is known, since it was confirmed; his land was on Black River "about fifteen miles above the mouth" of Current River, a place called by the French "Petit Barrel" and by the Americans "Peach Orchard."[66] McLeod helpfully noted that the location is near the present town of Peach Orchard in Clay County.[67] Claiming he had settled on it in 1800, LeMieux sold it in 1816 for only $40, which either indicates that he had little hope of seeing it confirmed or that he had long since abandoned it for other locations. The latter is supported, in fact, by McLeod's assertion of local tradition that LeMieux was the head of the French settlement at Clover Bend.[68] If true, then he had left his own grant to reside nearer the rest of the Janis family. It may not be too speculative to suggest that LeMieux and his family moved into a home left empty by the death of Antoine and François Janis in 1816, thus strengthening the Janis enclave.

Another member of the enclave was Joseph Guignolet, the possessor of

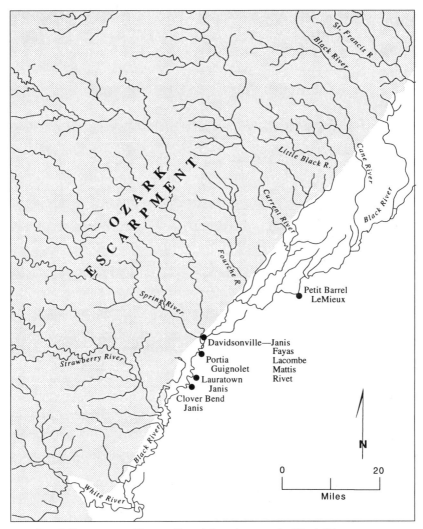

Ozark Escarpment. Known French locations on the Black River.

the other grant in the Janis list. Like Antoine Janis, he was on the Arkansas
Post censuses of 1794–98 as a bachelor, but Joseph Legrand noted that he
lived on his grant on the Black with a wife and child in 1803.[69] The location
of the grant is known to be at Portia, just above Lauratown.[70] Guignolet
was still living there in 1816, when he sold the rights to all of the grant except
"the place and preemption right where said Joseph now lives."[71] Two years
later, in 1818, he was ill and went to live with the Charboneaux family; when

he died he left his last property, sixteen head of cattle and three horses, to Michel Janis, Meno Charboneaux, and Marie Anne Janis.[72] His will was witnessed by Louis Lariver and Alexander Brident, both of whom also had land grants nearby. Lariver's claim was on the White, and he sold it in 1820.[73] Brident's claim on the White was validated by the Board of Land Commissioners in 1811.[74]

Antoine Janis's other son, Joseph, had embarked on another land venture, possibly earlier than the rest, since he was not even listed on the 1798 census of Arkansas Post. He apparently established close relations with four other men (hunters like himself), one of them his brother-in-law Jean Fayas, and they settled adjacent to each other on the west bank of the Black just above the junction with the Spring River. From the descriptions, the plots ran from the river bank straight back, side by side. The owners were Joseph Janis, Jean Fayas, Cola LaCombe, Jerôme Matis, and Augustine Rivet.[75]

Fayas (Jean LaBass *dit* Fayas) had served in the Arkansas Post militia in 1780 and was one of the delinquent hunters on the White in 1789. In 1793 the census listed him and three children, but he and his son Jean were alone listed in 1794–98 (unless "Madelena Thyase" in Charles Refeld's home in 1794 was one of the missing children).[76] In 1812 his grant on the Black was confirmed by the board.[77] When the Janis grants were being sold in 1818, he (or his son Jean) was shown as the husband of Louise Janis. This is somewhat confusing because only two years later two children of Jean Fayas and *Hélène* Janis were baptized.[78] The godfather of the children, also named Jean and Hélène, was Germain Charboneaux. Either two generations of Fayas men married Janis sisters, or there is another double-name problem.

Cola (diminutive for Nicholas) LaCombe was from Sainte Geneviève, where his father (?) Louis LaCombe was married in 1773 and bought a house in 1782.[79] Louis and Nicholas were granted New Bourbon lots in 1797, and two of Nicholas's children died there in 1799 and 1801.[80] Those deaths may have been the motivation to go south, for he next appears in the records in connection with the Black River land grant.

Jerôme Matis received a lot in New Bourbon in 1797, where he was living in 1801 when he and Cola LaCombe signed a petition by the inhabitants requesting that the Peorias be ordered to settle at least three miles distant from the village.[81] With seven thousand shingles delivered to the grantor in Sainte Geneviève, Matis bought another piece of land in New Bourbon in 1803, which makes it likely that he had not personally settled on the claim on the Black during the legal period set by Land Commission rules.[82]

Augustine Rivet was in the Arkansas area much earlier, for he was listed as a bachelor hunter in the censuses of 1794 and 1796.[83] Nothing more is known about him until he shows up in the records as the owner of the Black River claim with the others—Janis, Fayas, LaCombe, and Matis.

Their five adjacent plots were bought by de Mun and Company in 1815 as a way of creating a county seat for the newly created Lawrence County, Missouri Territory.[84] The purchase of the five grants, even unconfirmed, probably seemed safer than trying to wait for virgin land to be surveyed, and Lawrence County needed a county seat immediately. Moreover, the site just above the junction of the Spring and the Black must have seemed a likely site, liable to grow rapidly with the river as a highway. Thus came into existence the Anglo-American town of Davidsonville, destined to die after only fifteen years of existence.[85]

This aggregation of Spanish grants cannot be precisely plotted, for all of the locations, other than that they were on the White and Black Rivers, are not known (see map). Most of them were never finally confirmed by the United States, even after decades of litigation, so their very existence is now attested only in the scattered relics of sales of the "rights" to land specula-tors. It is only when they are pulled together in this sort of historical perspective that the size of the French occupation of the southeastern Ozarks can be appreciated. The grants which have been alluded to in the preceding pages, all connected with the Janis family in one way or another, number seventeen, all presumed to have been on the Black River. But there were yet others in North Arkansas. There was Jean Baptiste Graver, for example, who improved a grant on the Black beginning in the 1790s (he was listed in the Arkansas Post census of 1798 as "Crever").[86] Pierre Lefevre had a grant on the Cache River confirmed in 1812, which places yet another French settler in the area.[87] There were at least four Spanish grants on the White River in the thirty miles above the mouth of the Black, and the origi-nal grantees may have been part of the French enclave.

Antoine Bauvais was the focus of yet another group of the Kaskaskia/Sainte Geneviève French settlers. Thanks to a late (1832) registration of his Spanish grant by Richard Searcy, the location of Bauvais's settlement is identifiable. The U.S. survey had apparently ignored the grant boundaries, so Searcy translated it into a land call, locating it in Section 30 of T5N R8E, on the Mississippi River a little north of Memphis.[88] The exact relation of the Arkansas Antoine Bauvais to the family in Sainte Geneviève is not known, but it is probable that Antoine, born in 1732, was a son of the patri-arch, Jean Baptiste St. Gem Bauvais of Kaskaskia and Sainte Geneviève, "who became the richest man in the Illinois country."[89] Like Nicholas Janis, he had been there since the early days (in his case, before 1725) and had reared a large family.[90] His seven children, like Janis's, married into the other pioneer families of the Illinois. Marriage even brought an official link between the Janis and Bauvais families, for in 1776 his son Vital St. Gem Bauvais married Félicité Janis. He himself died in 1767, leaving a complex estate which took a decade to settle.[91] His children, especially Jean Baptiste and Vital, became leaders in the new Sainte Geneviève.

Antoine Bauvais appeared in the Arkansas records in 1789, when he signed a petition against the Osage.[92] In the 1791 and 1793 censuses he was listed along with his wife, Charlotte Levasseur, six children, and six slaves. He died the next year at the age of sixty-two, and the 1794 and 1796 censuses listed the Widow Bauvais and her family, who were continuing their substantial farming.[93] The family was missing from the 1798 census. Antoine Bauvais was also connected with others who were part of the Arkansas Post sphere. His wife Charlotte's father, Estanislas Levasseur (an "artisan"), and Levasseur's sons François and Etienne (and his wife Marie Larose) were all listed in the Arkansas Post records.[94] They, too, were from Kaskaskia. Antoine's sister (?) Marie was the wife of Jean Baptiste Desruisseaux, who signed the Osage petition in 1789, but died before the 1791 census, leaving his wife and three children to continue their farming.[95] Joseph Baugi, from Kaskaskia, was an important member of the Arkansas Post community, becoming "*Don* José Bougi" by the 1796 census. His wife was Marie du Placy (Plasy, Placide), whose brothers (?) Jean Baptiste, Joseph, and Louis were listed as hunters in Arkansas through the 1790s.[96] In 1805 in Sainte Geneviève, Joseph Bogy *fils* married Marie St. Gem Bauvais, daughter of Vital Bauvais and Félicité Janis, thus bringing together the Baugis, the Bauvais, and the Janis.[97]

There is no evidence that all these families were living close together in Spanish Arkansas, but there is a possibility that the Antoine Bauvais connections constituted another enclave similar to that of Antoine Janis, possibly on the Mississippi River. It is clear that they all were in the Arkansas area through the 1790s, and they may have continued there into the 1820s.

As a whole, all of these families—claiming at least twenty-four sites in Arkansas between the Post and Sainte Geneviève—produced a pattern of settlement which should probably be considered an immigration movement. Many of them were listed in the Kaskaskia census of 1787, and they thus were subject to the same motivations to leave American Illinois that were discussed above—anarchy, political despotism, economic losses, and American immigration pressure. Instead of going with their larger families to St. Charles, St. Louis, or Ste. Geneviève, however, this group went south into the sparsely settled region between the Missouri towns and Arkansas Post. They maintained their ties, to be sure, for their family connections lay in the towns of Spanish Illinois, but they began what amounts to a new colonization. Their governmental center was Arkansas Post, but their cultural connections were in Ste. Geneviève. The Janis enclave on the Black River was an impressive beginning, considering at least seventeen land grants (or settlements) there. It is instructive to recall that venerable Arkansas Post in 1749 had only seven households, and that the full census for the Arkansas district in 1796 listed only fifty-seven households—and the Kaskaskia group constituted at least ten of them.[98]

This new population center was doomed not to come to fruition. The reason for it, of course, was the passage of the vast region of Louisiana to the United States, and the particular mechanism which brought the "Illinark" to an end was the U.S. Land Commission. The problem was getting a colonial era settlement legitimated in the American system of land ownership. For the French living on their land, the difficulty lay primarily in the fact that their titles were incomplete. As Arnold and others have made clear, there were no grants to individuals during the French dominion,[99] and the full process of receiving a clear title under the Spanish was daunting. For people who lived far from the governmental centers, it seemed too difficult and expensive to bother with, especially in the sparsely settled areas. In fact, Arnold says, "There was not a single regular Spanish land title ever made out in the entire state of Arkansas."[100]

As long as the settlers remained under the Spanish flag, possession and improvement of the land was sufficient title, but the transition to U.S. territorial status in the opening decades of the nineteenth century forced the regularization of land titles. The Board of Land Commissioners found themselves having to determine "legitimacy" for prior land ownership. Their task was complicated by land fraud—and the belated attempts of some of the Spanish commandants to give settlers legal grants before the Americans took over. The board's response was to set strict standards which had to be met in order to show the legitimacy of a claim, including proof that the claimants were actually living on the land prior to December 1803, or even earlier, and that they were farming significant acreage. Both the standards and the process of providing proof were difficult for many of the French, and they saw little chance of success. Moreover, there may have been some anti-Gallic bias involved, for the board refused to confirm the joint ownership of the commons in the French towns, and thus voted against the European settlement pattern itself.[101] It is also possible that some of the grants were part of a French pattern of settlement seen in other places, such as the Mobile region, in which distant agricultural plots were held for summer residence, with the family in the town house for the remainder of the year.[102]

This process of the transition of land grants to U.S. deeds has been discussed in detail elsewhere and will not be resurveyed here.[103] It is enough to point to what the deed records of Lawrence County show—that the French settlers considered it much more likely that they could realize some profit out of their imperfect land titles by selling their claims (and thus the land itself, in the short run) to Anglo-American speculators, many of whom were lawyers who felt comfortable with the litigation which would be necessary to secure firm U.S. ownership. As it turned out, very few of the Spanish land grants were ultimately confirmed, and the deed records alone remain to mark the French presence in Northeast Arkansas in the colonial period.

What happened to the French colonial settlers? The deaths of the older generations came early in the nineteenth century. In Sainte Geneviève the patriarch Nicholas Janis died in 1808,[104] Vital Bauvais died in 1816,[105] the younger Jean Baptiste Janis died in 1830 and the elder in 1836.[106] François Janis preceded his brother in 1832,[107] and octogenarian Jean Baptiste St. Gem Bauvais died in 1833.[108] As mentioned above, in Arkansas Antoine Janis died in 1816. The family did not all vanish from Arkansas, however, at least not immediately. In 1825 the Lawrence County Circuit Court appointed a commission to mark a road from "Janis mill" on Janis Creek to the county seat at Davidsonville.[109]

Pierre LeMieux *pére* died in 1818,[110] and the younger Pierre was still in Lawrence County in 1829 when he, his wife, three sons and a daughter were listed in the Sheriff's Census.[111] He was the administrator in 1834 when his brother (or son) Antoine died.[112] He himself died in 1840, at Clover Bend, suggesting a continuing French community for at least another two decades.[113]

John LaBass (Jean Fayas) revealed his accommodation to the new regime in an 1816 deed granting a small piece of land to a ferry owner across the Spring River "opposite the place where I now live."[114] He had successfully sold his plot on the Black (Davidsonville) and was living nearby on another plot, adapting to the U.S. system. The elder Jean LaBass died in 1826, and his son Jean was one of the administrators.[115] The only member of the family listed in the Sheriff's Census of 1829 was "Mary LaBasq" and her family.[116] The continuation of the LaBass name in the area suggests that at least some of Jean's descendants became part of the new order and stayed there. The others, having realized whatever profit they could from their years on the Black, probably moved to Ste. Geneviève or St. Louis, many of them—those born in Arkansas—thereby finding themselves in the context of a French community for the first time.

Thus ended a barely discerned immigration of the French from the Illinois into the area between Spanish Illinois and Arkansas Post, inland from the Mississippi River. Given several generations more to develop and complete the evolution of villages, the 1790s French might well have created another urban focus for settlement on the Black River and adjacent areas, but that time was not granted. The French presence in Northeast Arkansas vanished, leaving some names on the land and some deeds in the records, but no ongoing contribution to life and culture. Even so, it is provocative to consider that the southeastern edge of the Ozarks was once almost "Illinark."

Between a Rock and a Hard Place

The Indian Trade in Spanish Arkansas

GILBERT C. DIN

Of the functions Arkansas Post served during the Spanish era, one of the most important was the Indian trade and control of the native tribes.[1] Trade played a vital role in the domination of the natives, particularly through exchanging the goods they wanted (guns, munitions, alcohol, clothing, and ironware) for the skins, furs, and other forest products they collected. With few soldiers in Louisiana, Spain needed the cooperation and loyalty of the Mississippi's west bank Indians to help guard its territory. Therefore, it was essential to maintain friendly relations with the tribes. Virtually the only natives living in what is now the state of Arkansas were the Quapaws, who resided in three villages on the Arkansas River. But through the eighteenth century, other tribes entered this region in increasing numbers to exploit its abundant game and escape from the Americans who were seizing their lands. Some of the natives, however, also killed and robbed white hunters, which made hunting in Arkansas a hazardous occupation. First established by the French in 1686 and refounded by them in 1721, Arkansas Post was taken over by the Spaniards in the 1760s after the Seven Years' War and constituted the only white settlement in the region.[2]

Throughout the Spanish era in Louisiana (1763–1804), Arkansas Post was essentially a fort and a trading center. Most of its few inhabitants were hunters and traders.[3] From the governorship of Luis de Unzaga y Amezaga, Spanish governors of Louisiana[4] repeatedly instructed Arkansas Post commandants[5] to wean the *coureurs de bois* away from hunting and toward farming in order to develop a permanent population that would be useful in protecting the province against outsiders. These admonitions, however, fell on deaf ears because agriculture in Arkansas was not remunerative. Instead both Indians and whites engaged in hunting. As early as the 1720s, numerous whites flocked to the region to gather the animal resources of the forest and prairie. These seasonal expeditions continued throughout the eighteenth century. They supplied New Orleans with large quantities of salted meat (usually bison), tallow, bear oil, furs, and animal skins; and the city became dependent on them.[6]

At Arkansas Post the Spaniards presented the Indians of the district, the Quapaws,[7] with annual presents, reported on other Europeans in the area, tried to reduce the warring tribes to peace, and conducted trade.[8] But besides the legal commerce, renegade or "vagabond" traders often illicitly supplied the Indians. Many of them were military deserters from the French era, fugitive criminals, and assorted whites who had "gone native." Their illicit trade with the tribes weakened Indian subordination to legitimate authorities.[9]

The Spanish governors of Louisiana did little to alter the existing French pattern of trade at Arkansas Post. The first governor, Antonio de Ulloa, issued lengthy orders to the St. Louis commandant that reflected his wish for good relations with the natives, but he said little about the Indian trade. One of Ulloa's few actions concerning Arkansas Post was appointing elderly Capt. Alexandre de Clouet commandant. He took over in early 1768.[10] When Lt. Gen. Alejandro O'Reilly arrived in Louisiana in August 1769 to suppress the Creole revolt of the year before that ousted Ulloa and his men, the general introduced Spanish laws and institutions. He reorganized the colony from top to bottom. He created two lieutenant governors for the Mississippi's west bank, one at St. Louis for Missouri (the Spaniards called it Spanish Illinois, which was an area larger than the present state of Missouri), and the other at Natchitoches. O'Reilly wrote out extensive orders for the two lieutenant governors, giving both important roles in controlling the natives of their respective jurisdictions.[11]

Not as lengthy were O'Reilly's instructions for Arkansas Post. Of the orders' twelve articles, only four dealt with the Indians. The commandant was to ensure that the natives left their arms at the gate of the fort when they entered to see him and, in order to avoid drunk and disorderly conduct, that they did not imbibe spirituous beverages at the Post. The king would provide annual gifts to the natives, who were to recognize only him, his provincial governor, and his post commandant. These were the only gifts they would receive from the king. The natives were to arrest itinerant traders and fugitives and take them to the Post, and they were to be on guard against a surprise attack. Trade at Arkansas Post was open to all residents, but New Orleans merchants could have a clerk there. The presence of traders would ensure that the natives could exchange their animal skins and oils quickly for needed European goods.[12]

Because of the limited Indian trade at Arkansas Post, fewer merchants lived there than at St. Louis or Natchitoches. They did not commerce exclusively with the natives, but also supplied the numerous white hunters. In 1777 there were between thirty-five and forty hunting parties on the Arkansas River with others on the White and St. Francis Rivers. In 1787 the Post commandant reported two hundred European hunters on the Arkansas River. While they were not exclusively of French origin, the majority were. A few of them were Spaniards (discharged soldiers who elected to remain in Arkansas), Anglo-Americans, and perhaps a few other nationalities.[13]

Among the merchants present in the Spanish era were François and Pierre Ménard, Andrés López, Marcos Olivares, Jean Baptiste Duchasin, François Vaugine, Joseph Bougy, and Pierre Nitar. The Ménard family was prominent in the early and middle years of the Spanish regime. In later years, Joseph Bougy was a leading merchant, and he was helped in large measure by the Arkansas Post commandant, Carlos de Vilemont, who was also his son-in-law. Bougy had arrived about 1787 from Kaskaskia, and Vilemont established a liaison with Bougy's daughter Catalina (Catherine) not long after he settled at Arkansas Post in 1794.[14]

While both the St. Louis and Natchitoches districts had numerous natives, Arkansas had few of them. At times the Quapaw trade was reserved for the Post commandant, who needed to earn additional money to offset the expenses he incurred, often in entertaining visiting Indians. The gifts given to the natives by the Post commandant were in addition to the annual presents provided by the governor in the name of the king. The governor in New Orleans was also expected to provide visiting Indians with entertainment, alcoholic drinks, food, shelter, and more gifts during their visits and to pay for these out of his personal funds. Needless to say, the governors sent repeated instructions for Post commandants to discourage Indians from going to the city.[15] The natives expected these gifts, which were essential for maintaining friendly relations. The commandant's salary did not cover the cost of presents, and he was not provided with additional funds to pay for them. A trade monopoly with the Indians might help offset these expenses, but it was not always forthcoming. Commandant Joseph Vallière complained in 1787 that he did not have the Quapaw trade that year because the tribe commerced with the local merchants. How long this had been going on is uncertain because commandants were usually given the Quapaw monopoly, or at least a part of it, in the 1760s and 1770s.[16]

When Vallière asked for a trade monopoly with a group of Delawares in 1787 who were then living in the Arkansas district, Governor Estevan Miró denied it, stating it would not be fair to the other traders or merchants.

Miró's refusal to award the trade to Vallière may have stemmed from the latter's unsavory reputation for making money any way he could, including selling supplies to soldiers at the fort at inflated prices and lending them money, which increased their indebtedness. Regimental Commandant Francisco Bouligny told Vallière's successor, Ignacio Delinó: "You cannot ignore that the soldiers' limited salary is unable to sustain exorbitant charges and that their officer's principal concern should be to free them from debt and even to liquidate it entirely." Vallière's money-making schemes made him unpopular with his men and the other inhabitants at Arkansas Post. Perhaps that explains why he was relieved of his command ahead of the normal term post commandants usually served.[17]

Because Arkansas commandants did not keep records as faithfully as did the lieutenant governors in St. Louis, the distribution of licenses for trade is not fully known. They also failed to record the quantities of pelts and other forest products sent out of the district. Given the numerous hunters, these no doubt amounted to a considerable quantity. To cite two examples of what the forest and prairie yielded: Commandant Fernando de Leyba shipped twenty-eight hundred *potes* (fifty-six hundred liters) of oil and five hundred pounds of tallow to New Orleans in 1772. Commandant José Orieta reported that in the first several months of 1776, the English had obtained twelve thousand deerskins and six thousand pounds of beaver furs on the White and St. Francis Rivers.[18]

As part of their Indian policy, the Spaniards wanted peaceful relations both with the natives and between the natives. To achieve these goals, they supplied friendly tribes with annual gifts as the French had done; provided the Indians with needed trade goods but, at the same time, tried to limit guns, munitions, and sometimes alcoholic beverages; and gave Indian chiefs and leaders symbols of authority such as medals, flags, commissions (printed or hand-lettered certificates of the Indian's rank), uniforms (coats and hats), and staffs of office. These symbols of authority gave greatly prized status to tribal members.[19]

Among the goods the Indians prized most were guns, gunpowder, and shot. These were used primarily for warfare against hostile tribes rather than hunting.[20] The weapons traded to the natives were inferior in quality to the fusils the soldiers used and often needed repair, as evidenced by the frequency with which the natives sought gunsmiths.[21] Although Spanish policy tried to limit the number available to the Indians, in 1801 Lieut. Gov. Carlos Dehault de Luzières Delassus of St. Louis gave the Osages a large gift of one hundred guns, three hundred pounds of gunpowder, and three hundred pounds of shot. Acting Governor Casa-Calvo upbraided Delassus for being so generous.[22] The Spaniards tried to limit the goods traded with friendly Indians to a minimal level, and had no intention of permitting them to supply firearms to possibly hostile nations.

Traders to the Indians were important auxiliaries in carrying out official policy. It was their duty to inform the government about noteworthy events occurring at Indian villages, take the yearly gifts from New Orleans to Arkansas Post, convey the governor's messages to the natives, and be fair in their business dealings with the tribes.[23] The governor granted licenses to merchants to commerce with specific tribes; these were really monopolies that stated how much merchandise could be traded. Although the Spaniards said they wanted free trade with the Indian nations, it was thought to be easier to exercise control of the natives if they had only one supplier rather than many. If more than one traded with them, it would be difficult if not impossible to cut off trade with a tribe that committed a crime. In the case of a large group, such as the Big Osages, the Spaniards granted licenses to several traders who were limited in the quantity of goods each could exchange. Article sixty of Ulloa's instructions to the St. Louis commandant stated, "No person who does not carry a license signed by the governor shall be allowed to enter among the tribes dependent on the settlement (St. Louis) . . ." or to sell to them there.[24]

The earliest Spanish monopoly originated in the French era. In 1763 the French director of Louisiana, Jean Jacques Blaise d'Abbadie, granted an exclusive eight-year trade on the Missouri River and north to the Minnesota River to Maxent, Laclede and Company. It was terminated early.[25] Among the monopolies permitted to Arkansas traders, Governor Miró gave Francisco Martin an exclusive license to trade with the Arkansas Osages in 1785. But because Martin lacked sufficient capital for the enterprise, it was awarded to Claudio Bougard. The governor also granted an exclusive license the next year to a New Orleans merchant to trade with the Delawares who visited the Arkansas district. This occurred at about the same time that Miró refused Vallière's request for the same monopoly.[26]

Arkansas Post commandants sometimes expected to make considerable money from the fur trade and the sale of liquor.[27] Over the years, they traded with many of the tribes that either inhabited Arkansas or visited there. These included the Delaware, Chickasaw, Osage, Loup, and Cherokee nations, in addition to the Quapaw. Fernando de Leyba, who became commandant in May 1771, clearly expected to engage in commerce at the Post since he brought with him a large quantity of merchandise. Shortly after his arrival, he asked the governor not to give any other commercial licenses in Arkansas. The next year the Arkansas merchant Días accused Leyba of trying to organize trade as an exclusive privilege. Leyba had also sought a monopoly in supplying liquor at Arkansas Post, a request Governor Unzaga rejected.[28]

Balthazar de Villiers, who became commandant in 1776, was also deeply involved in trade at Arkansas Post. He borrowed large sums of money to acquire goods. To further his commercial dealings, he worked with an English merchant from Natchez in British West Florida, Jean Blommart, which probably violated Spanish law, and he tried to commerce with the Osage Indians, which was against established practice. He knew that Arkansas inhabitants traded illegally with the English, and he apparently did little to stop them because of his partnership with Blommart. In 1778 he requested a monopoly on the sale of *eau de vie*, declaring that it was dangerous to allow other persons to sell it. He was deeply in debt when he died in 1782, and his wife, Françoise Voisin de Bonaventure, attempted to liquidate their debts by continuing the trade. She had been as much a business partner as a spouse, and had journeyed frequently on the Mississippi between New Orleans and Arkansas Post, hauling merchandise upriver and returning with forest products. After her husband's death, several creditors sued to recover money lent to him, but they failed to collect fully.[29]

Commandant Carlos de Vilemont, who served at Arkansas Post in the last decade of Spanish rule, received a license to trade exclusively with the Cherokee and Loup Indians in the Arkansas district. When it expired in 1798, he sought a renewal, but Governor Manuel Gayoso de Lemos refused, as it would infringe on the economic interests of others. The governor believed in permitting anyone who wanted to trade to do so.[30]

Merchants and traders probably made more money outfitting white hunters than they did trading with the Indians. Hunts went on throughout the year, although winter pelts and skins had a greater value. But this was a risky business. Hunters were not always successful and often failed to repay the merchant's advance for other reasons. Sometimes Osage Indians attacked and forced them to retire to the safety of Arkansas Post or elsewhere. On numerous occasions, the Europeans reportedly lost the entire product of their hunt, guns, supplies, and even the clothes they were wearing to Osage raids. Other times, hunters simply chose not to return to the Post and, in violation of agreements, exchanged their product with itinerant traders who went upstream. It became customary for traders to travel upriver without taking goods in order to insure that merchants were not defrauded of their rightful earnings. Hunters were directed to return with their product, but because there were many interruptions in the hunt, rules were not always followed. Finally, the hunters, who were typically in debt, might not return in part because they felt no great loyalty to merchants who may have defrauded them by plying them with liquor or inducing them to gamble.[31]

Experience taught the Arkansas traders and hunters that they needed local regulations to carry out their work. Rules were perhaps developed as early as the French era. In time the observance of these "rules legalized by custom" embraced everyone, even the Post commandant.[32] Governors, who possessed the authority to grant licenses for trade with the natives, sometimes violated custom by giving individuals special favors. Governor Miró did this is 1784 and again in 1786. On the first occasion, he gave Francisco Ménard and Juan Baptista Ymvo permission to take merchandise upriver. Commandant Jacobo Dubreuil, however, questioned Ménard's ethical behavior and declared that if he went, Ménard would acquire all the hunters' furs and skins by selling goods to them. Dubreuil prevented him from going. Because no one was critical of Ymvo's conduct, the commandant allowed him to take his merchandise upriver.[33]

A furor broke out at Arkansas Post when it became known in 1786 that Miró had granted permission to traders Andrés López and Jean Diana to go upriver to meet returning hunters and collect debts. Three traders petitioned Commandant Dubreuil and implored him in the name of fairness to prevent privileged persons from going upriver. Dubreuil agreed not to violate the custom of the Post, which dictated that the last outfitter was to be paid first, after which other creditors would receive payment proportionally if the debt could not be satisfied in full.[34]

This system failed, however, and in January 1798, six Arkansas merchants drew up a new document of five articles, which became binding on the Post's traders and hunters. The commandant was to bear witness to all agreements made. In order to avoid entanglements, only one trader was to outfit a hunter, and he was to receive payment first. If a hunter could not repay his creditor due to accidental circumstances, the latter would be expected to outfit him again. If a merchant found it necessary to collect from a hunter, he could go upriver to do so, but he could only obtain furs from those he had outfitted. A violation could cost him a two-hundred-peso fine, or if the peltry was worth more, a fine of four hundred pesos. Both hunters and traders were prohibited from shipping furs or merchandise clandestinely; violators faced a twenty-peso fine and fifteen days in jail. The six merchants (François Vaugine, Charles Refeld, Abenazar Pahom, Joseph Bougy, Louis Jardelat, and Andrés Fagot) promised to observe these rules.[35]

Only three months afterwards, Jardelat, one of the signatories, asked for a license to go upriver. Commandant Vilemont interpreted his request as a violation of the agreement and sought Governor Gayoso's advice. Vilemont explained that the traders' agreement was fair to all persons at the Post and that it was designed to avoid problems. He asked Gayoso to deny the license.[36]

Two other signatories, Vaugine and Bougy, were in New Orleans when Vilemont's letter with Jardelat's petition arrived; when they learned about the petition, they made their own appeal. They convinced Gayoso that the request was against the interest of traders. Moreover, they insisted that licenses to commerce with Indians be granted only at the post involved and not elsewhere. Gayoso accepted the first part of their argument and denied Jardelat's petition. But accepting the second part would have deprived the governor of the right to issue licenses, and he refused. Gayoso also made additional rules for persons at Arkansas Post to follow. He designated the Post as the district's only trading center and prohibited hunters from taking merchandise with them on their hunts. He limited the gunpowder and shot each could take to twenty and forty pounds respectively. At the end of the season, all hunters were to return to the Post where they were to observe the rules outlined in the January 1798 agreement.[37]

When Vilemont received the governor's regulations, he called a meeting of those concerned then present at the Post. They elected two traders and two hunters to form a committee; the election has been called the "only democratic sign in Spanish Arkansas."[38] The committee established fines and punishment for persons who violated both the January agreement and Gayoso's rules. Any hunter who took merchandise upriver was to be fined twenty-five pesos and jailed for one month. The merchant who provided the goods was to be fined five hundred pesos and imprisoned for three months. Any hunter who hid his pelts in the forest to cheat his outfitter and any merchant who bought them were also to suffer the same punishments. Governor Gayoso, however, believed the penalties to be excessive and reduced both the sentences and the fines.[39] These were the last formal rules created to regulate trade at Arkansas Post in the Spanish era.

Other problems confronted Spanish Arkansas with regard to the Indian trade. English rivals presented a major challenge and continued to do so until the American Revolution. When Spain acquired Louisiana west of the Mississippi River in 1763 with the conclusion of the Seven Years' War (French and Indian War), the British gained control of all of Canada and the eastern part of Louisiana (all of the Mississippi's east bank north of Bayou Manchac, which was also called the Iberville River, located about fifteen miles south of Baton Rouge). English traders had the use of the Mississippi and, with abundant and cheaper goods, often ventured west of the river. Their hunters occasionally came from as far away as the Carolinas to seek game on the Mississippi's east bank; they sometimes illegally crossed the river into Arkansas. Through the 1760s and 1770s, reports came of English hunters and traders penetrating the area and selling freely to the natives, even to the Quapaws. Besides cheap goods, they provided the Indians with copious quantities of alcoholic beverages; the English traded more liquor than other Europeans, and the illegal commerce went on at a time when the Spaniards had only an under-strength battalion (approximately six hundred men when at full strength) to guard the entire colony. Arkansas Post's commandant had strict orders not to send out parties of soldiers from the fort's small garrison for any reason, since it was feared that the reduced number of soldiers might lead to the fort's capture. The Quapaws, too, were of concern. About 1776, Angaska, the great chief of the three Quapaw villages, admitted making a secret alliance with English traders and accepting a medal and flag from them. The Spaniards punished him by withholding gifts to him that year.[40]

Among the English merchants who flagrantly entered Spanish Arkansas was a woman, "Dame Magdelon," who sold large quantities of alcohol, much of it to the Quapaws. Another daringly intruded as far as the Quapaw villages.[41] They also established the post of Concordia, consisting mainly of taverns that dispensed liquor freely, opposite the mouth of the Arkansas River. After Britain's American colonies declared their independence, a group of rebel soldiers led by the adventurer Capt. James Willing pillaged Concordia in February 1778. Although the English inhabitants returned, a fire destroyed all the buildings three months later, after which they abandoned the site. In November 1780, a year after the outbreak of war between Spain and England, Commandant Balthazar de Villiers led a party of soldiers to the former site of Concordia and claimed the east bank of the Mississippi for Spain. The English threat to Arkansas Post during the war proved to be virtually nonexistent except for the Loyalist band of James Colbert and its thwarted attack on the Spanish fort there in 1783.[42]

Spanish military weakness in Louisiana meant that it could do little to halt English hunters and merchants from penetrating the line of the Mississippi, but while English trading ventures alarmed Spanish authorities, diverted part of the forest products, and subverted some of the natives, they did not constitute a real threat to Spanish ownership. The English, the French, and later the Americans, all made liberal use of liquor in their trade with the Indians, creating a serious problem. The Spaniards, especially under Governor Ulloa, tried to limit consumption, but the natives wanted it. When in 1770 the Quapaws received their annual gifts without liquor, a disgruntled chief dispatched a message to the governor declaring that his people expected and demanded *tafia* (raw rum). By 1772, if not sooner, liquor was again part of the annual gift. That year the Quapaws received several barrels; in 1776 they got 48 *potes* (96 liters) of *tafia;* and in 1783 they received 150 *potes* (300 liters) of *aguardiente* (raw brandy). In the latter year, Commandant Dubreuil suggested setting the Quapaw liquor ration at three *barricas,* approximately 680 liters.[43]

In 1784 Governor Miró favored limiting the disbursement of alcohol to the natives. This was after he had issued it liberally at two Indian congresses held in Pensacola and Mobile that year. Problems had surfaced near Mobile and elsewhere in Spanish Louisiana, and Miró's effort to curb the use of liquor was not aimed exclusively at Arkansas. But by that time the Quapaws were showing the ravages of alcoholism, and in 1786 the Quapaw chiefs who traveled to New Orleans to see the governor begged him to prohibit its introduction in their district. They showed him a document in which Commandant Dubreuil had approved their request. However, Miró dissented and, thinking more of the benefits of trade, allowed it to continue. Besides, Spanish policy advocated moderation rather than abstinence.[44]

Dubreuil's successor at Arkansas Post, Joseph Vallière, quickly learned the consequences of Indian alcoholism. Five Quapaws died in drunken brawls in the first three months of his administration. A chief from one Quapaw village visited another village, where intoxicated Indians killed him and dumped his body in the river. The incident prompted Captain Vallière to write Miró: "Rum is the cause of it all. It would be of great benefit to this tribe if you would not permit anyone to bring rum to this post, because this tribe wishes to trade only for rum, and these Indians are all destitute."[45]

Vallière's description of the devastation produced by alcoholism at Arkansas Post finally had the desired effect on the governor. Miró banned liquor and made the commandant responsible for enforcing his order. Before the end of 1787, Vallière published the decree. Perhaps for a time no liquor came to Arkansas, but in 1789 the commandant complained that the trader Pierre Nitar was reintroducing it.[46] After this, nothing more was said about liquor for several years.

By 1790, alcoholic beverages were again available. In 1796 Commandant Vilemont asked that only "the indispensable amount" of liquor be allowed to come to Arkansas. Two years later, three traders at the Post, François Vaugine, Andrés Fagot, and Joseph Bougy, sent a memorial to the governor explaining how alcohol affected the Indians. Among other things they reported that when the natives became drunk, their rowdiness produced riots that were difficult to contain.[47] Despite the merchants' admonition about the ill effects of liquor, there is no indication that the trade declined.

Several reasons help to explain why alcohol sales flourished at Arkansas Post. First and foremost, the liquor trade, then as now, was profitable. Moreover, most Indians demanded it, and the Spaniards felt that if they did not supply it, others would and reap the benefits. In addition, Europeans were accustomed to drinking. In certain lines of work in Louisiana, it was traditional for employers to provide alcohol to their laborers. For example, rowers of crafts that plied the Mississippi were furnished with a daily *filet* (ration) of liquor. Finally, both hunters and soldiers at Arkansas Post consumed alcohol in immoderate quantities when money and opportunity made it available.[48] Despite the harm produced by alcoholism—disorder, injury, death, impoverishment, and dependency—the liquor trade in Arkansas continued.

Alcohol created many problems, but the Osage nation constituted the greatest obstacle to peaceful hunting in Arkansas, in addition to being the biggest problem overall for the Spaniards on the Mississippi's west bank.[49] Spain had little control over the tribes that warred against her Native American friends. Dealing with the Osages was difficult for several reasons. The nation was large, with numerous warriors (twelve and possibly fifteen hundred by the 1790s), and produced more furs and skins than any other west bank tribe.[50] Although they resided mainly in southwestern Missouri, the Osages roamed over a vast area from the Missouri River in the north to the Red River in the south. They engaged in almost constant warfare with other tribes, and this conflict enabled them to exploit the game in Arkansas (which was needed to trade for goods), steal horses and women among the Caddo and other neighboring nations of the Natchitoches district, and improve the tribal status of young warriors. The Osages also tried to prevent guns and munitions from reaching rival tribes on the western plains.[51]

An Osage custom that occasionally caused trouble with whites was the "Mourning War" ceremony. It dictated that when a notable Osage died, a mourning party would retaliate by taking the scalp of the first non-Osage it encountered. Although this custom was not always followed to the letter, enough whites were killed that the Spanish government in Louisiana often wanted to halt trade with the tribe until the guilty were punished or amends made.[52] But this created another problem that mitigated against punishment. If the Spaniards tried to discipline the tribe, the Osages might abandon them and support other whites, particularly the English or the Americans. Moreover, halting commerce with the tribe because of crimes would cause substantial losses for the St. Louis merchants since the Osage trade was the most lucrative in Missouri.[53]

The tribe's tendency to fragment also made controlling them difficult. The first known division occurred early in the eighteenth century when the Little Osages split off from the main group, or Big Osages. Later in the Spanish era, another faction broke away from the Big Osages and established itself on the Upper Arkansas River in what is now the northwestern part of the state. This group came to be called the Arkansas Osages and made repeated efforts to initiate trade with the Post.[54] They were also responsible for many of the killings of white and Indian hunters on the Arkansas, White, and St. Francis Rivers, settlers in Missouri, and Indians in the Natchitoches district. Miró described these Osages in the following way: "Every year parties of young (Osage) warriors break away from the body of the nation and descend to the neighborhood of the Arkansas and the St. Francis rivers. . . . If these young warriors encounter white hunters, they rob them of their peltries, and occasionally they have captured one of the hunters, who was never to be seen again."[55]

Spanish authorities in both New Orleans and St. Louis did not want the Osages trading with the Arkansas merchants because leverage on the tribe to compel it to do as the Spaniards wished would decrease if it had multiple suppliers, and St. Louis merchants would lose profit. By restricting trade with the Osages to one base, Spanish governors believed that the tribe could be induced to behave and the Indians responsible for crimes punished. But leverage rarely worked because of the desire to make money. So determined were the St. Louis merchants to commerce with the Osages that they continued it clandestinely when governors imposed trade embargoes.[56] And although it was against orders, Arkansas commandants occasionally sent traders to supply them. Vilemont, for example, supplied two Osage parties at Arkansas Post in July and September 1796. As a result, Governor Carondelet instructed him not to send traders to the Osages.[57]

Arkansas merchants looked at their rivals in St. Louis with envy and yearned for access to the Osage trade. They believed the tribe's killing and pillaging in their district would vanish if the Osages received the goods they wanted. However, the Osages killed whether they were supplied by surreptitious ("vagabond") traders or legitimate authorities. Moreover, other factors made it difficult, if not impossible, to implement Spanish efforts to reduce them to peace. Osage society, particularly in the Arkansas faction, was not based on maintaining peaceful relations with neighbors.[58]

Not all of the Osages were responsible for the killings and violence. The main group of Big Osages who followed their leaders was generally not liable. These chiefs frequently lamented their inability to control the dissident elements within the tribe, especially the Arkansas Osages, which included many of the younger men who wanted to use warfare to raise their standing within the tribe.[59]

Because they committed many depredations in the Natchitoches district and never sent delegations there asking for peace and trade, as they did to Arkansas Post and St. Louis, the lieutenant governors of Natchitoches spoke only of Osage annihilation. Chief among them was Athanase de Mézières who wanted the tribe destroyed. Similarly, the Caddo nation that inhabited the Natchitoches district and suffered numerous losses at Osage hands never spoke of peace. The Quapaws also generally favored war against the Osages because of their many broken promises.[60] The principal exponents of peace with the tribe, excluding St. Louis merchants, were commandants and merchants at Arkansas Post who wanted to increase economic opportunities through trade.

Nonetheless, on numerous occasions in the Spanish era, when Osage bands entered the Arkansas district, they pillaged and killed white hunters and natives. Peace rarely lasted long. When the government halted trade or threatened to, the Osages would arrive at Arkansas Post asking for reconciliation; they sent emissaries there in 1771, 1785, 1790, 1796, and 1802. In between were years of violence on the Arkansas, White, and St. Francis Rivers, when hunters and traders often fell victim to Osage depredations. When the Indians came to the Post offering the excuse that their violence resulted from being refused commerce, the commandant and the local merchants were inclined to believe them. Trade usually took place upriver, without official permission, at a site convenient to the Osages.[61] Despite the lapse Miró displayed in 1785 when he thought peace possible and sent a trader from Arkansas Post, Spanish policy officially prohibited the exchange of skins and furs with the tribe in Arkansas.

Because of these attacks on both whites and Indians, the Spaniards tried repeatedly to reduce the Osages to peace, make them punish criminal leaders (partisans who led war parties), return stolen goods, and supply hostages who would be responsible with their lives for the good conduct of the rest of the tribe. Often those deemed responsible for killings refused to surrender, and the chiefs lacked the authority to force them. Consequently, these efforts largely failed, although stolen horses were sometimes surrendered and several partisans spent months in jail in St. Louis. No Osage was ever executed in accordance with a "life for a life" agreement for murder negotiated with the tribe by Lieut. Gov. Pedro Piernas in St. Louis in 1773.[62] The absence of punishment, the lifting of trade embargoes soon after imposition, and clandestine trade no doubt dissuaded the belligerent Osages from altering their conduct. When American hunter Robert Gibson of Arkansas Post was murdered by a party of Quapaw and Delaware Indians, the commandant decreed that one person from each tribe who was in the party was to be executed, and they were. The agreement of a "head for a head" in cases of murder was sometimes carried out on the Mississippi's west bank during the Spanish period. While the records do not mention a white killing an Indian or being executed for murdering a native in Arkansas in compliance with this rule, it happened in West Florida. In 1792 a white (Antonio Beltrán) and a black (Leonardo de la Trinidad Poveda) were executed for killing two Indians. It occurred during the administration of Governor Carondelet, who was a stickler for enforcing agreements with the natives. Perhaps what made the executions possible was that both men were *presidarios* (prison inmates) who had escaped.[63]

The Spanish fear in the early years that the Osages would abandon them for the English, particularly in trade, gave way to a new fear in the 1780s and 1790s that Great Britain, France, the United States, or a combination of these nations, would invade Louisiana. Under Governor Carondelet, the Spaniards held out hope that Osage warriors would be employed to defend the province, but this was not founded on reality.[64]

In addition to defense "by the Osages," there was need for protection from them. Lieut. Gov. Manuel Pérez of St. Louis twice advocated building a fort near the Big Osage village on the Upper Osage River to keep the tribe peaceful. While Governor Miró ignored the proposals, former Arkansas commandant Joseph Vallière seized the idea to promote a fort on the Upper Arkansas River. He did so only after a new governor, the Barón de Carondelet, had replaced Miró.[65]

Early in 1792 Vallière discussed the fort with Carondelet before committing his ideas to writing. He suggested establishing it at Les Gallais, one hundred and fifty leagues upriver from Arkansas Post and, he claimed, a two-day journey to the Big Osage village. He alleged Arkansas hunters and traders believed it would prevent Osage thefts and incursions and convert the tribe to peaceful hunting. These whites would pay the costs of building the fort, which would be garrisoned by forty regular soldiers, five artillerymen, and one officer. The post would also promote trade with other Indians, particularly the Panis (Wichitas) and the Laytanes (Comanches).[66]

While Carondelet supported it, the proposal soon ran into opposition. Capt. Gen. Luis de las Casas of Cuba was against it because it would further divide the few Spanish soldiers in Louisiana. Nevertheless, he sent the plan to Spain for a decision there. When Commandant Ignacio Delinó heard about the suggested fort from the governor, he solicited opinions from hunters and traders, who were ignorant of the idea. They replied that the fort would provide only minimal protection since it could not shield them once they left it, and refused to pay for its construction. In Madrid former Governor Miró was consulted, and he also rejected the idea in a lengthy report he wrote about conditions in Louisiana.[67] Nothing ever came of the proposed fort on the Upper Arkansas.

Osage depredations continued unabated in 1793. Indian and white inhabitants from Missouri to Natchitoches felt their sting, but only in Arkansas was any effort made to fight back. In the spring of 1793, Commandant Delinó informed the governor that he was working to punish the Osages by raising a war party of 120 or 130 men, of whom 50 would be white hunters. Their expedition would begin in June. On receiving word, Carondelet heartily endorsed the project. He then conceived the idea of a joint venture with expeditions from Natchitoches, New Madrid, and St. Louis. However, he would only pay for gunpowder and bullets.[68]

Meanwhile at Arkansas Post on April 8, the hunters drew up a short agreement for their expedition, which was now scheduled to depart in early May. They appointed Michael Bonne, Baptiste Dardaine, and Louis Souligny as their leaders. All the booty seized from the Osages would be auctioned at Arkansas Post and distributed equally among the participants. If anyone lost a limb and became unable to hunt due to the expedition, each hunter agreed to pay him two pesos per year. Delinó reported that fifty or sixty hunters and sixty Quapaws would join the campaign.[69]

While the Arkansas expedition left in May to search for Osage war parties, no other district sent out forces. The lieutenant governor in St. Louis was in opposition and did nothing; it was not good for trade and the antagonized Osages might unleash new attacks on the dispersed settlers of Missouri.[70] In July, after two months of sloshing through rain-soaked woods, suffering from widespread illnesses, and catching no sight of raiders, the weary expedition returned. Delinó concluded that the tribe had not left its village that summer and possibly had been warned.[72] The Arkansas attempt of 1793 was the closest the Spaniards came to unleashing a punitive expedition against the Osages.

Because of the many injuries sustained by hunters in Arkansas, it was only natural that officials there rather than those in Missouri should plan to strike back. But it was a St. Louis merchant who revived the idea of a new fort to contain the Osages. In the spring of 1794, the St. Louis merchant and trader Auguste Chouteau led a party of Big and Little Osage chiefs to New Orleans to negotiate peace with Governor Carondelet. They agreed to let Chouteau build a fort near the Big Osage village, which he named "Fort Carondelet of the Osages" and garrisoned with twenty militiamen (in reality Chouteau employees) paid by the government. Chouteau promised to keep the Indians peaceful and to punish any who committed crimes. In return, he received a monopoly contract to trade with the tribe for six years. For much of the period from 1794 to 1797, the presence of Chouteau's fort contributed to keeping the Osages generally peaceful. But it was not absolute peace since Arkansas continued to suffer from their random violence.[72]

Although from 1797 to 1801 an uneasy peace existed, Osage attacks began to increase, usually by the dissident Arkansas faction. These attacks compelled hunters to flee for their lives in the fall of 1797. In the spring of 1799, a large band of raiders entered the Arkansas River valley, where it divided into three parties and committed many depredations. As Commandant Vilemont explained it, their violence resulted from being denied trade, and he recommended allowing Arkansas merchant Joseph Bougy to trade with them. But because Chouteau had the monopoly, Bougy did not receive the appointment.[73]

When in 1802 Capt. Francisco Caso y Luengo took command at Arkansas Post, he sent the governor a report on conditions there. He noted the poverty of the hunters and traders, almost all of whom owed money to local or New Orleans merchants. He, too, wanted peace in the district in order to improve its economic situation. Indian warfare, he claimed, was responsible each year for the deaths of several Arkansas hunters. He issued a call for peace talks with the tribes that frequented the district—the Quapaw, Osage, Chickasaw, Choctaw, and Cherokee nations.[74]

When the Osages appeared in late August, Caso y Luengo used the opportunity to promote peace rather than demand satisfaction for earlier misdeeds in order to reconcile the tribe with the other nations present. The Osages repeatedly expressed their profoundest desires for peace, extended their hand in friendship, danced, and accepted gifts from the commandant. Their behavior pleased Caso y Luengo since he wanted friendly relations, but inexperience caused him to err.[75]

The Choctaws, who at first seemed willing to initiate peaceful relations with the Osages, three days later were seeking their scalps. When the commandant rebuked them, they answered with "frivolous excuses." Only by bribing them with gifts did he restrain them from attacking. Respecting the custom of hospitality, the Quapaws escorted the Osages for two days when the latter returned to their village. In reporting the incident to the governor, Caso y Luengo deplored the way the Choctaws had behaved. He noted that hundreds of them were then in Arkansas, many roaming about without a chief, acting as lords of the land, and on the verge of causing harm. He preferred not to trade with them but feared that denying them goods might provoke an attack on the warehouse or on the district's white inhabitants.[76]

Little is known about the Osage activity during the last year or two of the Spanish era. Caso y Luengo did not mention them again, and Natchitoches was also quiet about them. In Missouri they made occasional depredations, mostly stealing horses with an occasional murder.[77] But the Osages were not faring well there because Native American foes were effectively raiding them.[78]

A problem of long standing that affected Arkansas commerce was the entry of numerous Indians from east of the Mississippi. United States pressure on the tribes forced many of them to flee westward, and some entered Arkansas.[79] While the Spaniards were tolerant of small tribes coming in, they were not as charitable to the larger nations with whom they had fought on occasion. Within Arkansas, however, the newcomers represented economic opportunities for the Post's traders and merchants.

As early as the 1760s and 1770s, outside tribes occasionally sent bands into Arkansas to trade.[80] In 1780 the Spaniards encouraged Illinois Indians to settle on lands, including Arkansas, on the White and St. Francis Rivers. Soon Delaware and Shawnee Indians began accepting the offer. Throughout the decade, they slowly settled in Arkansas. Usually small bands from a tribe entered individually. For example, groups of Delawares arrived in the 1780s, many of them settling in northern Arkansas. Further north, at Cape Girardeau, the Shawnees settled under the supervision of the local commandant, Louis Lorimier.[81] At the end of the 1780s, many more tribes were moving onto the Mississippi, particularly to the Ouachita district south of the Arkansas.[82]

Of the many tribes that came to the region, the Spaniards were most apprehensive about the Chickasaws and the Choctaws. The Chickasaws had been long-time English allies and had robbed Arkansas hunters on many occasions while the Choctaws were hostile to the Caddos. Numerous and often belligerent, they seemed willing to fight the local warriors, but they usually contented themselves with taking the scalps of peaceful Indians. In the 1790s Governor Carondelet wanted to form a coalition of west bank tribes, including the Osages, against the Choctaws, but past hostilities between would-be allies made that impossible. Moreover, it was Spanish policy to stay out of purely Indian quarrels. No resolution was found to the problem of east bank Indians moving west and warring or committing acts of violence on the established tribes.[83]

Nevertheless, the presence of new Indian groups in the Arkansas district represented fresh trading opportunities. Among the inhabitants who got licenses to commerce with them was Anselmo Billet, a hunter, who was given the right to trade with a group of Chickasaws in 1784. Billet was the son-in-law of the merchant François Ménard.[84]

A New Orleans merchant received a monopoly in 1786 to trade with the Delawares who visited Arkansas, and Commandant Vilemont also enjoyed a monopoly trade with the Cherokee and Loup Indians in the 1790s. Among others who received the right to trade with these newcomers were Joseph Bougy and Francisco Vinseman. On March 11, 1801, Bougy petitioned Governor Casa-Calvo for the Indian trade on the St. Francis River for a period of three years. He explained that his depressed financial predicament resulted from not being repaid for loans he had made in the war against Great Britain and from six slaves who ran away. In addition, providing for his numerous family contributed to his needy economic situation. Eight days later Casa-Calvo approved his request.[85] On March 8, 1801, the governor gave Andrés Fagot the trade with the Cherokees settled on the White River for two years. But learning that Fagot lacked the resources to carry out the trade, on March 30 Casa-Calvo permitted Vinseman to commerce there with goods worth fifteen hundred pesos.[86]

These are but a few of the trading licenses granted to Arkansas inhabitants. While on the one hand the addition of new waves of Native Americans constituted a counterweight to the Osages, on the other hand they had a disturbing effect on the established colonial and Indian populations. In the late Spanish period, whites were at last growing slightly in numbers because the district was witnessing a small influx of American farmers. Still, after eight decades of settlement, whites totaled less than five hundred by 1804.[87]

Because of its sparse population, Arkansas would continue to be a region known primarily for hunting in the first years of the American era. The Indian trade as well as commerce with white hunters had grown during the Spanish years, despite the favoritism official policy showed to Missouri and the disquieting effect outside natives, such as the Osages (who remained the chief obstacle to peaceful hunting in the early nineteenth century), Chickasaws, and Choctaws, had on the Arkansas district. Other factors, too, such as isolation, periodic flooding, and a small white population, contributed to the region's sluggish economic growth in the Spanish era.[88]

Unfortunately, because Arkansas Post commandants failed to report the quantities of furs, skins, oil, tallow, salted meat, and other products that left their jurisdiction, it is impossible to determine just how remunerative hunting was during the Spanish regime. Moreover, illicit trade removed products that never reached the Post and would not have been counted. Therefore it can only be assumed that hunting yielded more at the beginning of the nineteenth century than it did in the 1760s. But what is known to be true was that Arkansas ended the Spanish era much as it had started it, as a region where the Indian trade and forest products still accounted for the largest economic activity.

The Significance of Arkansas's Colonial Experience

MORRIS S. ARNOLD

To speak of the gentry of colonial Arkansas may seem to be doubly oxymoronic: first, because the phrase "colonial Arkansas" itself has an odd ring in the ears, summoning up pictures of sturdy hill folk outfitted in tricornered hats; and, second, because we have all learned that eighteenth-century Arkansas Post gave shelter mainly to hunters and vagabonds of small means and less cultivation. It is nevertheless the case that there were a number of persons of gentle birth who made their way to the Arkansas wilderness in colonial times to assume such positions of prominence as were available here at the time.

Most of these people were attached to the military and many were the Post commandants to whom the colonial administration entrusted both the civil and military government of the Arkansas River region. But there is an aspect of their careers that needs to be emphasized so that they may be appreciated as the men and women of parts that they truly were. The French and Spanish colonial administrations attracted persons of their quality to the forest posts of Louisiana by allowing them to engage in business and trade: they were, in many respects, merchant-capitalists first and military officers second. For instance, Pierre de Coulange, who reestablished the Arkansas garrison in 1732, came upriver from New Orleans to be commandant before he had even received his ensign's commission from Louis XV.[1] Sometimes, as an inducement, Arkansas commandants sought and received monopoly rights to the trade with certain tribes. Not infrequently, the government expected in return that the commandant would make loans to it to defray governmental costs or even to pay expenses that would never be reimbursed. It may be, for instance, that Lieutenant Paul Augustin de La Houssaye built the fort begun on the Arkansas River in 1751 out of his own private funds.[2] It is certain, at any rate, that a number of Post commandants found themselves stuck with the bills for the entertainment of visiting Indian dignitaries and sometimes had to advance the salaries of their soldiers out of their own pockets or their individual stores. It is therefore not an exaggeration to say that government in eighteenth-century Arkansas was sometimes farmed out to private enterprise in exchange for trading rights. Thus we often need to think of the commandants not as government officials who were coincidentally in business, but as businessmen who were coincidentally in the government.

Many of these sojourning entrepreneurs fared quite well financially in the Arkansas country. Pierre-Joseph Favrot, for example, a well-educated member of one of Louisiana's most prominent colonial families who spent some years at the Post in the early Spanish period, vigorously (though unsuccessfully) sought appointment as commandant of Arkansas Post in the 1790s, presumably because he had found the region quite lucrative.[3] Ignace Delinó de Chalmette amassed such a trading fortune here and at Natchez that the New Orleans grandee the Baron de Pontalba affected for a time to regard it as in some manner scandalous.[4] Others, of course, were not so lucky: Balthazar de Villiers, for instance, died bankrupt due to trade losses, some of which he incurred when he outfitted a band of refugees from the American Revolution who disappeared into the woods never to return.

When viewed in the fullness of their context, the activities of Arkansas's colonial gentry take on an interesting texture. It is instructive, for instance, to see how often the self-interests of the governing class corresponded with governmental interests. For example, commandants were expected to encourage immigration into their bailiwick; and this was a duty that they could have been expected enthusiastically to pursue, for a larger population might well mean more business for them. Improved Indian relations, one of the main aims of the colonial administration, would also help increase their trade accounts. Commandants were expected to keep out English intruders from across the mighty river, and the extent of their success in this would decrease foreign competition for the Indian trade. The encouragement of the agricultural and mechanical arts would also redound to the financial benefit of the commandants. Colonial administrators thus cleverly linked private and public interests to reduce the cost of government. Self-interest was drafted to promote the public good; the chamber of commerce was the government.

Of course, this method of staffing and financing a government runs completely contrary to current notions of fairness, for we are socialized to

Pierre-Joseph Favrot.

Courtesy of Mr. Richmond G. Favrot, New Orleans.

think that disinterestedness is the *sine qua non* of equitable government. Our liberal, republican, and bureaucratic ideals, however, were far too expensive for colonial Arkansas, because they would have required taxation to support a civil-servant class; and the colonial Louisiana administration kept taxes virtually nonexistent in order to encourage immigration. But in any case, all was not rosy in this political picture, since self-interest could sometimes undermine the fairness of governmental functions. For example, Arkansas commandants had to serve as civil judges, and the cases that came before them had mainly to do with trade debts and labor relations. That meant that litigants were often direct business competitors of the judge, a situation that would rightly be considered scandalous today. An excellent instance of the dangers of this kind of conflict of interest occurred in the 1770s when Commandant Balthazar de Villiers was called upon to decide a matter involving one François Ménard, the richest man at the Post. The records of the case reveal that de Villiers cordially hated Ménard and considered him an archvillain because he regularly breached local trading regulations.[5] Perhaps de Villiers was correct about Ménard's character; but since they were frequently embroiled with each other in trade disputes, de Villiers could hardly qualify as an impartial judge.

Self-interest nevertheless very frequently induced commandants to attend to affairs of state with an admirable devotion, for reasons already adumbrated. In accomplishing the objectives of the Louisiana colonial administration, it turns out, they mainly failed, not because of the vices to which the pursuit of personal happiness sometimes leads, but because of large forces over which they could not have hoped realistically to gain an ascendancy. Economic development in Arkansas simply proved an elusive and unachievable goal. As late as 1768, for instance, a good three or four generations after Europeans had been settling in the Arkansas region, Alexandre de Clouet reported that not a single one of his residents had one of those outdoor ovens with which civilized Louisiana communities had abounded from early times. He did, he claimed, finally succeed in getting four of these built; and he even tried to convince his inhabitants to build a common fence to make possible the kind of communal agriculture that brought a measure of prosperity to the Illinois country. (In this last venture, however, he appears to have been unsuccessful.)[6] It was not until 1791, moreover, that we first hear of horse-powered grist mills, almost one hundred years after they had appeared in Illinois.[7] The Post's first sawmill barely predated the American takeover in 1804;[8] and Arkansas's first cotton gin was probably not erected until 1805,[9] though gins were common in other parts of the colony long before.

The early history of Arkansas is full of intrinsic interest and its study does not need to be justified by showing that it is somehow relevant to our present condition. In fact, it greatly narrows and seriously misconstrues the function of historical studies to insist that they must necessarily help us understand how we got where we are. Nevertheless, there is certainly nothing wrong with studies that do just that, and we shall now turn to an effort to establish a nexus between the lack of success of Arkansas's colonial leadership and some of our present predicaments.

Forty-five years ago, John Gould Fletcher, the brilliant Arkansas poet and writer, in his history of Arkansas, shrugged off the colonial experience with a single nonchalant sentence: "Life in Arkansas Post under the French regime seemed to me to have little to do with the main story of Arkansas, and so I omitted it."[10] But there is evidence that, on the contrary, many of the recurrent themes of Arkansas history, especially its persistent poverty and relative cultural backwardness, have their roots deep in the eighteenth century. More specifically, it is becoming clear that Arkansas was undeveloped compared to its neighbors in the rest of Louisiana during the colonial epoch; that its territorial period continued to be influenced by that relative backwardness; and that the frustration that is felt even today, because the state seems always to be struggling to catch up with the rest of the nation, can be partly laid to the activities of colonial Louisiana authorities.

For a starting point, it will be instructive to wonder why Arkansas Post, founded by the same generation of European expansionists that established Philadelphia and Charleston, never attained anything approaching prominence in any respect, while the achievements of those other two settlements were of the greatest importance. Better yet, compare three French Louisiana settlements: why is it that New Orleans, founded thirty-five years after Arkansas Post, and St. Louis, established forty-five years later still, are cities of stature and attainment, while Arkansas Post no longer exists as a real town? It will be necessary to admit to the complexity of the forces that work in combination to produce large and sophisticated communities. For instance, immigration was long retarded into Arkansas because of the primitive condition of its roads and the fear of Indians. Geography, too, has been extremely important: it is hardly fortuitous that Charleston, Philadelphia, St. Louis, and New Orleans are (or were) great port cities and thus natural creators of wealth and culture.

It is best to begin a consideration of the importance of Arkansas's remote colonial past with a cursory examination of its topography. There is very little high ground suitable for the establishment of towns along Arkansas's eastern border, the Mississippi River. The same is true of the Arkansas River: one has, even today, to go well up it, all the way to that little detached part of the Grand Prairie near where the tiny Arkansas County

Henri de Tonty.

community called Nady is now situated, before a good settlement site is encountered. This, in fact, was where Henri de Tonty decided, in the summer of 1686, to locate his isolated fur-trading concern—the first Arkansas Post. Here also, in 1721, a couple of decades after the failure of Tonty's venture, John Law's abortive Alsatian colony collapsed.

In 1726 the first description of the nature of Arkansas's European population appeared, and it is full of portent: "The people are all poor," the census-taker lamented, "and they live only by the hunting of wild animals."[11] This first, terse, and epigrammatic description of colonial Arkansans would be expatiated on during the rest of the century, but its essential message would remain unaltered. A 1746 report on Louisiana said of the twelve *habitant* families at the Post that "their principal occupation is hunting, curing meat, and commerce in tallow and bear oil."[12] Two decades later, the Englishman Philip Pittman remarked that "on account of the sandiness of the soil, and the lowness of the situation, which makes it subject to be overflowed," agriculture was impossible at the downriver location of the Post. Therefore, he concluded, "[t]hese people subsist mostly by hunting, and every season send to New Orleans great quantities of bear's oil, tallow, salted buffaloe meat, and a few skins."[13] In 1777, Captain de Villiers reported to his superiors in New Orleans that his Post was "a place of residence for merchants and a supply point for the hunters who come here to equip themselves."[14] As late as 1796, Commandant de Vilemont wrote that all his *habitants* were hunters.[15]

This kind of description of Arkansas's population persisted into the nineteenth century. For instance, in 1802 François Marie Perrin du Lac said that the inhabitants "of the *Village des Arkansas . . .* are hunters by profession. . . ." "More than half the year," he went on, "one finds in this village only women, children, and old people. The men go to hunt deer, the skins of which are less valued than those from the northern country; buffalo which they salt for their use; and some beaver which they still find at a little distance."[16] Six years later, Fortescue Cuming could still write that the Post "consists chiefly of hunters and Indian traders, [and] of course is a poor place, as settlers of this description never look for anything beyond the mere necessities of life, except whiskey."[17]

Some contemporaneous evaluations illuminate the moral and cultural condition of these hunters who formed the bulk of Arkansas's colonial denizens. De Villiers grumbled in 1777 that they were mostly people of evil doings who could soon be replaced by useful agricultural colonists if only a suitable town site were provided.[18] The lieutenant governor at Natchitoches, Athanase de Mézières, said that the Arkansas hunters were murderers, rapists, and fugitives from justice, and he suspected them of encouraging the Osages to raid the Caddo and Natchitoches regions to steal women, children, and horses.[19] The most sustained and stinging denunciation of the Arkansas hunters, however, came from Juan Fihliol of Ouachita Post (modern Monroe, Louisiana) in 1786. He thought most white

Arkansans were outlaws seeking asylum in the woods. "These men," he said, "consist of scum of all kinds of nations . . . who . . . have become stuck here through their fondness for idleness and independence. . . . Their customs correspond to their origins. Hardly do they know whether they are Christians. They excel in all the vices and their kind of life is a real scandal. The savages, though uncivilized, hold them in contempt. . . . The women are as vicious as the men, and are worthy companions of their husbands."[20] Fihliol's attempts to herd his South Arkansas vagabonds into an ordered agrarian settlement met with almost no success. In 1768, Commandant de Clouet of Arkansas Post also despaired of ever convincing his population "that the land yielded every good thing to those who were not lazy."[21] And Perrin du Lac noted that every year when the hunters returned to the Post, "they pass their time playing games, dancing, drinking, or doing nothing, similar in this as in other things to the savage peoples with whom they pass the greater part of their lives, whose habits and customs they acquire."[22]

In sum, the reputation in Louisiana of Arkansas colonials was that they were for the most part lazy and shiftless, given to excess drinking and libertinage, and irredeemably lawless and amoral. It is, of course, entirely natural that that reputation would subsist well into the American period. For instance, William Darby, in his influential *Emigrant's Guide* published just before Arkansas became a territory, described Arkansas Post "as poor and inconsiderable, like all other places where the inhabitants depend upon hunting and trade with savages for their subsistence."[23] This assessment is indistinguishable from the one that the Louisiana census taker had ventured almost a century earlier. Furthermore, it is no step at all from the numerous descriptions of colonial Arkansas already alluded to to the predominant antebellum image of Arkansas as the "bear state," the refuge of outlaws, and the home of "the Arkansas toothpick," or Bowie knife.[24] Charles Bolton's admirable book *Territorial Ambition* provides a sophisticated correction to the unrelentingly bleak picture of territorial Arkansas that most historians have served up.[25] But the point remains unblunted that Arkansas, whatever net progress it was able to generate in the early nineteenth century, got off to a bad start which it never managed to overcome. Is it not obvious that Arkansas's colonial reputation very materially contributed to a reluctance on the part of respectable American immigrants to settle the region during the territorial period?

The consequences of Arkansas's eighteenth-century reputation alone would make its colonial epoch of great relevance to the state's present condition, for most historians would agree that there is a certain continuity between antebellum Arkansas and modern times. The first suggestion, therefore, is that this continuity can readily be extended back to the very beginning of European settlement in the state. But there is more: the sad truth is that the relative lack of cultural and commercial sophistication in the Arkansas region in the eighteenth century was the direct and sometimes intended consequence of French and Spanish colonial governmental policy. This is a matter of some complexity, but at least three instances where that policy had demonstrably dire consequences for Arkansas's development come readily to mind.

First of all, the French government in 1756 ordered the removal of Arkansas Post from the fertile highlands of the Grand Prairie to the swamps of present Desha County so that it would be more convenient to the convoys plying the Mississippi between the Illinois country and New Orleans.[26] It is likely that this change of venue was made necessary by the beginning of the Seven Years' War. Whatever the reason for the move, the new location was entirely unsuited for farming; indeed, as Captain Pittman lamented in 1765, "on account of the sandiness of the soil, and the lowness of the situation, which makes it subject to be overflowed, [the Post inhabitants] do not raise their necessary provisions."[27] (In fact, in 1766 the Quapaws became so discouraged by the hopelessness of their situation that they asked the governor in New Orleans to be allowed to migrate to the Red River region.) Two years later, Alexandre de Clouet wrote that there had been no crop at all in the previous four years and de Villiers reported precisely the same thing in 1779.[28] It is therefore abundantly plain that no real settlement could gather around the little water-logged fort while the Post was in the delta of Desha County from 1756 to 1779, a critical period in the history of Louisiana immigration and settlement.

A second example, and probably an even more important one, occurred after the Post moved back upriver in 1779. It seems that St. Louis commercial interests exerted pressure on the colonial government to inhibit and retard the economic development of the Arkansas region because they did not want the competition that Arkansas would represent. St. Louis was not founded until 1764, but it was established in reliance on the French colonial government's express promise to bestow on its proprietors a trade monopoly with the Osage Indians. The Arkansas merchants quite naturally wanted a piece of this lucrative market, but when the government forbade it in order to protect the St. Louis monopoly, the Osages attacked, robbed, and sometimes killed the Arkansas hunters. It was said that this violence was because the Post would not send the Osages a trader, and this seems to have been true: it is possible that the Osages considered the Post population

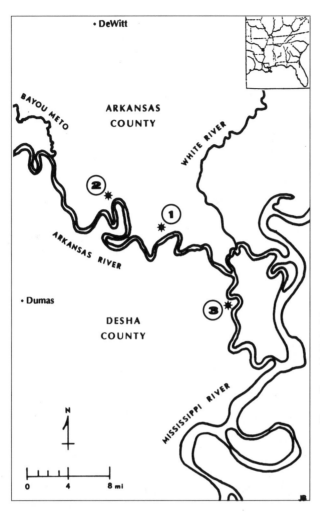

Locations of Arkansas Post, 1686–present:
1. 1686–99; 1721–49.
2. 1749–56; 1779–present.
3. 1756–79.

Map by John Baldwin. Courtesy of Arkansas Historical Association.

as a kind of separate tribe of whites; and among some of the indigenous peoples of North America it was a rule of behavior that if a tribe was not trading it was *ipso facto* hostile and a state of war existed with it. Though the colonial governors wanted to wage war on the Osages because of their depredations in Arkansas, the St. Louis lieutenant governors had no enthusiasm for such a project because it would undermine the commercial foundation of their town. St. Louis magnates exhibited a callous indifference towards the Arkansas hunters, whom they termed "scum" whose interests were not even worth consulting when compared to the economic well-being of their own prosperous trading community. When the Arkansas commandant raged that this attitude amounted to sealing commerce with the blood of the innocents, the governor had no ready reply.[29]

A third example, this one the most ironic, will suffice to make the point: economic growth in Arkansas was actually stymied by the colonial government's effort to stimulate population growth. Because of the fear of being overrun by the westering American republic, a panicked Spanish government very late in the eighteenth century began making huge land grants in Arkansas to encourage the influx of a population to act as a buffer to American expansion. Two of the largest of these grants were made to one Elisha Winter and his associates and to Commandant Carlos de Vilemont: Winter's grant contained upwards of a million acres north of the Arkansas River, and he was supposed to establish a cattle ranch on it; de Vilemont's grant was in modern Chicot County. Though Winter did make some perfunctory efforts to establish himself in the eighteenth century, no real progress was ever made toward settling his grant; and de Vilemont did nothing whatever with his until some years after the American takeover.[30] The result was that there was a cloud on the title to much of the arable land in Arkansas's delta well into the nineteenth century, and this naturally retarded immigration. As Thomas Nuttall explained in 1819, "[t]he improvement and settlement of this place proceeded slowly, owing, in some measure, as I am informed, to the uncertain titles of the neighboring lands. Several enormous Spanish grants remained still undecided. . . ."[31] He specifically mentioned Elisha Winter's grant and lamented that this "enormous claim . . . containing about a million of acres of this territory, and which will yet probably for some time remain undetermined, proves a considerable bar to the progress of the settlement."[32]

After fifteen years of studying this fascinating and neglected aspect of Arkansas's past, it does not seem at all fanciful to say that what Arkansas Post was (and was not) may turn out to have been as important to Arkansas's modern condition as Williamsburg was to Virginia's and Charleston was to South Carolina's. More research of course needs to be done, but the matters outlined briefly above would seem to demonstrate that Arkansas's colonial past is connected to the present in important ways that have not been properly appreciated. These matters deserve serious attention from future scholars; they certainly cannot conscionably continue to be ignored.

Indian Signs on the Land

SAMUEL D. DICKINSON

Indians left lasting marks on Arkansas. Most conspicuous is the name of both the state itself and the big river that crosses it diagonally. In all parts of Arkansas there are places with names that came from tribal languages. Some are prominent, others are significant only locally.

These names may be divided into two categories: imported and native. The former—such as Pocahontas, Powhatan, Osceola, and Etowah—were affixed by white settlers either to honor Indians or in remembrance of communities with those names in other states from which the settlers had migrated. The etymology of these names does not enter into this discussion, for they are secondhand, and their origins for the most part are well known.

In contrast, meanings of Arkansas's native Indian place names usually are obscure. Corrupted spellings in some cases have made their derivation uncertain, and exact linguistic identification is not always possible. All these names, however, were clinging to the land before the Indians had to abandon it. Designating streams, lakes, mountains, hills, prairies, and a few communities, they today bear witness to the aboriginal peoples who practiced different customs, who spoke different languages, yet who all strived to live in harmony with nature if not with each other. It is fitting as well as fortunate for us that the land still testifies to their former presence.

These names follow in alphabetical order:

AIAITA was the old name of Choctaw Prairie, bordering the Arkansas River directly southwest of Altus, Franklin County. This word is a variant of the Choctaw *Aiataia*, "landing" or "a place to rest upon."[1] This prairie was included in a grant made to Jean-Baptiste Dardenne, a trader and farmer, April 20, 1816.[2]

ARKANSAS, as is commonly recognized, perpetuates a name of the Quapaw tribe whom French explorers found living on the banks of the Mississippi and Arkansas Rivers in the area of their confluence. But the word is not from the Quapaw language. When Père Jacques Marquette's and Louis Jolliet's party visited the Kappa village of the Quapaws in 1673, a young Illinois Indian served as interpreter.[3] He used the Illinois, or Algonquian, name for the Quapaws as he was accustomed to doing. This name was recorded as *Akamsea* in Marquette's journal and on his map. It means "South Wind People." The Illinois root is *Ak-akon-ca* or *Ak-akan-ze*.[4]

Akancea, Acansea, Acansa and *Accancea* were customary variations of the name in accounts written by Frenchmen who descended the Mississippi from Canada. Those who sailed to Mobile and New Orleans directly from the motherland added *r* and a terminal *s* to the name, as Stanley Faye pointed out.[5] For instance, André-Joseph Pénigaut in his narrative of his journey with Pierre-Charles de Sueur up the Mississippi in 1700 referred to *la Rivière des Arkansas* and *la nation des Arkansas*.[6] The *des* as well as the *s* indicates that he had the plural in mind.

Spaniards favored a *z* instead of the terminal *s*. Officials were prone to abbreviate names in their reports. Their abbreviation *Arc* for *Arcansas* was mistaken for a similar French word meaning "bow" by some nineteenth-century writers.

The French *aux Arcansas*, meaning "to" or "at Arkansas Post," was shortened to *aux Arc*, which, because of the sound when elided, eventually gave the corruption, *Ozark*.[7] John Pope in recounting his travels in 1791 mentioned both the "Osarque River" and the "Osarque Indians."[8]

The Quapaws, according to their own tradition, before migrating to Arkansas had lived with their Dhegiha Siouan relatives on the Ohio River. Their kinsmen were ancestors of the Osages, Kansas, Poncas, and Omahas. Illinois tribes called all these people the *Alkansa* or the *Acansas*, and they identified the river with them. The 1718 N. de Fer map of Louisiana designated this stream as *Rivière d'Oubache ou Akansea Sipi*.

Leaving their homeland, perhaps forced by the Iroquois, these Dhegiha Sioux, on reaching the mouth of the river, separated. Those who became Quapaws descended the Mississippi and consequently acquired the name *Okáȟpa*, "Downstream People," while those who went up the Mississippi thereafter were known as the *Omaha*, "Upstream People." Dr. Robert L. Rankin of the University of Kansas Department of Linguistics, the authority on the Quapaw language, says that the root of *Okáȟpa* is *Káȟpa*, the term for "south" or "downstream."[9]

Obviously, the word "Quapaw" is a corruption of *Okáȟpa*. Arkansas Territorial Governor George Izard attributed it to the Americans.[10] Presumably he meant English-speaking Americans. French and Spanish corruptions were different. Père Pierre F. X. de Charlevoix in 1721 referred to the tribe as the *Ouyapes*.[11] They were known to Mexicans as the *Mahas*.[12]

Quapaws were occupying four villages in 1682 at the time René-Robert Cavelier, Sieur de La Salle, explored the Mississippi. To Dr. Rankin we are indebted for an explanation of their names.

Kappa, he says, was the way the French spelled *Okáȟpa*. "Modern Quapaws have replaced the *k* of *Okáȟpa* with a *g* sound, so it is pronounced *Ogáȟpa* nowadays," he remarks.

Osotouy was a French spelling for *Ozó-tiohi* which Dr. Rankin breaks down into *ozó*, "tree-covered bottom land along a river," *ti*, "dwelling," and *ohi*, a suffix denoting location. So he translates this name as "dwelling(s) in the bottom lands."

Tonguenga, the French form of *Toⁿwaⁿjinga*, according to Dr. Rankin, was compounded from *toⁿwaⁿ*, "town," and *jinga*, "little." Thus, he confirms the meaning, "Little Town," that Henri Joutel learned from Jean Couture in 1687.

Tourima signified *Pommes de Terres*, "Indian Potatoes," Jean-Baptiste Bénard de La Harpe wrote in his report of his investigation of the Arkansas River country in 1722.[13] The name of the same village is recorded in other memoirs as *Touriman* and *Thoriman*. *To* in all Siouan languages, Dr. Rankin notes, does mean "Indian potato." Nevertheless, he questions La Harpe's interpretation, because the Reverend J. Owen Dorsey, a Smithsonian Institution ethnologist who studied Dhegiha-Siouan tribes in the 1880s, insisted that the correct form of the word was *Ti-oadimaⁿ*. *Ti* is the pan-Siouan word for "dwelling," Dr. Rankin says. Unfortunately, nothing in his data or in Dorsey's indicates the meaning of *oadimaⁿ*.[14]

Although the Quapaws claimed as their hunting grounds lands from the mouth of the Arkansas River to the Canadian River and from the Mississippi to the Red, very few of their place names have survived. In modern times a historic district in Little Rock, a Hot Springs bathhouse, and various enterprises have adopted the name "Quapaw," but no geographic feature in the state retains that name from the Indians themselves. There is, however, Quapaw Bayou near Shreveport, Louisiana, attesting to the presence of a Quapaw band that moved down Red River from the Sulphur River in the early 1820s.

BAYOU, the term applied to a sluggish stream, often an abandoned river channel, came from the Choctaw *bayuk*, sometimes confused with *bok*, meaning "a stream smaller than a river" in Choctaw.[15]

BODCAW, a bayou originating in Nevada and Hempstead Counties, gave its name to a Nevada County community. On some modern Louisiana maps the name is spelled *Bodcau*. Governor General Estevan Miró of the Province of Louisiana in 1779 referred to it as *Batea*. Early nineteenth-century spellings were *Badkah* and *Bodeau*.[16] Since this stream is in the heart of what once was Caddo territory, one would expect the name to be Caddoan. But a Choctaw origin seems more probable, though the Choctaw language does not have a *d* as does the Caddo. Choctaws hunted along this bayou in the late eighteenth and early nineteenth centuries. Perhaps this name was corrupted from *bokko*, their word for "mound," "hillock," "bank."[17] A large flat-topped mound, dating back to the early Caddo or Coles Creek culture, stands near this stream in Nevada County. There were other mounds, Indian-made and natural, along its course to the Red River in Louisiana.

CADDO, a river rising in mountains of the same name in Montgomery County, recalls the confederation of ten Caddoan tribes that occupied present Southwest Arkansas, East Texas, Northeast Oklahoma, and Northwest Louisiana. The old town of Caddo Gap, Montgomery County, is located where the river breaks through a range. Caddo Valley, Clark County, is a relatively new community where highways converge near the river several miles above its mouth on the Ouachita River.

There is no record of a Caddo village on this river during the historic period unless Tula, whose inhabitants fiercely attacked Hernando de Soto's army on October 8, 1541, was at or near this gap as the United States De Soto Expedition Commission believed. Commission chairman, Dr. John R. Swanton of the Smithsonian Institution, identified the Indians as Caddos, yet he was unable to determine the origin of the name.[18] Dr. Charles H. Hudson Jr., of the University of Georgia, in the latest study of the de Soto entrada, relocates Tula near the present Bluffton, Yell County.[19] He likewise thinks the Indians were Caddos. However, this writer suspects they were Wichita, kin to the Caddos.

Indians who accompanied the Spaniards might have been responsible for the name. Maybe they took it from Choctaw, Chickasaw, or the Mobilian trade jargon that was spoken throughout the Southeast. If it were from the last, it means "to fall down" or "to lie down."[20] On the other hand, it is possible that Padre José Antonio Pichardo was right in guessing that the

Spaniards bestowed the name of the Toltec capital on these Indians.[21] That pre-Aztec city-state took its name from the Nahua *tule*, "cane," "reed."

The most important Caddos in the Red River country called themselves the *Ka dohada cho*, "Great Chiefs."[22] From their villages in the great bend they influenced distant tribes as well as those related to them. French writers spelled their names *Cadodaquois*, *Cadodaquioux*, *Caddodacchos*, and *Kados*. The short form was the French plural of *caddi*, ka-edi, "chief."[23] *Caudachos*, *Grand Cadaux*, *Cados d'Acquioux*, and *Cadaux-dakioux* were common Spanish spellings.

In 1719 Jean-Baptiste Bénard de La Harpe founded Fort Breton at the Nassonis, a neighbor tribe to the Kadohadacho proper and a member of that division of the Caddos. Eventually the fort became the Spanish post of San Luis de Cadodachos. Relics that have been unearthed at Rosborough Lake, Bowie County, Texas, just northwest of Texarkana, indicate this was the location of the settlement. The Caddo Trace ran from great bend villages to the Quapaws on the Lower Arkansas River.

CAHAYNOHOUA was the name of Indians who in the seventeenth century were living beside the Caddo Trace on a stream west of the trace crossing on the Ouachita River at modern Camden. Henri Joutel, a guest of these Indians in July 1687, failed to record the meaning of their name. However, he did say that their chief's name, Hinma Koapemiche, meant "Big Knife."[24] Geographer N. de Fer added another village, Cayoaho, to his 1718 map. Guillaume Delisle's map done in the same year shows only the village of Cahinoa on the Ouachita. Jean-Bernard Bossu in 1777 referred to the tribe as the *Kanoatino*. *Cahinnio* has become the standard spelling in archaeological publications. This tribe disappeared from the Arkansas region in the eighteenth century, leaving no place name.

CHAFFIE or CHEFFIE Creek, immediately south of Camden, acquired its name from Cheffo, son of Chief LeBum or Lebun of a band of Choctaws who lived in the present Ouachita County in the early 1800s. These Indians were associated with a larger group living several miles southwest of modern Monroe, Louisiana. Cheffo likely was a corruption of the Choctaw *chafa*, "runner," "exile," "flier."[25] Obviously the chief's name was a corruption either from the French or from the Choctaw language itself. The first person singular in Choctaw is *le*, *la*, *li*. It follows the verb, so it is in the wrong place to be joined to *bonna*, "rolled up," which otherwise might have been the origin of Bum or Bun.[26] Maybe the chief was the son of a Frenchman by a Choctaw mother and took his father's name, *Bon*, "Good."

The Daughters of the American Revolution erected a monument at what is believed to be the Indian's grave.

CHATAUGNA Mountain on White River above Batesville marked the eastern boundary of the land given to the Cherokees by the U.S. government as authorized by the treaty of July 8, 1817. In historical records the name also was spelled *Chatunga, Cathoochee,* and *Catouch.* The last form evidently is a corruption of the Cherokee *gadusi*, "hill,"[27] which seems to be related to the name, *Chattanooga*, meaning "a rock that goes up to a point."[28] *Chataugna* may be a variation of Chattanooga.

CHEROKEE Settlement, consisting of villages on the north bank of the Arkansas River from Point Remove to Mulberry River, appeared on an 1820 map of *Countries Bordering On the Mississippi and Missouri.* The Indians whom we call Cherokee called themselves *Tsalagi.* Maybe it means "ancient tobacco people." However, their older name for themselves was *Ani-Yun wiya*, "Principal People."[29] The Choctaw noun, *couluk,* or *chiluk,* "well," or "cave," seems to have given rise to the word, "Cherokee."[30] It was appropriate, because so many of the tribe lived originally in the mountains of Kentucky, eastern Tennessee, northern Georgia, North and South Carolina, northern Alabama, Virginia, and West Virginia, where there were caves and sink holes.

After the American Revolution, disputes between Cherokees and whites led to violence. Attacks invited reprisals. Duwala, a chief whom whites called "Chief Bowl," or "The Bowl," and his Chickamauga warriors killed white immigrants at Muscle Shoals. Fearing retaliation, he brought his family and associates to the St. Francis River in 1794.

In 1811 another chief, Skaquaw, "The Swan," announced to those Cherokees that he had a vision one night while he was leaning against a stump and gazing at a comet. Lightning, he claimed, suddenly flashed from four directions and formed a small light at his feet. He picked it up on a wood chip. It did not burn his hand, because it was "tame fire." A child came from the East and another approached from the West. They perfumed the air, and he fell asleep. Then the Great Spirit advised him to warn his people to leave the St. Francis before disaster befell them. When the Great Spirit finished talking one of the children blew out the fire, and Skaquaw awakened. He informed the Cherokees of what he had learned, and they hastened to depart. Thus, they escaped the New Madrid earthquakes.[31]

Some of them stopped on the White River, but most went on to the Arkansas River. From the U.S. government they received lands between the

White and Arkansas Rivers in exchange for their old lands east of the Mississippi. They had possession only until they signed the treaty of May 6, 1828, by which they relinquished all claims in return for lands further west.

CHICKALAH, the name of a creek, mountain, and rural community in Yell County, is a variation of *Chikileh*, the name of a Cherokee chief who was noted for his oratory. His speech in favor of peace persuaded his fellow chiefs to agree to bury the hatchet with their old enemies, the Osages.[32] His name was derived from *Tsgwa-legwala*, "Whipperwill."[33]

CHICKANINNY Prairie stretches from Boyd Hill, six miles southwest of Lewisville, Lafayette County, toward the Red River. The name is an anglicized form of the Caddo *Cha-kani-ne*, "the place of crying," the mythical location of the emergence of people and animals on the surface of the earth. The hill, so the Caddos believed, once had a cave extending to the Underworld. Through it the first inhabitants of the world and the first animals issued. An old man, carrying a pipe and fire in one hand and a drum in the other, appeared first. His wife, bearing seeds of corn and pumpkins, followed. Before all the other folk below and the remaining animals could climb out, a wolf closed the cave opening. The people outside wept for those who never would be able to join them. Thereafter Caddos considered the hill sacred.[34]

CHICKASAW Crossing was the name that early nineteenth-century pioneers gave to the place on White River where Augusta, Woodruff County, stands today.[35] Indians who traveled a path from the Chickasaw Bluff, at the site of Memphis, forded the river here. The Chickasaws, whose lands included what is now North Mississippi and West Tennessee, were hereditary foes of the Quapaws. While the latter were allies first of the French and then of the Spanish, the Chickasaws were aligned with the British, who encouraged them to attack the Quapaws, and even Arkansas Post. According to tradition, the Chickasaws originally were members of the Choctaw tribe. Their name confirms it. It was compounded from the Choctaw *chikkih*, "not a very great while ago," and *ashachi*, "to leave."[36] As game declined on the east bank of the Mississippi during the late 1700s, Chickasaws crossed the river to hunt in the St. Francis bottoms. In 1790 warriors pursued a party of Miami Indians into the Caddo country and killed their chief, thereby arousing widespread alarm among Arkansas's Indians. Both the Chickasaw and Choctaw spoke a Muskhogean dialect. Sometimes they went to war together.

CHICKASAWBA Mound in Mississippi County is supposed to have been named for Chickasawha, chief of a Chickasaw band of forty families that were living in the vicinity as late as 1836.[37] *Ha* in Choctaw is the equivalent of a^n, a determinative particle which means "the" and is placed after nouns to specify or emphasize. *Ba* is an adverb meaning "certainly," "surely," and "merely."[38] It, likewise, follows the verb. The suffix affirms the Chickasaw presence at the mound.

CHOBOHOLLAY was the English spelling of *Shoboli*, "Smoky," the Choctaw name for the St. Francis River.[39] This place name is obsolete in Arkansas.

CHOCTAW is the name of a bayou and mound in Desha County, a lake in Prairie County, a township in Lincoln County, and a crossing on Little Red River in White County. The origin of the name is uncertain. Some linguists believe that the Creek word, *cate*, "red," was the source while others are inclined to derive the name from the Spanish *chato*, "flat."[40] The Choctaws flattened the heads of infants.

In about 1763, with permission of the Spanish government, Choctaws began leaving their homeland in Mississippi and Alabama to hunt in the Ouachita River basin. After the American Revolution and under pressure from land-hungry whites, Choctaw bands sought new homes on the west side of the Mississippi River.

Besides the aforementioned village near modern Camden, other villages are known to have been on the Lower Arkansas River, on the St. Francis and in present Hempstead County before the United States ceded to Choctaws territory in Arkansas. The grant was west of a line running from Point Remove on the Arkansas River to Red River three miles below the mouth of Little River. Five years later the Choctaws gave back land east of a line starting one hundred paces east of Fort Smith on the Arkansas River and extending due south to Red River.

During the removal of Choctaws from east of the Mississippi in compliance with the Treaty of Dancing Rabbit, September 27, 1830, many of the Indians traveled the route long known as the Choctaw Trace that crossed the Mississippi into Chicot County and ran through South Arkansas by way of Washington, Hempstead County, to Indian Territory. Approximately seventy-eight Choctaws left the Camden area in 1832 to live with the kinsmen who had already migrated.[41] However, some Choctaws, who had married blacks, remained in Arkansas and thereafter were considered Negroes.

CHULA, the Choctaw word for "fox,"[42] is the name of a creek and community in Yell County.

COLOTOCHES, the name of a bayou tributary of the Cache River in Prairie County, and *Callachee*, the name of a bay there, are variations of the same Creek word. It was reported in 1825 that an Indian chief, Callaches, once had a village on a hill near the bay.[43] That name is a corruption of *Kealedji*, a branch of the Tukabahohee Creeks. It refers to a headdress.[44] About 1770 a band of Creeks from the present state of Alabama settled among the Quapaws, and in later years Creeks hunted in several river valleys of the Arkansas region.

COUNCIL BEND, an oxbow lake in Lee County, is a remnant of a Mississippi River meander that once was divided by Council Island. The place takes its name from an Indian assembly that was held there.[45] This council convened before 1793, because Pierre George Rousseau, commanding general of Spanish galleys on the Mississippi, in his log of the galliot *La Fleche*, mentioned passing the "Great Council Island" on February 14 of that year.[46] Probably it was a meeting of representatives of various tribes in early April 1791, to decide whether to make war on the Osages. Arkansas Post commandant Juan Ignace Delino learned from hunters, who had it from Abenakis, that the Abenakis, Shawnees, Sauks, Chickasaws, Cherokees, and Mascoutens were to hold a council for that purpose somewhere above the mouth of the St. Francis.[47]

DELAWARE Creek in Yell County indicates the general location of a village of the Delaware Indians who were associated with the Cherokees. The Delaware tribe called itself *Leni-Lenape*, "men of our nation," or simply *Lenape*, "our men."[48] These Indians, nevertheless, were fated to be known in history by the title of an English governor, Lord De La Warr, for whom the river, on whose banks they originally lived, was named by the colonists. In the mid-eighteenth century the Indians migrated into the Ohio River valley. There they aligned themselves with the Shawnees. Both tribes, with permission of the Spanish government, moved west of the Mississippi. A band of Delawares and perhaps some Shawnees joined the Cherokees in the St. Francis bottoms. In 1824, two hundred families of Delawares and Shawnees asked the Cherokee Indian agent to allow them to settle on White River below the mouth of the Buffalo. (That was within Cherokee territory.) Delawares and Shawnees were said to have lived also in the present Carroll and Marion Counties.

Before 1817 Delawares migrated to the Red River. They established villages a considerable distance up the west side of the Red River above the mouth of Sulphur River. A site on an old channel of the Red in Lafayette County that archaeologists have tested is believed to have been occupied by Delawares.

DORCHEAT Bayou, which rises in Nevada County and empties into Lake Bistineau, Louisiana, seems to have taken its name from the Caddos. Other spellings in old records and on early maps are "Dacheet," "Dauchite," "Datache," and "Dorchite." Dr. William A. Read of Louisiana State University, an authority on Indian place names in that state, thought the source word might have meant "people" in Caddo.[49] François Grappé, an interpreter for that tribe, in 1806, said that *Dorcheat* meant "a place where a bear had gnawed a gap in a log." Dr. Read, finding no linguistic evidence for that interpretation, dismissed it as folklore.[50]

DUTCH Creek, heading in Scott County and flowing into Petit Jean River in Yell County, retains the name of a Cherokee chief, Tahchee, who was known to the whites as "Captain William Dutch." In the early 1800s he led a band of Cherokees from Tennessee to join those already in Arkansas. He settled on the south side of the Arkansas River, probably on this creek. When the U.S. government ordered the Cherokees south of the river to move to the other side, he refused. Still angry about that, he left Arkansas the next year and chose a site at the mouth of the Kiamichi River for his new home.

Later he went to the Osage country, made friends of former enemies, and married one of their women. Included in their war parties, he distinguished himself in daring exploits. Then his wife committed a crime for which the Osages executed her. Infuriated, Captain Dutch returned to the Kiamichi and declared war on the entire tribe. Even he lost count of the number of Osages he killed and scalped. But the Cherokees acclaimed him and elected him to their national council. He died November 24, 1848.[51]

ENTE NOUEPA WATTISHKA, "Bayou of the Marshes," was the Quapaw name for Moro Bayou,[52] a Ouachita River tributary that forms the boundary between Cleveland and Dallas Counties, as well as Bradley and Calhoun Counties. This place name was forgotten after the Quapaws left Arkansas.

GALLEY in Pope County is an area about two miles along the Arkansas River extending back about five miles. Galla Rock overlooking the river and Galla Creek flowing into it obviously bear a variation of the name. Rock formations exposed in the bluff and back in the hills are pebbly.[53] Dr. John C. Branner concluded that *galets*, French for "pebbles," was the source of the name.[54]

There is no known record of French association with the area. But Cherokees lived here. The Galley, Thomas Nuttall wrote, was the first Cherokee village that he encountered as he ascended the Arkansas River in 1819. He visited a settlement of about twelve families at Galley Hills. Approximately ten miles upstream he still could see "the low ridge, which originated this fanciful name."[55] Because of the Cherokee occupations, there is good reason to believe that the name came from their word *ga laga*, "climb."[56]

HATCHIECOON Bayou in Poinsett County received its name from Choctaws. The name means "Young Cane River," having been derived from *hacha*, "river," and *kuni*, "young cane."[57]

HECKATOO, a Lincoln County community, was named in honor of the principal Quapaw chieftain during the tribe's final years in Arkansas Territory. "Heckaton" is the spelling that appears in historical records. Thomas Nuttall said that the name means "Dry Man."[58] That same meaning was written beside the chief's name and mark on a treaty with the United States.[59] In view of that interpretation one might assume that the chief either was a teetotaler or else his skin needed a moistener cream or lotion. That assumption would be wrong. This name continued in use long after the chief died. Dr. Dorsey learned from the Quapaws themselves that it meant "Turkey Buzzard." Dr. Rankin has confirmed it.[60]

ILLINOIS Bayou in Pope County and Illinois River in Washington County might have been named by French or English speaking persons from the Illinois country. However, it is likely that these streams took their names from the Illinois tribe or from tribes belonging to the Illinois confederation. The name "Illinois" came from the Algonquian *ilini*, "man,"[61] which the French made plural by adding *s*. Throughout the historic period the Quapaw and Illinois tribes were friends. Bands of Kaskaskia, Peoria, Miami, Kickapoo, and Illinois proper all visited Arkansas Post during the 1700s. Some of these Indians might have remained on the Arkansas River and ventured to other streams.

KESHOTEE Island in Little River, Mississippi County, according to legend, keeps the name of an Indian who was murdered there by another Indian named Chuckalee.[62] The victim's name seems to be one of several corruptions of *Koasiti*, the name of an Upper Creek tribe meaning "White Reed Brake." This name was composed from Choctaw *kusha* or *kushak*, "reed," "reed brake," and *hata*, "white".[63] The tribe commonly was known as Coushatta. In the late 1700s most of them migrated from Alabama to Red River and Bayou Chicot in Louisiana while one band went to Arkansas.

Chuckalee means "plucked out" or "pulled out," with reference either to hair or grass. The Choctaw spelling was *chukali*.[64]

KOROA, a small tribe apparently of the Tunican linguistic stock, had villages in present Southeast Arkansas, Northeast Louisiana, and West Central Mississippi. Henri de Tonty sent two men in 1690 to a Koroa village on Bayou Bartholomew. Other spellings of the name were *Coroa, Courrois, Couroyes, Coloa, Icouera, Ikouera,* and *Akora.* The *Coligua,* or *Colima,* Indians of the de Soto narratives probably were Koroa. The meaning of the name is unknown. No landmark in Arkansas carries any reminder of the tribe, but Bayou Colewa in Northeast Louisiana evidently took its name from the Koroa, though the pronunciation is "Cole-wa" now.[65]

MENTOS were the easternmost group of Wichitas. De Tonty, who called them the *Maintou,* said in a letter he wrote September 12, 1693, that their village was ten leagues from the Ozotoue village near Arkansas Post and forty leagues from Cadodaquio. That location would be in Southeast Arkansas, perhaps near modern McGehee. The band went back up the Arkansas River in the early 1700s. *Mentous, Mentons, Manton, Mauton,* and *Matora* were other French spellings of their name. Its origin has not been found. It might have come from some other Indian language. The word *Wichita* was of Choctaw origin. The Paneassa acquired their name from the French who incorrectly spelled the Siouan name for them, meaning "Black Pawnee."[66] Could the Osage word, *manka,* "black," have been the origin of *Mento?*

MISSISSIPPI River, as is well known, received its name from Algonquian-speaking Indians. For example, in Ojibway *missi* is "big" and *sippi* is "river." The Algonquian term, *Meact-Chassipi,* was said to mean "The Ancient Father of Rivers."[67] Caddos called the stream *Ba hat sasin,* "Mother River" and *Ba hathai mi,* "Big River."[68] *Ny-Tonka,* "Great River," was the Quapaw name for both the Mississippi and the Ohio.[69]

MITCHEGAMAS or MITCHEGAMIAS, a large lake running parallel to the St. Francis from its mouth upstream a considerable distance, was outlined on eighteenth-century maps.[70] The lake took its name from Mitchigamea Indians who stopped Père Marquette and his companions on the Mississippi there. In addition to their village on the bank of the Mississippi, the Marquette map shows a second one inland to the northwest. A site which the Arkansas Archeological Survey excavated in Greene County has yielded material that indicates the place was the location of that second village.

The Mitchigamea, whose name means "Great Waters,"[71] belonged to the Illinois confederacy. The St. Francis lake disappeared in the early 1800s, but Lake Michigan and the state of Michigan retain a corruption of the tribal name.

NETTA BOC Creek in Sevier County was called *nita*, "bear," *boc*, "creek," by Choctaws.[72] A nineteenth-century post office was given that name.

NISKA, the Quapaw name for the White River, was formed from *Ny*, "river," and *skah*, "white."[73]

NY-JITTEH, "Red River" was the Quapaw name for the Arkansas River.[74] *Napestle*,[75] an eighteenth-century Spanish name, apparently was an extreme corruption of the Quapaw term.

NY-WHOUTTEH-JUNKA, "Little Muddy River," was the Quapaw name for the St. Francis River.[76]

OSAGE Creek and Osage Prairie in Benton County are reminders that the Osage tribe included Northwest Arkansas in its hunting grounds. These Indians called themselves the *Wazhazhe* which the French corrupted to "Osage."[77] The meaning is not known. Although they were kinsmen of the Quapaws, they made war on them as well as the Caddos. Osage war parties ventured as far south as present Pike, Clark, and Hempstead Counties. Osage horsemen traveled a path down the White River so much that they beat out a trail known as the Osage Path. Through the treaties of 1808 and 1818, the tribe ceded their Arkansas lands to the U.S. government.

OUACHITA River, which heads in mountains of the same name, took the name of a small Caddo tribe whose village the Sieur de Bienville visited on that stream in Louisiana March 28, 1700. The name is believed to mean "Cow River People."[78] "Cow" in this instance refers to buffalo. There were many American bison in the Ouachita basin then. When the tribe broke up most members joined the Natchitoches Caddos. Others disappeared among the Wichitas,[79] perhaps having traveled up the Arkansas with the Mentos.

PEMISCOT Bayou, Mississippi County, carries a name of a band of Algonquian Indians whose home originally was on a river in Maine named for them. This group came to Missouri during the Spanish regime and in all likelihood hunted along this bayou. The name is a corruption of the Algonquian term, *penoonskeook*, "at the fall of the rocks," referring to the location of their village on Pemiscot River.[80] In colonial records the Missouri band sometimes was called the *Abenakis*, which was a generic term for Algonquian tribes of Maine and New Brunswick. It means "easterners."

SARASSA Mounds, Lincoln County, may really belong in a list of French colonial place names instead of here. The origin of this name is much in doubt. It may be assumed that it was derived from *Sarasin*, the name of the half-breed Quapaw war chief who became a folk hero at Pine Bluff. He must have been related to François Saracen, or Sarrazin, French interpreter for the Quapaws. But the last syllable of the mounds' name sounds Indian. Pronunciation of it does not correspond to the way the final syllable of the war chief's name is pronounced in either English or French. Quapaws probably occupied this site.[81]

SHAWNEE, a community in Mississippi County, marks the general location of a Shawnee village about 1800. *Shawnugoi*, the Algonquian word which was corrupted into Shawnee, denotes "southerners."[82] The history of this tribe is a record of migrations. Probably the Ohio River valley was the original home. Forced out by the Iroquois, the Shawnees went to the present states of South Carolina, Georgia, and Alabama. Toward the end of the seventeenth century they migrated to the Delaware country and into the present state of Tennessee. Next they moved to Kentucky and back to the Ohio River. During the American Revolution they were British allies, and afterward they entered the New Madrid district of Spanish Missouri. From there they came to Arkansas to live a few years before going to Texas.

SHOAL Creek, a Logan County tributary of the Arkansas River, is included in this study because of its association with the Cherokee chief, Duwala, "The Bowl." He and his band settled here after leaving the St. Francis River.[83] The Cherokee name for this creek has been lost. Doubtless there were shallows to account for the English name. Nevertheless, it is remarkable that the stream name repeats in part Muscle Shoals, Alabama, site of the massacre which caused The Bowl to migrate westward. Could it be just a coincidence?

In 1817 The Bowl conducted his band to the east side of the Red River probably in the vicinity of present Garland City, Lafayette County. Because they were disturbed by white traders and liquor dealers, they moved across the river to Lost Prairie, Miller County. In July 1820 the Arkansas militia made them migrate to Texas where they established themselves on the Sabine. After a Cherokee battle with the Texas Army in 1839, The Bowl was fatally wounded.

Several Cherokee sites on the Red River have been identified by the Arkansas Archeological Survey.

SOLGOHACHIA, a Conway County community, continues the name of an Indian village that preceded it, according to local legend. There was a Creek village by this name in the present state of Alabama in 1760. While settlers called a creek near that village "Rattle Creek," a translation from the Creek *sougo*, "cymbal," and *hatche*, "creek."[84]

TANICO, a dispersed Indian village near a pool of warm and brackish water, first saw Europeans September 16, 1541, when Hernando de Soto, leading a party of horsemen, arrived. The U.S. De Soto Expedition Commission in 1939 located Tanico in the Hot Springs area. Dr. Charles Hudson of the University of Georgia and several Arkansas archaeologists now place it in Carden Bottoms, Yell County. The Marquette map shows the Tanika west of the Quapaws in 1673. These Indians were of the Tunica tribe whose villages in 1699–1706 were located on the Lower Yazoo River. Before the Quapaws drove them out, the Tunica lived in present Eastern Arkansas and probably on the Arkansas River. In the late 1600s there were Tunica salt makers and traders on the Ouachita River. Remnants of the tribe have been at Marksville on the Red River in Louisiana since about 1790. Their name means "The People."[85]

TENSAS River, which heads in Chicot County and in Louisiana and joins the Little River and the Ouachita River to form the Black River, acquired its name from a small tribe of Taensa Indians who moved to it in 1744. In 1682 the La Salle expedition encountered the tribe on the banks of Lake Saint Joseph in the present Tensas Parish. The last known survivors were reported on Tensas Bayou near Grand Lake, Saint Martin Parish, in the 1800s.[86] The meaning of *Taensa* is unknown. No relics of those people have been identified in Arkansas.

TUYAHHOSAH, Cherokee name for Lee Creek, Crawford County, signifies "where something died." The word comes from *ayochusga*, "to die."[87] According to legend, Lee, a white man, fighting nearby with Cherokees against Osages, was mortally wounded. He crawled to the creek and died.[88]

WABBASEKA, the name of a bayou and a community in Jefferson County, appears to be of Quapaw derivation, though its origin has not been ascertained. Maybe this stream is the one that the Quapaws called *Wadittesha Wattishka*, "Black Salt Lick Bayou."[89]

WAPANOCCA Bayou in Crittenden County retains a corrupted form of *Wapanachki*, "easterners," a term that western Algonquian tribes applied to Delawares and other woodland Indians of the Upper Atlantic coast.[90] This name was spelled *Wappanocka* in a grant of 640 arpents the Spanish government made to Benjamin Fooy December 15, 1802.

WATTENSAW Bayou in Lonoke and Prairie Counties probably owes its name to Quapaws. An early nineteenth-century spelling was *Ouatensaw*. The meaning is unknown.

WATTISHKA JINKA, "Little Bayou," was the Quapaw name for the Saline River.[91] In the Quapaw glossary recorded by Governor Izard, "bayou" is spelled *uahtisychka*.[92]

Some place names purposely were left out of this study. Most of those in the de Soto narratives were excluded because they are to be considered in a future essay concerning Padre Pichardo's theory that the Spaniards named certain chiefdoms after places in Latin America. Tyronza and a few other names, which are said to be Indian but may not be, also have been excluded. There may be Indian names known only locally that have been overlooked in this investigation. Still, the substantial number evident on any good map of the state permanently links Arkansas to its Indian past.

Notes

THE EXPEDITION OF HERNANDO DE SOTO

1. Hakluyt entitled it *Virginia richly valued by the Description of the Mainland of Florida, her next Neighbor*. It has received two modern translations: that of Buckingham Smith, in Edward Gaylor Bourne, ed., *Narratives of the Career of Hernando de Soto*, 2 vols. (New York: A. S. Barnes, 1904); and James A. Robertson, trans., *True relation of the hardships suffered by Governor Fernando de Soto & certain Portuguese gentlemen during the discovery of the province of Florida . . .* (Deland: Florida State Historical Society , 1932–33). The latter, rare in the original, blindingly difficult to read in the microprint edition (Lost Cause Press: 1961), but very valuable for the quality of its translation and for its detailed bibliographical and annotative information, is now much more accessible thanks to its inclusion in Lawrence A. Clayton, Vernon James Knight, and Edward C. Moore, eds., *The De Soto Chronicles: The Expedition of Hernando de Soto to North America in 1539–1543* (Tuscaloosa: The University of Alabama Press, 1993), 1:19–219, with footnotes brought up to date by John H. Hann.

2. Clayton, Knight, and Moore, *De Soto Chronicles*, 69, 82, 122–23, 152.

3. Ibid., 136.

4. Ibid., 108–9.

5. The French translation was done by Henri Ternaux Compans, a multilingual Parisian with a doctoral degree from Gottingen and a passion for Spanish America. His *Recueil de pièces sur la Floride* was the twentieth volume in a series of sources on Spain in America that he published at his own expense, many items of which were either unknown or long forgotten. See Henry R. Wagner, "Henri Ternaux Compans: The First Collector of Hispanic Americana," *Revista Interamericana de Bibliografia* 4 (October 1954): 283–94. The translation used here is John E. Worth in Clayton, Knight, and Moore, *De Soto Chronicles*, 1:225–46.

6. Clayton, Knight, and Moore, *De Soto Chronicles*, 1:243. Laconic Biedma was, but not non-committal: how often does a subordinate report that his commander has died of confusion?

7. The *Historia General y Natural de las Indias* was first published in its entirety in 1851, under the direction of José Amador de los Rios. It is reprinted in *Biblioteca de Autores Espanoles*, vols. 117–21 (Madrid: Edicones Atlas, 1959). Biographical information has been taken from Juan Perez de Tudela Bueso's lengthy and informative introduction in *Biblioteca*, 117:vii–clxxv. It has been available in English only in this century. The first English translation was done by Edward Bourne, and appeared in Bourne, *Narratives*, 2:41–149. References made here are to the translation by John E. Worth in Clayton, Knight, and Moore, *De Soto Chronicles*, 1:247–306.

8. Clayton, Knight, and Moore, *De Soto Chronicles*, 1:253, 259–60, 302–3.

9. Ibid., 1:282–85; on prostitution: 1:282, 285, 289, 291. The Gentleman of Elvas does make one passing reference to "female slaves" of an Indian ruler. He does not say what their fate was to be. Ibid., 1:85.

10. Ibid., 1:267, where Ranjel refers to the Apalachees in the area of the first winter encampment (in the vicinity of Tallahassee) as "the most valiant of men [with] great spirit and boldness," is an example. He also notes the quality of the thread that Indian women made from what he identified as mulberry bark. Ibid., 1:271.

11.   Ibid., 1:301. The question of what the twelve priests did with their days during this expedition has been an ongoing puzzle. They appear prominently twice: when they perform a "dry mass" after their ceremonial materials are destroyed in battle, and when they help raise a huge cross at Casqui shortly after crossing the Mississippi River. Aside from that, they seem to have been somewhat less than energetic in their mission. The two efforts to emphasize their activities inadvertently underscore the opposite point. See Michael Kenny, *The Romance of the Floridas: The Finding and the Founding* (1934; reprint, New York: AMS Press, 1970), 39–52, and Francis Borgia Steck, "Neglected Aspects of the De Soto Expedition," *Mid-America*, 4 (July 1952): 3–26.

12.   Salas, "Fernández de Oviedo," in *Tres Cronistas de Indias, Pedro Mártir de Anglería, Gonzalo Fernández de Oviedo, Fray Bartolomé de las Casas* (Mexico City: Fondo de Cultura Económica, 1959), 83.

13.   As Concepción Bravo has recently emphasized, Ranjel had played a very large role in organizing the expedition. See Bravo, *Hernando de Soto* (Madrid: Historia 16—Quorum, 1987), 93–98.

14.   Clayton, Knight, and Moore, *De Soto Chronicles*, 1:256. When Oviedo speaks in the first person, it is clear that he intends the reader to understand that that is his own voice and not Ranjel's, but the judgmental passages are not always so indicated.

15.   Ibid., 1:289. This sentiment, so near to those of his contemporary Bartolomé de Las Casas, the great opponent of the conquistadors, implies an affinity between the two men that did not exist. The enemy of my enemy was, in this case, still my enemy.

16.   Salas, 110–11.

17.   First published in Lisbon in 1605 as *La Florida del Ynca. Historia del Adelantado Hernando de Soto, Governador y capitan general del Reyno de la Florida, y de otros heroicos cavalleros Españoles è Indios*, and reprinted in 1723 and many times thereafter. Although parts of the work had been available in English since the mid-nineteenth century, the first complete edition was John Grier Varner and Jeannette Johnson Varner, trans., *The Florida of the Inca, A History of the Adelantado, Hernando de Soto, Governor and Captain General of the kingdom of Florida, and of other heroic Spanish and Indian Cavaliers, written by the Inca, Garcilaso de la Vega, an officer of His Majesty, and a native of the great city of Cuzco, capital of the realms and provinces of Peru* (Austin: University of Texas Press, 1951). References here are to the Charmion Shelby translation, originally done for the United States De Soto Commission and now available in Clayton, Knight, and Moore, *The De Soto Chronicles*, 2:25–559.

18.   The literature on this fascinating man is immense, though the focus has often been on the body of his work relating to the conquest of Peru rather than on the de Soto expedition. The standard biography in Spanish is Aurelio Miró Quesada y Sosa, *El Inca Garcilaso* (Madrid: Instituto de Cultura Económico, 1948); but there is a more recent biography in English: John Varner, *El Inca: The Life and Times of Garcilaso de la Vega* (Austin: University of Texas Press, 1968). Prepared by the translator of *La Florida del Ynca*, it contains a great deal of information about that part of Garcilaso's life and work.

19.   Clayton, Knight, and Moore, *De Soto Chronicles*, 2:55–56.

20.   Such as the figure Juan de Vega, who appears in ibid., 2:55–56, 469–70.

21.   Varner is so convinced not only of Silvestre's role, but of his "strict supervision" that he refers to Garcilaso as Silvestre's "Peruvian amanuensis," though the evidence he gives does not make clear from where such a firm conviction arises (Varner, *Garcilaso*, 291–340, and esp. 336n; quotations from 297 and 310 respectively). Silvestre's being sent as a negotiator for more supplies for building the ships to carry the expedition down the Mississippi (Clayton, Knight, and Moore, *De Soto Chronicles*, 2:490–93) is a case of his being the only likely witness to an event.

22.   Clayton, Knight, and Moore, *De Soto Chronicles*, 2:332-33.

23.   Ibid., 2:334–35.

24. Ibid., 2:298–307.

25. Ibid., 1:280: "In the temple or oratory of Talimeco, there were breastplates, as well as corselets and helmets, made from raw and hairless hides of cows . . . and very good shields." End of description.

26. Ibid., 2:205.

27. Ibid., 2:176, 219, 285–86, 299, 462–64. Carmen de Mora Valcárcel, "Semblanza del Adelantado Hernando de Soto en *La Florida Del Inca*," *Anuario de estudios americanos* 42 (1985): 645–56. Valcárcel argues that Garcilaso was compelled by his historicoliterary perspective to create a proper tension between the heroic and the human; hence it was necessary for him to minimize the description of other characters, to juxtapose de Soto's virtues against the defects of other individuals and of the army as a whole, and to reveal the weaknesses only after the strengths were established, even if the price was historical accuracy. The details of the account do fit the thesis.

28. *Historia General de los Castellanos en las Islas y Tierra Firme del Mar Oceano* (1601–15; reprint, Madrid: Tipografía de Archivos, 1954). Herrera says at one point (Dec. 7, lib. 1, cap. 15) that he obtained information for part of the account ("esta relación y lo que adelante se verá") from a monk who had encountered a member of the expedition ("y el religioso dixo que la traía de Mexico adonde la escribió uno de los Capitanes que se hallaron en esta jornada"). Theodore Irving, to whose work in the nineteenth century we shall turn presently, thought the informant to be Gonzalo de Silvestre once again, but Varner considers this unlikely (Varner, *Garcilaso*, 366n). In either case, the friar was not a direct witness. It seems odd that the religious figures on the expedition would not have left accounts, perhaps in the form of reports to a superior, but if such exist, they have not yet been located.

29. *Journal Historique de l'etablissement des Français à la Louisiane* (New Orleans: A.-L. Boinaire, 1831), 1: "ce qu'il y a de certain, c'est que ces découvreurs n'y firent qu'une espèce d'apparition et qu'ils n'y formirent aucune colonie. . . ." An artifact is mentioned on page 10. Bénard de La Harpe was in the area in 1719, when the French and Spanish were at war. Marcel Giraud, *Histoire de la Louisiane Français*, 3 vols. (Paris: Presses Universitaires de France, 1953–66), 3:170, 297–315.

30. *Histoire et Description Generale de la Nouvelle France avec le Journal historique d'un Voyage fait par order des Roi dans l'Amerique Septentrionale* (Paris: Rollins fils, 1744), 1:23; 2:xx, xlv (where he judges Garcilaso, his main source, to be good on the expedition but hyperbolic on the wealth and power of the aboriginals), liii, 257, 411–12; 3:408, 410, 420, 426. Charlevoix's letters (appearing as the third volume of the above work, and published separately as well) described a trip he had taken through eastern North America in 1720–22. They appeared in an English translation in 1761.

31. Las Casas's *Brevísima Relación de la Destrucción de las Indias*, the cornerstone of the Black Legend, was first translated into English in 1656 under the title *Tears of the Indians*. A reprint of an American edition of the work published in 1898 in support of the Spanish-American War is available in Lewis Hanke, intro., *Tears of the Indians, by Bartolemé de Las Casas & The Life of Las Casas By Sir Arthur Helps, K.C.B.* (Williamstown, Mass.: J. Lilburne, 1970). The quotation is from page 66. The uses made of Las Casas in England are reviewed in William S. Maltby, *The Black Legend in England* (Durham, N.C.: Duke University Press, 1971), 12–28.

32. William Roberts, *An Account of the First Discovery, and Natural History of Florida. . . .* (London, 1763), 5, 33–80.

33. William Robertson, *History of America*, 4 vols. (London, 1796[?]).

34. William Robertson, *History of America* (London: A. Strahan, 1800), vi.

35. Idem, *History of America*, 4 vols. (reprint, New York: Derby and Jackson, 1856).

36. Theodore Irving, *The Conquest of Florida by Hernando de Soto* (1835; reprint, New York, 1857).

37. Theodore's uncle encouraged his work, though he did not seem to hold out much hope for a literary career for his nephew. He tried to get him a career in the navy, then in the law; just months before the work was published he still thought Theodore was doing a work of translation, not a history. Washington Irving to Martin Van Buren, January 2, 1833, in Richard B. Rust, gen. ed., *The Complete Works of Washington Irving* 30 vols. (Boston: Twayne Publishers, 1979–89), *Letters*, 2:174; same to same, July 25, 1833, ibid., 2:769; Irving to Louis McLane, January 20, 1834, ibid., 2:785–86; Irving to William Irving, April 3, 1834, ibid., 2:792. Theodore eventually became a college professor, and later entered the ministry. S. Austin Allibone, *A Critical Dictionary of English Literature and British and American Authors* . . . (Philadelphia, 1886), 955.

38. Irving, *Conquest*, xii.

39. As at ibid., 74, and constantly thereafter.

40. Ibid., 219n. In this particular case he suspects Garcilaso of doing so in his estimates of the power of the famous "princess" of Cofitachequi and of the size of her "dominions."

41. Ibid., 284–86, 346; quote at 284 (emphasis added).

42. Ibid., 360, 374, 379, 410.

43. Ibid., xiii, 447.

44. Ibid., xiii.

45. Ibid., 305n.

46. His notes are a good indication of the large amount of activity of local scholarship. See ibid., 38–39n, 104n, 111n, 128–29n, 130n, 198n, 234n, 251, 342n.

47. As well as one of the most popular: new editions appeared regularly throughout the nineteenth century, the last in 1888.

48. "The Epochs and Events of American History, as Suited to the Purposes of Art in Fiction," *Views and Reviews in American Literature History and Fiction*, ed. C. Hugh Holman (1845; reprint, Cambridge, Mass.: Belknap Press, 1962), 34n.

49. William Gilmore Simms, *History of South Carolina* (Charleston, 1840), 13–14.

50. Holman, *Views and Reviews*, xxxv; William Gilmore Simms, "The Early Spanish Voyagers—Hernando de Soto as a Subject for Romance," in ibid., 87–98.

51. William Gilmore Simms, *Vasconcelos* (Chicago., n.d.), 1–2. The work was first published in 1853, with new editions in 1857, 1882, and 1885.

52. David Levin draws upon Simms's treatment of the Indians in the latter's novel *The Yemassee* to illustrate how within the Romantic framework one may admire a race, yet not mourn its passing. Levin, *History as a Romantic Art: Bancroft, Prescott, Motley, and Parkman* (Stanford, Calif.: Stanford University Press, 1959), 130.

53. Simms, *Vasconcelos*, 180, 181.

54. Ibid., 1.

55. Clayton, Knight, and Moore, *De Soto Chronicles*, 1:87. The only eyewitness to notice the Queen's heart is the Gentleman of Elvas, who reports her having taken up with a black slave of André de Vasconcelos—to have been a fly on the wall when Simms came across *that* piece of information!

56. John C. Guilds , "Simms's Use of History: Theory and Practice," *Mississippi Quarterly* 30 (fall 1977): 505–11; Guilds reasserts on Simms's behalf the claim of a commitment to historical accuracy, pointing in particular to his characterization of Amerindian culture: "It is now generally recognized that Simms's picture of the Indian is the most historically accurate, the most warmly humanized, in nineteenth century American literature." The case would be easier to maintain if *Vasconcelos* had not been written.

57. *The Life, Travels and Adventures of Ferdinand de Soto, Discoverer of the Mississippi* (Philadelphia: J. T. Lloyd, 1859). Biographical information from James Grant Wilson and John Fiske, eds., *Appleton's Cyclopaedia of American Biography*, 6 vols., (New York, 1888–89), 6:543.

58. Wilmer, *Life*, 1–5. How he could judge the use of sources he had not seen is not explained.

59. Ibid., 22–23, 79, 184–86, 410.

60. Reproduced in its entirety at ibid., 77–79.

61. Ibid., 507–18.

62. Ibid., 251.

63. Ibid., unnumbered end page.

64. Theodore Maynard, working on de Soto nearly a century later, saw Wilmer's book as a continuing malignancy. See Maynard, *De Soto and the Conquistadores* (London and New York: Longmans, Green & Co., 1930), viii–ix.

65. John S. C. Abbot, *Ferdinand de Soto, Discoverer of the Mississippi* (New York, 1873); biographical information from Benson John Lossing, ed., *Harper's Encyclopedia of United States History* 10 vols. (New York and London, 1902), 1:3.

66. Abbott, *Ferdinand de Soto*, 70–71, 102, 153, 188. De Soto's conscience was also pricked by his wife, whose supposed letter on moral matters Abbott borrowed from Wilmer, *Life*, 214–15, 278.

67. Abbott, *Ferdinand de Soto,* 249.

68. Ibid., 56–57, 128, 143.

69. Ibid., 159.

70. Edward T. James, et al., eds., *Notable American Women, 1607–1950: A Biographical Dictionary* (Cambridge, Mass.: Belknap Press, 1971), 2:331–32.

71. Grace King, *De Soto and His Men in the Land of Florida* (New York, 1898), vii–ix.

72. Ibid., 127–43, 177, 246–54.

73. Robert Bontine Cunninghame Graham, *Hernando de Soto: Together With an Account of One of His Captains, Gonçalo Silvestre* (1902; reprint, New York, 1924).

74. Graham has been the subject of almost as many biographers as de Soto. The two most recent ones are: Cedric Watts and Laurence Davies, *Cunninghame Graham: A Critical Biography* (Cambridge: Cambridge University Press, 1979); and Alicia Jurado, *El Escocès Errante* (Buenos Aires: Emecé Editores, 1978). Biographical material has been drawn from both.

75. Graham, *Hernando de Soto*, vii.

76. Ibid., 12, 16, 149n. Graham is aware of Oviedo as a source, and makes periodic use of him, but the criticisms to be found there he dismisses with the peculiar remark that de Soto must be judged "by the standards of his time" (196). It is difficult to see how the remarks of a man who shared de Soto's historical moment, particularly one whose life and thought is often chosen as paradigmatic of that moment ("[S]i se me obligara a escoger una figura a través de cuya biographía debiera definirse el momento de la floración imperial española, acaso prefiriera la de Gonzalo Fernández de Oviedo" [Perez de Tudela Bueso, aforementioned introduction to Oviedo, vii–x]; "Pocas existencias habrá tan típicas, tan representativas de la generación excelente que se forma en España en el último cuarto del siglo XV, como la de Gonzalo Fernández de Oviedo," Ramón Iglesia, *Cronistas e Historiadores de la Conquista de México* (México, D.F., 1942), 79) could be dismissed as anachronistic. Graham does not elaborate.

77. Graham, *Hernando de Soto*, 35–36, 152. He rationalized Spanish abuses, observes Jurado, but condemned the same behavior in others: "cualquier otra nación . . . que obrase de idéntica manera, resultaría a sus ojos cobarde, desalmada, y opresora." Jurado, *Escocés Errante*, 172.

78. Graham, *Hernando de Soto*, 152. Pages 141, 143n, 172, and 193 provide a good sampling of his views on Christianity. Later, however (and perhaps inevitably), he would defend what was for most Englishmen of his time the least defensible branch of the faith in *A Vanished Arcadia: Being Some Account of the Jesuits of Paraguay, 1607–1767* (London, 1901).

79. Graham is too quotable for this chapter's good, but perhaps one relevant to this point will be allowed. On an Indian who preferred suicide to surrender: "One wonders that some freedom-loving millionaire of Alabama does not perpetuate himself and this brave Indian in some misshapen bronze, or cheap Carrera marble effigy, with due inscription on the pediment." *Hernando de Soto*, 148.

80. Watts and Davies note perceptively that Graham's "good" conquistador had "a rebellious tendency to abuse his patronage by some act of brutality.... Over so much of the conquest there hangs an atmosphere of moral derangement which Graham's judgments frequently probe but never completely penetrate"; Davies, *Cunnighame Grahame*, 212.

81. See, for example, the contrast drawn with the Amerindians of his own day. Graham, *Hernando de Soto*, 99.

82. By his own account, Malone was drawn to the subject because of the similarity he perceived between de Soto, the "King of Pioneers," and modern Americans: "De Soto's age was in truth like our own, and De Soto was himself a type of the American of to-day,—one ever striding onward, heedless of difficulties, and despairing of nothing as impossible"; Malone, *Hernando de Soto* (New York and London, 1914), xi, xiii, 531. The six-hundred-page poem is mainly a first person narrative of de Soto's life up through the Battle of Mauvila, told to the chief of the Chickasaws on cold winter nights around the campfire. This is preceded by a short narrative by Juan Ortiz, and followed by a third-person account of the rest of the expedition. The poem builds to a mystic vision in which the *adelantado* sees the development of mankind and learns that self-reliance is the primary virtue. Malone predicted that his "exercise in temerity" would go unread, but persisted out of a conviction that the epic form had proved too durable over the centuries for its present decline to be anything but temporary. Thus far he has been wrong. Not only did the poem disappear, its author did too: Malone appeared in the *Dictionary of American Biography* (1943), but gets no mention in either of the more specialized modern works on the South, *The Encyclopedia of Southern History* (1979) and *The Encyclopedia of Southern Culture* (1989).

Daly's *Adventures of Roget L'Etrange* (London, 1896) presents the expedition through the eyes of a young English Catholic aristocrat who joins up with de Soto after having been persecuted out of his homeland. It is faithful to the basic facts of the expedition, and constructs an ingenious case for the possibility of a drastic short-term alteration of the aboriginal situation by a single European. Less imaginative is Charles E. Knowles, *In Quest of Gold* (New York, 1912).

83. Frederick Ober, *Ferdinand de Soto and the Invasion of Florida* (New York and London, 1906); Oscar Fay Adams, *A Dictionary of American Authors,* 5th ed. (Boston and New York, 1904).

84. Theodore Maynard, *De Soto and the Conquistadores* (London and New York: Lincoln MacVeagh, 1930).

85. *Who's Who in America* (New York, 1930–31), 16:1484.

86. Maynard, *De Soto,* vii–ix; Robertson, *True relation* , 2:423.

87. Alfred W. Crosby, "The Columbian Voyages, The Columbian Exchange, and Their Historians," in American Historical Association, *Essays on Global and Comparative History* (Washington, D.C., 1987).

88. Andrew Lytle, *At the Moon's Inn* (Indianapolis: Bobbs-Merrill Co., 1941).

89. John Jennings, *The Golden Eagle* (New York: G. P. Putnam's Sons, 1958). The big and lusty claim was made in the paperback edition (New York: Dell Publishing Co., Inc., 1959).

90. Lily Peter, *The Great Riding: The Story of De Soto in America* (Fayetteville: University of Arkansas Press, 1983).

91. Janice Evans, "Lily Peter," in *Horizons: 100 Arkansas Women of Achievement* (Little Rock: Rose Publishing Company, 1980), 128–29.

92. F. Blanco Castilla, *Hernando de Soto, El Centauro de las Indias* (Madrid: Editorial Carrera del Castillo, [cover 1955]).

93. Ibid., 7. Interest in El Cid in pre–Charlton Heston America is not immediately obvious. Where Blanco Castilla found it he does not say.

94. Ibid., 9 ("en el concepto moderno la Biographía viene a ser como árbol que hunde sus raíces en la tierra firme de la Historia y expande sus ramas en la voluble atmósfera de la Literatura, para dar sombra y frutos no solamente a la escasa minor erudita, sino también a la multitud lectora").

95. Ibid., 159. "Al cabo, fué el amor la más penetrante lanza, el *requerimiento* más eficaz, la doctrina más persuasiva en la conquista de aquel nuevo mundo; porque el amor es el único lenguaje universal."

96. Miguel Albarnoz, *Hernando de Soto, El Amadís de La Florida* (Madrid: Ediciones Castilla, 1971). Amadís was the hero of the most popular chivalric romance of de Soto's time.

97. Guillermo de Zéndequi, "The Amadis of Florida," *Americas* 5 (May, 1974), 30–33.

98. Don Luis Villanueva y Cañeo, *Hernando de Soto* (1892; 2nd ed., Badajoz: A. Arqueros, 1929), 20–21.

99. Carried to its reductionist end, such an argument can conclude that this was a world so unique as to be completely irretrievable. This was the position recently taken by a commentator on a recent film documentary of Spanish exploration: the sixteenth century was an age of action, never to be understood by cloistered scholars in an age of reflection. *España Estuvo Allí,* Capitulo 3, "Espanoles en el golfo de Méjico" (Princeton: N.J.: Films for the Humanities, 1986). It may or may not be irrelevant to observe that the commentator who took this position was wearing heavily tinted glasses indoors.

This raises the pertinent larger point of how to measure the influence of contemporary information upon the commentators whose accounts have shaped our understanding of the expedition. For example, some years ago Irving A. Leonard, in his careful analysis of the writings most likely to have been read, or otherwise absorbed, by the conquistadors was particularly impressed by the widespread, uncritical belief in Amazon women; Leonard, *Books of the Brave* (Cambridge, Mass.: Harvard University Press, 1949), 36–64. How does one understand the "Queen of Cofitachequi" and other accounts of aboriginal women and of gender relations within this context? It is a subject not yet adequately explored.

100. One finds the same approach, in a more muted form, in a short biography produced for a Spanish Columbian quincentennial series: Concepción Bravo *Hernando de Soto* (Madrid: Historia 16—Quorum, 1987). Bravo returns to Thomas Carlyle's nineteenth century romanticist notion of the heroic figure as destiny's tot for a conceptual framework ("la fidelidad a su proprio destino"), supplementing it with José Ortega y Gasset's idea of a heroic "drive for singularity" ("querer ser uno mismo, negándose a repetir los gestos de la costumbre y la tradición, o aquello que sus instintos biológicos lo fuerzan a hacer"). Ibid., 6.

101. Richard Langworth and Consumer Guide, *Encyclopedia of American Cars,* 1940–70 (New York: Beekman House, 1980), 125–51. Curiously, the hood ornament was a lady until 1949, when she was replaced by a glow-in-the-dark bust of the car's namesake. Equally curious is the decision to make Coronado, de Soto's equally famous contemporary, only a model in the line.

102. The novel that appeared coincidentally, Mary Brabson Littleton's *By the King's Command: A Romance of Hernando de Soto* (New York: P. J. Kenedy & Sons, 1928), would only have helped, as it barely got Soto across the Atlantic.

103. The success of the automobile also determined, in the United States anyway, that its namesake would forever be called *de* Soto, although the name makes no sense.

104. Simms versus Pickett, a quintessential expression of the diverging approaches, is covered in Charles S. Watson, "De Soto's Expedition: Contrasting Treatments in Pickett's *History of Alabama* and Simms's *Vasconcelos,*" *Alabama Review* 31 (July 1978): 199–208.

105. That this was not an easy transition is perhaps best illustrated by the ambivalence in the mind of the man selected here as a harbinger of the change. Pickett had a great interest in fiction, and a desire to try his hand at it. He resisted the impulse, in part because, as he confided to his friend Charles Gayarré, to do so might undermine his reputation as an historian, just as Simms ". . . never could gain reputation as a grave & accurate historian, after having produced so many works of fancy- and *half*-truth if I may be allowed the expression." Pickett to Gayarré, November 25, 1852. Charles Gayarré Papers, Louisiana and Lower Mississippi Collections, LSU Libraries, Louisiana State University. My thanks to Professor Michael O'Brien for providing me with this information and with a copy of his informative essay, "On the Writing of History in the Old South," in *Rewriting the South: History and Fiction*, eds. Lothar Hönnighausen and Valeria Gennaro (Tübingen: Francke, 1993), 141–66.

106. "Ancient Florida," in *Narrative and Critical History of America*, ed. Justin Winsor, 8 vols. (Boston and New York: Houghton, Mifflin and Company, 1884–89), 2:283–98.

107. Woodbury Lowery, *The Spanish Settlements within the Present Limits of the United States* (New York and London: G. P. Putnam's Sons, 1901).

108. John R. Swanton, ed., *The Final Report of the United States De Soto Expedition Commission* (1939; reprint, Washington, D.C.: Smithsonian Institution Press, 1985). This edition, part of the *Classics of Smithsonian Anthropology* series (the title is revealing both on the significance of the work and on the relative contributions of historians and anthropologists to the subject in this century), contains a fine summary by Jeffrey Brain of the ongoing controversy on the route of the expedition.

109. Ibid., 1. Garcilaso had predicted as much in the sixteenth century: "[I have not made] a definitive statement of the direction that our people took, because . . . though I endeavored to ascertain it, it was not possible for me to do so. The one who gave me the account, since he was not a cosmographer or a mariner, did not know it, and the army carried no instruments for determining the latitude, nor was there anyone who would attempt to do so or interest himself in it because they were all so disappointed at not finding gold or silver that they thought of nothing else." Clayton, Knight, and Moore, *De Soto Chronicles*, 2:436.

110. Swanton, *Final Report*, xxv.

111. Shipwreck survivors alone may have numbered over ten thousand in the sixteenth century, according to the recent estimate in J. Leitch Wright, *The Only Land They Knew: The Tragic Story of the American Indians in the Old South* (New York: The Free Press, 1981), 42. The extent of contact prior to the de Soto expedition is one of the subjects covered in a brilliant new reformulation of early exploration and colonization; Paul E. Hoffman; *A New Andalucia and a Way to the Orient: The American Southeast During the Sixteenth Century* (Baton Rouge: Louisiana State University Press, 1990).

112. Carl Sauer, *Sixteenth Century North America: The Land and The People as Seen by the Europeans* (Berkeley: University of California Press, 1971), 175. Sauer was, to my knowledge, the first to observe that the royal grant not only countenanced looting, but committed the expedition to it, making the project ". . . remarkable in the annals of colonialism for the shameless manner in which it announced its objective as unlimited plunder"; ibid., 158–59. This brilliant, idiosyncratic scholar's account of the expedition is a fascinating mix: in its concentration upon the march as a window into the aboriginal world, it is very new; in its bitterly judgmental tone, it is as old as Oviedo and Las Casas.

113. The artifact was conjured up (wryly) by State Archaeologist Hester Davis in a conversation with the author.

114. Anthropologist George Sabo has suggested that this may have been true in an even broader sense: having once made a careful observation of a phenomenon, be it biological, geological, or whatever, it may have seemed unnecessary to the chroniclers to remark upon it again (conversation with the author). Whatever the reason, there is less eyewitness information available after the Mississippi crossing. The expedition was in the trans-Mississippi

area about forty percent of the time. While the Elvas account actually favors that part of the expedition in terms of space, and while Biedma's short account is evenly distributed, Garcilaso grants nearly seventy percent to the earlier period, and Ranjel eighty percent.

115.   I exclude here the theory that the expedition came in above all these rivers at a point near Memphis. This theory, popular in the nineteenth century, depended heavily on the translation of Ranjel's *monte* as "mountain," which Swanton rejected in favor of the alternative definition of "forest," partly on the ground that Ranjel had used the same term earlier in situations where "mountain" would clearly have been nonsensical. It would seem that this extreme northern possibility could become part of the debate once again only with the discovery of artifacts. This illustration of how much can depend on a word is good evidence of the need to follow David Henige's admonition that all scholars consult accounts in the original, or in the nearest form to it as possible; David Henige, "Proxy Data, Historical Method, and the de Soto Expedition," in *The Expedition of Hernando de Soto West of the Mississippi, 1541–1543: Proceedings of the de Soto Symposia, 1988 and 1990*, eds. Gloria A. Young and Michael P. Hoffman (Fayetteville: University of Arkansas Press, 1993), 155–72. But since that argument can be extended to require any scholar to be an expert in everything, perhaps the careful, literal translations of all the accounts in Clayton, Knight, and Moore, *De Soto Chronicles*, will become the accepted standard.

116.   The beds themselves are not so large a problem as may first appear. The Mississippi being one of the most carefully studied rivers in the world, its movement has been very carefully plotted back through time. Where the Mississippi was likely to have been *around* the time of de Soto is therefore plottable, but of course there can be no certainty, since the historical moment is so brief. The matter is considered in some detail in David Dye, "Reconstruction of the De Soto Route in Arkansas: the Mississippi Alluvial Plain," in Young and Hoffman, *Expedition of de Soto*, 36–57.

117.   John McPhee, *The Control of Nature* (New York: Noonday Press, 1989), notes that a recent professional appraisal of the war between the river and the Corps of Engineers concluded as much.

118.   There is yet another problem with the rivers worth mentioning: was what an observer saw at a single historical moment at all typical of a particular river? Much has been made of Elvas's comparison of the "River of Coligua" with a river that he had observed in Spain, the Caia, the conclusion being that the river Elvas described was much too small to be the Arkansas (Charles M. Hudson, "Reconstructing the Route West of the Mississippi: Summary and Contents," in Young and Hoffman, *Expedition of de Soto*, 146). But one is forced to rely upon an observation that may have been made at an extraordinary moment in the river's history with a memory of another river that Elvas may have observed many times, or a few, or perhaps only once, and then at an atypical moment. We do not know.

119.   Frank Schambach, "The End of the Trail: Reconstruction of the Route of Hernando de Soto's Army through Southwest Arkansas and East Texas," in Young and Hoffman, *Expedition of de Soto*, 78–105.

120.   Swanton, *Final Report*, 1, 234. Swanton's collaborator and the vice-chairman of the commission, John R. Fordyce of Hot Springs, a long-time student of the route question, had rejected the Commerce Landing possibility at least as early as 1929 and was committed to Camden and Hot Springs as anchor points by 1931. Harry J. Lemley to J. L. Stuart, August 15, 1929, Fordyce Papers, series 3, box 6, Special Collections, Mullins Library, University of Arkansas, Fayetteville; undated, unidentified newspaper clipping (Camden, c. July 24, 1931), ibid.; Fordyce to J. R. Swanton, December 21, 1931, ibid.

121.   A point made by many scholars, most recently by Ann Early, "Finding the Middle Passage: The Spanish Journey from the Swamplands to Caddo Country," in Young and Hoffman, *Expedition of de Soto*, 68–77.

122.   The theory, developed by University of Chicago chemistry professor Willard Libby,

did not appear in published form until 1949. Sheridan Bowman, *Radiocarbon Dating* (Berkeley and Los Angeles: University of California Press/British Museum, 1990), 9–10.

123.   There has been vigorous discussion, however, since the early part of the century. See, for example, Dunbar Rowland, ed., *A Symposium on the Place of the Discovery of the Mississippi by Hernando de Soto* (Jackson, Miss.: Publications of the Mississippi Historical Society, 1927).

124.   *Archaeological Survey in the Lower Mississippi Valley, 1940–1947* Papers of the Peabody Museum of Archaeology and Ethnology, vol. 25, (Cambridge, Mass., 1951), esp. 361–81.

125.   It would be useful, of course, if the "document" would expand, and in a limited way it has: Ignacio Avellaneda has provided much new and interesting material in his *Los Sobrevivientes de la Florida: The Survivors of the De Soto Expedition* (Gainesville: University of Florida Libraries, 1990), including the intriguing speculation that the literacy rate here was higher than that of the Pizarro expedition, see page 70; Eugene Lyon's discovery of a fragment of another eyewitness account of the expedition, the whole of which was still extant late in the sixteenth century, holds out the possibility that more original sources may still lie undiscovered. Lyon, "The Cañete Fragment," in *The Hernando de Soto Expedition*, ed. Jerald D. Milanich (New York and London: Garland Publishing, 1991), 453–54. It may also be found in Clayton, Knight, and Moore, *De Soto Chronicles*, 1:307–10.

126.   "Refinements in Hernando De Soto's Route through Georgia and South Carolina," in *Columbian Consequences: Archaeological and Historical Perspectives on the Spanish Borderlands East*, ed. David Hurst Thomas (Washington, D.C.: Smithsonian Institution Press, 1990), 108.

127.   The earliest trans-Mississippi projection of the Hudson reconstruction appeared in "De Soto in Arkansas: A Brief Synopsis," *Field Notes* (July/August 1985). This was done at the invitation of State Archaeologist Hester A. Davis, the idea being to stimulate interest and to elicit information. That journal has since carried a series of articles relevant to the subject. In 1988, and again in 1990, the University of Arkansas at Fayetteville sponsored conferences on the subject. Many of the papers delivered at those conferences are contained in the previously cited volume edited by Gloria A. Young and Michael P. Hoffman. The statement of method is from Dan F. Morse, "Archaeology and the Population of Arkansas in 1541–1543," in Young and Hoffman, *Expedition of de Soto*, 29–35.

128.   Phyllis A. Morse, "The Parkin Archaeological Site and its Role in Determining the Route of the De Soto Expedition," in Young and Hoffman, *Expedition of de Soto*, 58–67. Morse finds this "amazing", but does not use the word to suggest skepticism.

129.   Elsewhere, anti-Hudsonism appears to have reached the proportions of a minor industry, even spawning a journal (*The Soto States Anthropologist*, which first appeared in July, 1990). One finds in the pages of that journal the strong undercurrent of hostility between amateur and professional that has been a problem for the discipline of scientific anthropology since its inception. A good, accessible example of more measured criticism (though even this illustrates the peculiar rule that anthropologists seem to have adopted, which is to avoid the use of adjectives except when talking about each other) may be found in Keith J. Little and Caleb Curren, "Conquest Archaeology of Alabama," in *Columbian Consequences*, 169–95.

130.   Samuel Dickinson, who for many years has been a force in the study of native peoples in Arkansas, provided an early critique, "The River of Cayas, the Ouachita or the Arkansas River?" *Field Notes*, (March/April 1986): 5–10. He centered upon the dangers of relying upon aboriginal sites for which dates were uncertain, and has continued to be one of the most vigorous critics of the Hudson reconstruction. See also Henige, "Proxy Data, Historical Method, and the de Soto Expedition"; his criticism concentrates upon problems with the use of literary evidence that apply to the entire reconstruction.

131.   See Dickinson, "River of Cayas," 6.

132.   Swanton, *Final Report*, 234.

133.   There is a good discussion of the point in Early, "Finding the Middle Passage," 55–71.

134. Which, to allow a political reality to creep into the scholarly world, is partly the result of state funding policies. In the eyes of the committees of the Arkansas State Senate, all sites are not created equal.

135. The chief critic has been Jeffrey Brain, whose arguments are summarized in his introduction to Swanton, *Final Report*, xxxix–xl.

136. The matter of artifacts-as-evidence is raised often in the literature. The exchange between David Henige and Charles Hudson, et. al., in Young and Hoffman, *Expedition of de Soto*, is characteristic of the positions to be taken.

137. Hudson, oral presentation at the De Soto Conference, University of Arkansas, Fayetteville, Arkansas, October 3, 1988.

138. Thomas Kuhn, *The Structure of Scientific Revolutions* (Chicago: The University of Chicago Press, 1962).

139. Early, "Finding the Middle Passage," 88–94.

140. Schambach, "End of the Trail," 102. The ability of the aboriginal populations to support large groups of invading human parasites has been one part of the conquest literature to which modern scholars have been most sensitive. It was not always so: Adam Smith, observing the phenomenon in the eighteenth century with an eye for invidious comparisons between "primitive" economies and his own projection, saw it differently. "The famines which [the Spanish armies] are said to have occasioned almost wherever they went, in countries too which at the same time are represented as very populous and well-cultivated," he concluded, "sufficiently demonstrate that the story of this populousness and high cultivation is in a great measure fabulous." Adam Smith, *An Inquiry into the Nature and Causes of the Wealth of Nations* (1776; reprint,. Indianapolis, Ind.: Liberty Classics, 1981), 1:221.

141. Good points of entry into this very large literature are Russell Thornton, *American Indian: Holocaust and Survival, A Population History Since 1492* (Norman: University of Oklahoma Press, 1987), Ann Ramenofsky, *Vectors of Death: The Archaeology of European Contact* (Albuquerque: University of New Mexico Press, 1987); and for the area of the de Soto expedition (but only east of the Mississippi River), Marvin T. Smith, *Archaeology of Aboriginal Cultural Change in the Interior Southeast: Depopulation During the Early Historic Period* (Gainesville: University of Florida Press/The Florida State Museum, 1987).

142. Dan F. Morse and Phyllis F. Morse, "The Spanish Exploration of Arkansas," in Thomas, *Columbian Consequences*, 199, 208. This is in line with the estimates for the Lower Mississippi valley area made earlier by Philip Phillips, James Ford, and James B. Griffin, *Archaeological Survey*, 419. The same position is taken by Ann Ramenofsky, one of the most important theorists of the demographic impact of epidemic disease. She argues that smallpox, tuberculosis, and trichinosis *could* have existed in transmittable states. Her at times forceful, at times tentative assertion of a role for the de Soto expedition is itself an interesting statement of the problematic nature of the subject and the evidence; *Vectors of Death*, 42–71. Her earlier and more specific assertion that smallpox, tuberculosis, and trichinosis could have existed in transmittable states ("The Archaeology of Population Collapse: Native American Response to the Introduction of Infectious Diseases [Ann Arbor, Mich.: University Microfilms International, 1984], 253–61) does not find its way into the later work: there Ramenofsky states that she "cannot stipulate specific diseases," but holds firmly to the position that "the sixteenth century is the diseases century in the Southeast"; *Vectors of Death*, 69. Much of the best recent literature on this subject has been brought together in Clark Spencer Larsen, ed., *Native American Demography and the Spanish Borderlands*, 2 vols. (New York and London: Garland Publishing, 1991).

143. The references come from fairly early in the expedition's progress, when it was in the territory of the "Queen of Cofitachequi." Elvas notes that "two years ago there had been a plague in the land and they [the Indians] had moved to other towns," without making clear whether he is talking about crop diseases or something affecting humans directly; Clayton,

Knight, and Moore, *De Soto Chronicles*, 1:83. Biedma reports hearing about sickness in the Ayllón expedition; ibid., 1:231. Elvas also mentions that some of the one hundred and two Spaniards who had died prior to Mauvila had succumbed to illnesses; ibid., 1:104. There is also the matter of de Soto's own death from what Garcilaso described as "severe fever"; ibid., 2:447, and as a "fever" by Elvas; ibid., 1:134. None of the accounts make any mention of his illness spreading either to his troops or to the Indians, although this was a long period of close contact.

144. Barbara A. Burnett and Katherine A. Murray, "Death, Drought, and de Soto: The Bioarchaeology of Depopulation," in Young and Hoffman, *Expedition of de Soto*, 227–36. They suggest that a long drought, lasting from 1549 to 1577, started a decline that was then accelerated by European diseases. For support for this position, together with a careful analysis of the problem, see Michael P. Hoffman, "The Depopulation and Abandonment of Northeastern Arkansas in the Protohistoric Period" in *Archaeology of Eastern North America: Papers in Honor of Stephen Williams;* ed. James B. Stoltman (Jackson: Mississippi Department of Archives and History, 1993).

145. "American Archaeology as Native History: A Review Essay," *William and Mary Quarterly*, 3rd ser., 60 (July, 1983), 414–42.

146. See, for example, Timothy Perttula, "The Long-term Effects of the Entrada on Aboriginal Caddoan Populations," in Young and Hoffman, *Expedition of de Soto*, 237–54.

147. The possibilities are evident (and the difficulties are apparent) in Michael P. Hoffman, "Identification of Ethnic Groups Contacted by the de Soto Expedition in Arkansas"; Robert L. Rankin, "Language Affiliations of Some de Soto Place Names in Arkansas"; and Wallace Chafe, "Caddo Names in the de Soto Documents"; Young and Hoffman, *Expedition of de Soto*, 132–42, 210–21, 222–26 respectively.

148. "Child of the Sun: The Expedition of Hernando de Soto—a series for Public Radio," NEH grant application by Robert Clem, Project Director of the Foundation for New Mew Media (March, 1992).

149. "Españoles in el golfo de Méjico"; *Lost in Time,* Auburn Television (Auburn, Ala.: Auburn University).

150. George Sabo III, *Paths of Our Children: Historic Indians of Arkansas,* Arkansas Archaeological Survey, 3 (Fayetteville, 1992).

LIVING IN A GRAVEYARD: NATIVE AMERICANS IN COLONIAL ARKANSAS

1. Alfred W. Crosby, *Ecological Imperialism: The Biological Expansion of Europe, 900–1900* (Cambridge: Cambridge University Press, 1986; reprint, 1990), 210–13.

2. Lawrence A. Clayton, Vernon James Knight, and Edward C. Moore, eds., *The De Soto Chronicles: The Expedition of Hernando de Soto to North America in 1539–1543* (Tuscaloosa: University of Alabama Press, 1993), 1:114, 125, 128, 131.

3. Ibid., 1:241.

4. Ibid., 1:301, 304–5.

5. Barbara A. Burnett and Katherine A. Murray, "Death, Drought, and de Soto: The Bioarcheology of Depopulation," in *The Expedition of Hernando de Soto West of the Mississippi, 1541–1543: Proceedings of the De Soto Symposia 1988 and 1990*, ed. Gloria A. Young and Michael P. Hoffman (Fayetteville: University of Arkansas Press, 1993), 227–36.

6. Stanley Faye, "The Arkansas Post of Louisiana: French Domination," *The Louisiana Historical Quarterly* 26 (July 1943): 635.

7. Burnett and Murray, "Death, Drought, and de Soto," 236.

8. Timothy K. Perttula, *The Caddo Nation: Archaeological and Ethnohistoric Perspectives* (Austin: University of Texas Press, 1992): 11–24; Helen Hornbeck Tanner, "The Territory of

the Caddo Tribe of Oklahoma," in *The Southern Caddo: An Anthology*, ed. H. F. Gregory (New York: Garland Press, 1986), 19–31.

9. Robert L. Rankin, "Language Affiliations of some de Soto Place Names in Arkansas," in Young and Hoffman, *Expedition of de Soto*, 210–21; David Baird, *The Quapaw Indians: A History of the Downstream People* (Norman: University of Oklahoma Press, 1980), 1–23.

10. Richard White to author, Salt Lake City, November 23, 1983.

11. Crosby, *Ecological Imperialism*, 213.

12. Nancy M. Miller Surrey, *The Commerce of Louisiana During the French Régime, 1699–1763* (New York: Columbia University Press, 1916), 282, 301–2, 350–51, 357–58; Daniel H. Usner Jr., *Indians, Settlers, and Slaves in a Frontier Exchange Economy: The Lower Mississippi Valley Before 1783* (Chapel Hill: University of North Carolina Press, 1990), 244–75.

13. Charles M. Hudson, *The Southeastern Indians* (Knoxville: University of Tennessee Press, 1976), 279; John R. Swanton, *The Indians of the Southeastern United States*, Bureau of American Ethnology Bulletin 137 (Washington, D.C.: Government Printing Office, 1946; reprint, New York: Greenwood Press, 1969), 324–28; Perttula, "The Caddo Nation," 69, 226; Nancy Adele Kenmotsu, James E. Bruseth, and James E. Corbin, "Moscoso and the Route in Texas: A Reconstruction," in Young and Hoffman, *Expedition of de Soto*, 127–28.

14. W. W. Newcomb Jr., *The Indians of Texas: From Prehistoric to Modern Times* (Austin: University of Texas Press, 1961; reprint, 1978), 293.

15. Bruce D. Smith, "Middle Mississippian Exploitation of Animal Populations," Anthropological Papers, Museum of Anthropology, University of Michigan, 57 (Ann Arbor: University of Michigan Press, 1975), 82–83.

16. Ibid., 20–22, 41; Amelia W. Williams and Eugene C. Barker, eds., *The Writings of Sam Houston, 1813–1836*, (Austin: University of Texas Press, 1938), 1:273; *Arkansas Gazette*, 9 December 1823.

17. Smith, "Middle Mississippian Exploitation of Animal Populations," 20–21, 41.

18 Ibid., 116–17.

19. William J. Eccles, "The Fur Trade and Eighteenth-Century Imperialism," *William and Mary Quarterly*, 3d ser., 40 (July 1983): 344–45, 349–50.

20. Burnett and Murray, "Death, Drought and de Soto," 243; John C. Ewers, "The Influence of Epidemics on the Indian Populations and Cultures of Texas," *Plain Anthropologist* 18 (1973): 104–15; Faye, "Arkansas Post: French Domination," 636.

21. William J. Eccles, *The Canadian Frontier, 1534–1760* (Albuquerque: University of New Mexico Press, 1969; revised edition, 1983), 124–25; Eccles, "Fur Trade and Imperialism," 341.

22. Eccles, "Fur Trade and Imperialism," 341–45; Gilbert J. Garraghan, *Chapters in Frontier History: Research Studies in the Making of the West* (Milwaukee: Bruce Publishing Co., 1934), 60, 78–84.

23. Marcel Giraud, *A History of French Louisiana*, vol. 1 of *The Reign of Louis XIV, 1698–1715*, trans. Joseph C. Lambert (Baton Rouge: Louisiana State University Press, 1974), 141–67, 223–45.

24. Mildred Mott Wedel, "J. -B. Bénard, Sieur De La Harpe: Visitor to the Wichitas in 1719," *Great Plains Journal* 10 (spring 1971): 43; Tanner, "Territory of the Caddo," 40–41.

25. Ralph A. Smith, ed. and trans., "Account of the Journey of Bérnard de la Harpe: Discovery Made by Him of Several Nations Situated in the West," *Southwestern Historical Quarterly* 62 (April 1959): 533.

26. Wedel, "La Harpe: Visitor to the Wichitas," 56–57.

27. Eccles, "Fur Trade and Imperialism," 341–45.

28. Usner, *Frontier Exchange Economy*, 191–218.

29. Verner W. Crane, *The Southern Frontier, 1670–1732* (1929; reprint, Ann Arbor:

University of Michigan Press, 1956), 66, 111; Giraud, *Reign of Louis XIV*, 81–82; Verner W. Crane, "The Tennessee River as the Road to Carolina: The Beginnings of Exploration and Trade," *The Mississippi Valley Historical Review* 3 (June 1916): 3–18; Almon Wheeler Lauber, *Indian Slavery in Colonial Times Within the Present Limits of the United States*, Studies in History, Economics and Public Law, vol. 54 (Williamstown, Mass.: Corner House Publishers, 1970), 26–33, 63–102; John P. Reid, *A Better Kind of Hatchet: Law, Trade, and Diplomacy in the Cherokee Nation During the Early Years of European Contact* (University Park: Pennsylvania State University Press, 1976), 27–30; Elizabeth A. H. John, *Storms Brewed in Other Men's Worlds: The Confrontation of Indians, Spanish, and French in the Southwest, 1540–1795* (College Station: Texas A&M Press, 1975; reprint, Lincoln: University of Nebraska Press, 1981), 383; Surrey, *Commerce of Louisiana*, 227–28.

30. John, *Storms Brewed*, 339–42.

31. Richard White, *The Middle Ground: Indians, Empires, and Republicans in the Great Lakes Region, 1650–1815* (Cambridge: Cambridge University Press, 1991), 1–50.

32. John C. Ewers, "Symbols of Chiefly Authority in Spanish Louisiana," in *The Spanish in the Mississippi Valley, 1762–1804*, ed. John Francis McDermott (Urbana: University of Illinois Press, 1974), 273.

33. Elizabeth Ann Harper, "The Taovayas Indians in Frontier Trade and Diplomacy, 1769–1779," *Southwestern Historical Quarterly* 57 (October 1953): 181–85.

34. Stanley Faye, "The Arkansas Post of Louisiana: Spanish Domination," *The Louisiana Historical Quarterly* 17 (July 1944): 631.

35. Athanase de Mézières, the commander at Natchitoches, constantly complained about the Arkansas region. "But that river of the Akansa [Arkansas] having become infested by the concourse of malefactors of which I have spoken, they soon came to know the Osages, and incited them with powder, balls, fusils, and other munitions (which are furnished them by merchants who go annually with passports to visit them) to attack those of this district, for the purpose of stealing women, whom they would buy to satisfy their brutal appetites; Indian children, to aid them in their hunting; horses, on which to hunt wild cattle [buffalo]; and mules, on which to carry the fat and the flesh. Thus, all at once this district has become a pitiful theater of outrageous robberies and bloody encounters, and it has come to pass that in despair the Tuacanas, Yscanis, Tancaoüeys, and Quitseys have retreated toward the south until they are now in the neighborhood of the presidios of San Saba, Bexar, and Espíritu Santo." Herbert E. Bolton, ed., *Athanase de Mézières and the Louisiana-Texas Frontier, 1768–1780*, (Cleveland: Arthur H. Clark Co., 1914), 1:167.

36. Ibid.

37. Étienne de Vaugine to Esteban Miró, 12 April 1783, Manuscript Collection of Abraham P. Nasatir in San Diego, California, entitled "Imperial Osages: A Documentary History of the Osage Indians During the Spanish Regime," 3:48 (referred to hereafter as Nasatir Papers); John, *Storms Brewed*, 409, 411; John Joseph Mathews, *The Osage: Children of the Middle Waters* (Norman: University of Oklahoma Press, 1961; reprint, 1982), 236.

38. John, *Storms Brewed*, 429–30.

39. Balthazar De Villiers to Monsieur (Unzaga), 16 January 1774, Nasatir Papers, 2:111.

40. Elizabeth Ann Harper, "The Taovayas Indians in Frontier Trade and Diplomacy, 1719–1835," *Panhandle-Plains Historical Review* 23 (October 1953): 14.

41. At times the Osage destroyed their rivals' goods. In April 1786, the Osage were reported as "destroying the entire hunt by cutting the deerskins and bison tongues, and dumping out the bear fat and tallow," Miró to Joseph Vallière, 17 May 1789, Nasatir Papers, 2:239; The commander at Arkansas Post, Balthazar de Villiers, observed that the Quapaw were dwindling, many were drinking, their trade had almost disappeared, and that "having, in my opinion, the same origin as the Osages, since their language is the same, there being only a little difference according to all that I have seen and heard, there is no appearance

that they would go to war against them; that if three or four have recently joined the Chickasaws, it is again testimony of their weakness in that they have not dared to disoblige them." De Villiers to Bernardo de Gálvez, 11 June 1778, 2:205–8.

42. "By order of January 30, last, Your Excellency orders me that whenever any Indian tribe or nation presents itself with the intention of transmigrating themselves from [to] this side that they be permitted to do so." Zenon Trudeau to Francois Luis Hector, Baron de Carondelet, 16 May 1787, Nasatir Papers, 4:154; Vallière to Miró, 3 June 1787, ibid., 3:174–75; Vallière to Miró, 22 December 1788, ibid., 3:234; Vallière to Filhiol, 10 September 1789, ibid., 3:244–45.

43. Gilbert C. Din and Abraham P. Nasatir, *The Imperial Osages: Spanish-Indian Diplomacy in the Mississippi Valley* (Norman: University of Oklahoma Press, 1983), 190.

44. James Mooney, "Myths of the Cherokee and Sacred Formulas of the Cherokee," in *Nineteenth Annual Report, 1897–1898*, Bureau of American Ethnology (Washington, D.C.: Government Printing Office, 1900), 390–91.

PROTOHISTORIC TUNICAN INDIANS IN ARKANSAS

1. Dan F. Morse and Phyllis A. Morse, *Archaeology of the Central Mississippi Valley* (New York: Academic Press, 1983), 271–314.

2. Barbara A. Burnett and Katherine A. Murray, "Death, Drought and De Soto: The Bioarcheology of Depopulation" (Paper presented at the De Soto in Arkansas Symposium, University of Arkansas Museum, Fayetteville, Arkansas, 1989).

3. John R. Swanton, *Indian Tribes of the Lower Mississippi Valley and Adjacent Coast of the Gulf of Mexico*, Bureau of American Ethnology Bulletin 43 (Washington D.C. 1911), 333–37.

4. See Jeffrey P. Brain, "Tunica Archeology," *Papers of the Peabody Museum of Archaeology and Ethnology* 78 (1988).

5. Mary R. Haas, "Tunica Dictionary," *University of California Publications in Linguistics* 9 (1953): 175–332.

6. Swanton, *Indian Tribes*, 306–26.

7. See Haas, "Tunica Dictionary"; Haas, "Tunica Texts," *University of California Publications in Linguistics* 6 (1950): 1–174; and Haas, "The Solar Deity of the Tunica," *Papers of the Michigan Academy of Science, Arts and Letters* 28 (1942): 531–35.

8. See Brain, "Tunica Archaeology."

9. Ibid., 65.

10. Ibid., 264–80.

11. Ibid., 246.

12. Swanton, *Indian Tribes*, 306; and Samuel D. Dickinson, "Historic Tribes of the Ouachita Drainage System in Arkansas," *Arkansas Archeologist* 21 (1980): 1–11.

13. Marvin Jeter, "Tunicans West of the Mississippi: A Summary of Early Historic and Archeological Evidence," in *The Protohistoric Period in the Mid-South, 1500–1700*, ed. David H. Dye and R. C. Brister, Mississippi Department of History and Archives Report No. 18 (Jackson, Miss., 1986); Marvin Jeter, Katherine H. Cande, and John J. Mintz, "Goldsmith Oliver 2 (3PU306): A Protohistoric Archeological Site Near Little Rock, Arkansas" (Draft report to the Federal Aviation Administration, Southwest Region, Arkansas Archeological Survey, Fayetteville, Arkansas, 1989).

14. Robert L. Rankin, "Language Affiliations of Some De Soto Place Names in Arkansas" (Paper presented at the De Soto in Arkansas Symposium, University of Arkansas Museum, Fayetteville, Arkansas, 1988).

15. See, for example, Michael P. Hoffman, "The Kinkead-Mainard Site, 3PU2: A Late Prehistoric Quapaw Phase Site near Little Rock, Arkansas," *Arkansas Archeologist* 16–18 (1977):

1–41; "The Protohistoric Period in the Lower and Central Arkansas River Valley in Arkansas," in Dye and Brister, *Protohistoric Period in the Mid South*, 24–37; "An Examination of the Evidence for the Tunica People on the Arkansas River" (Paper presented at the annual meeting of the Mid-South Folklore Association, Clarksville, Arkansas, 1987); "Identification of Ethnic Groups Contacted by the de Soto Expedition in Arkansas" (Paper presented at the De Soto in Arkansas Symposium, University of Arkansas Museum, Fayetteville, Arkansas, 1988); "The Terminal Mississippian Period in the Arkansas River Valley and Quapaw Ethnogenesis," in *Towns and Temples Along the Mississippi*, ed. David H. Dye and Cheryl Anne Cox (Tuscaloosa: University of Alabama Press, 1990), 208–26; and "Quapaw Structures, 1673–1834, and Their Comparative Significance," in *Arkansas Before the Americans*, ed. Hester A. Davis, Arkansas Archeological Survey Research Series, No. 40 (Fayetteville, Arkansas, 1991), 55–68.

16. Samuel D. Dickinson and Samuel C. Dellinger, "A Survey of the Historic Earthenware of the Lower Arkansas Valley," *Texas Archeological and Paleontological Society Bulletin* 12 (1940): 1–11; James A. Ford, "Menard Site: The Quapaw Village of Osotouy on the Lower Arkansas River," *Anthropological Papers of the American Museum of Natural History* 48 (1961): 133–91; Charles R. McGimsey III, "A Report on the Quapaw in Arkansas Immediately Prior to the Treaty of 1818" (Miami, Oklahoma: Quapaw Tribal Council, 1964); Philip Phillips, "Archaeological Survey on the Lower Yazoo Basin, Mississippi, 1949–1955," *Papers of the Peabody Museum of Archaeology and Ethnology* 60 (1970): 943–44; Hoffman, "Kinkead-Mainard Site"; and, Morse and Morse, *Central Mississippi Valley*, 318–20.

17. See Ford, "Menard Site."

18. Phillips, "Lower Yazoo," 943–44.

19. See Phyllis M. Clancy, "The Carden's Bottoms Puzzle Elucidated" (M.A. thesis, University of Arkansas, Fayetteville, 1985).

20. Hoffman, "Protohistoric Period," 30–34; John H. House, "The Mississippian Sequence in the Menard Locality, Eastern Arkansas," in Davis, *Arkansas Before the Americans*, 6–39; and Jeter, Cande, and Mintz, "Goldsmith Oliver 2," 32–96.

21. Philip Phillips, James A. Ford, and James B. Griffin, "Archaeological Survey in the Lower Mississippi Alluvial Valley, 1940–1947," *Papers of the Peabody Museum of Archaeology and Ethnology* 25 (1951): 401.

22. Hoffman, "Quapaw Structures," 58.

23. House, "Mississippian Sequence," 20; Jeter, Cande, and Mintz, "Goldsmith Oliver 2," 43–45.

24. Phillips, Ford, and Griffin, "Lower Mississippi Valley Survey," fig. 71.

25. See Rankin, "Language Affiliations."

26. Jeter, Cande, and Mintz, "Goldsmith Oliver 2," 54.

27. David W. Bizzell, "A Report on the Quapaw: The Letters of Governor George Izard to the American Philosophical Society, 1825–1827," *Pulaski County Historical Review* 29 (1981): 72.

28. W. David Baird, *The Quapaw Indians: A History of the Downstream People* (Norman: University of Oklahoma Press, 1980), 228.

29. Morse and Morse, *Central Mississippi Valley*, 307; Charles Hudson, "De Soto in Arkansas: A Brief Synopsis," *Arkansas Archeological Society Field Notes* 205 (1985): 3–12.

30. Hudson, "De Soto in Arkansas," 5.

31. See Jeter, Cande, and Mintz, "Goldsmith Oliver 2," 531; Rankin, "Language Affiliations"; and Hoffman, "Tunica People."

32. Jeter, Cande, and Mintz, "Goldsmith Oliver 2," 531.

33. Clancy, "Carden's Bottoms Puzzle," 236–40.

34. Clarence Bloomfield Moore, "Certain Mounds of Arkansas and Mississippi, Part 1: Mounds and Cemeteries of the Lower Arkansas River," *Journal of the Academy of Natural*

Sciences of Philadelphia 14 (1908): 254–364; see also Dickinson and Dellinger, "Earthenware of Lower Arkansas Valley"; Ford, "Menard Site"; and Hoffman, "Kinkead-Mainard Site."

35. Jeter, Cande, and Mintz, "Goldsmith Oliver 2."

36. Ibid., 519.

37. Ibid., 134.

38. Martin T. Smith, "Glass Beads from the Goldsmith Oliver Site," in ibid., 217.

39. Barbara A. Burnett, "Bioarcheology of the Goldsmith Oliver 2 Site and the Protohistoric Period in Arkansas," in ibid., 216.

40. Jeffrey P. Brain, "The Tunica Treasure," *Papers of the Peabody Museum of Archaeology and Ethnology* 71 (1979): 234; Jeter, "Tunicas West," 53; Hoffman, "Kinkead-Mainard Site," fig. 9.

41. Hoffman, "Protohistoric Period," 28.

42. See John R. Swanton, *The Final Report of the United States De Soto Expedition Commission,* 76th Cong., 1st sess., H. Doc. 71, 1939; Jeffrey P. Brain, "Introduction: Update of De Soto Studies Since the United States De Soto Commission Report," in *The Final Report of the United States De Soto Expedition Commission* (1939; reprint, Washington, D.C.: Smithsonian Institution Press, 1985), xxxiii–xlvi; Dickinson, "Historic Tribes," 1–11.

43. Morse and Morse, *Central Mississippi Valley*, 305–15.

44. See Rankin, "Language Affiliations"; and Swanton, *Final Report*, 52.

45. See Rankin, "Language Affiliations."

46. Dan F. Morse, "On the Possible Origins of the Quapaws in Northeastern Arkansas," in Davis, *Arkansas Before the Americans*, 54.

47. Morse and Morse, *Central Mississippi Valley*, 305–15.

48. Ibid., 286, 297–98; Hoffman, "Quapaw Structures," 66–67; Phyllis A. Morse, *Parkin: The 1978–79 Archeological Investigations of a Cross County, Arkansas Site* (Arkansas Archeological Survey Research Series, No. 40, Fayetteville, 1981), 23; Charles H. Nash and Rodney Gates Jr., "Chucalissa," *Tennessee Historical Quarterly* 22 (1962): 7.

49. Brain, "Tunica Treasure," 234–40; and "Tunica Archaeology," 264–85.

50. Jeter, Cande, and Mintz, "Goldsmith Oliver 2," 523–37.

51. See Jeter, "Tunicans West."

52. Dickinson, "Historic Tribes," 6; Jeter, "Tunicans West," 42.

53. Dickinson, "Historic Tribes," 6.

54. Jeter, "Tunicans West," 45.

55. See Hoffman, "Identification of Ethnic Groups."

56. Jeter, "Tunicans West," 41.

57. Ibid.; Jeter, Cande, and Mintz, "Goldsmith Oliver 2," 95.

58. Jeter, "Tunicans West," 49–58.

59. Ibid., 49.

60. Tristram R. Kidder, "The Koroa Indians of the Lower Mississippi Valley," *Mississippi Archaeology* 23 (1988): 1–42.

61. Morse and Morse, *Central Mississippi Valley*, 314; see also, Burnett and Murray, "Death, Drought, and De Soto."

62. See Burnett and Murray, "Death, Drought and De Soto."

63. Swanton, *Indian Tribes*, 242.

64. Brain, "Tunica Archaeology," 262.

65. Ibid., 281–82.

66. Marvin D. Jeter, "Review of Brain: Tunica Archaeology," *Southeastern Archaeology* 9 (1990): 147–148.

67. Jeter, Cande, and Mintz, "Goldsmith Oliver 2," 528-35.

68. Frank F. Schambach, "The Place of Spiro in Southeastern Prehistory: Is It Caddoan or Mississippian?" *Southeastern Archaeology* 9 (1990): 67–68.

69. See Katherine A. Murray, "Bioarchaeology of the Post Contact Mississippi and Arkansas River Valleys, 1500–1700 A.D." (M.A. thesis, University of Arkansas, Fayetteville, 1989); and Burnett, "Bioarcheology, Goldsmith Oliver 2," 146–213.

70. See Jeffrey P. Brain, *The Tunica-Biloxi* (New York, 1990).

71. Ibid., 70.

72. Ibid., 93.

73. Ibid., 92.

RITUALS OF ENCOUNTER: INTERPRETING NATIVE AMERICAN VIEWS OF EUROPEAN EXPLORERS.

1. Historical and ethnographic information on the Quapaws can be found in W. David Baird, *The Quapaw: A History of the Downstream People* (Norman: University of Oklahoma Press, 1980). For the Caddos, see John R. Swanton, *Source Material on the History and Ethnology of the Caddo Indians*. Bureau of American Ethnology Bulletin 132 (Washington, D.C.: Government Printing Office 1942).

2. Isaac Joslin Cox, ed., *The Journeys of Réné Robert Cavelier, Sieur de La Salle* (New York: Allerton Books, 1922), 1:xvi.

3. In the translated "Memoir on La Salle's Discoveries, by Tonty, 1678–1690 [1693]," in *Early Narratives of the Northwest, 1634–1699*, ed. Louise Phelps Kellogg (New York: Barnes and Noble, 1917), 298, Tonty identifies the village name as "Capa." The name of the village is given as "Kapaha" in the *procès-verbal* account written by the expedition's notary, Jacques de la Métairie, as printed in Pierre Margry, ed., *Découvertes et établissements des français dans l'ouest et dans le sud de l'Amérique septentrionale (1614–1764)* 6 vols., (Paris: Maisonneuve, 1876–86), 2:181. The inhabitants of this village and three nearby villages (named Tongigua, Tourima, and Osotouy, or variants thereof), are usually identified in early French accounts as the Akamsea or Akansas, later as the Arkansas. By the nineteenth century, these people are most frequently referred to as the Quapaws.

4. "Letter of Father Zénobe Membré," translated in Marion A. Habig, *The Franciscan Père Marquette: A Critical Biography of Father Zénobe Membré, O.F.M., La Salle's Chaplain and Missionary Companion* (New York: Joseph F. Wagner, 1934), 209; Melville B. Anderson, ed. and trans., *Relation of Henri de Tonty Concerning the Explorations of La Salle* (Chicago: Caxton Club, 1898), 71–74; "Voyage Made from Canada Inland Going Southward during the Year 1682" by Minet, translated by Ann Linda Bell and annotated by Patricia Galloway in *La Salle, the Mississippi, and the Gulf*, ed. Robert S. Weddle (College Station: Texas A&M University Press, 1987), 46; Melville B. Anderson, ed. and trans., *Relation of the Discovery of the Mississippi River, Written from the Narrative of Nicolas de la Salle* (Chicago: Caxton Club, 1898), 18–20.

5. Of the nine first hand accounts of La Salle's 1682 voyage, the relations of the cartographer Minet and Nicolas de La Salle provide the most detailed descriptions of the greeting ceremonies performed by the Quapaws for La Salle and his companions. Since Minet credits Nicholas as a primary source of information, the latter's relation is quoted to describe the Quapaw greeting ceremony. For a critical evaluation of these accounts, see Patricia K. Galloway, "Sources for the La Salle Expedition of 1682," in *La Salle and His Legacy: Frenchmen and Indians in the Lower Mississippi Valley*, ed. Patricia K. Galloway (Jackson: University of Mississippi Press, 1982), 11–40; Patricia K. Galloway, "The Minet Relation: Journey by River," in Weddle, *La Salle*, 17–27.

6.   Anderson, *Relation of the Discovery of the Mississippi River*, 20–22. See also, Minet, "Voyage Made from Canada Inland," 46–47.

7.   *Procès-verbal* in Margry, *Découvertes*, 2:183–84.

8.   Anderson, *Relation of the Discovery of the Mississippi River*, 23–29; Minet, "Voyage Made from Canada Inland," 47–51.

9.   Anderson, *Relation of the Discovery of the Mississippi River*, 64; Minet, "Voyage Made from Canada Inland," 62; "Letter of Father Zénobe Membré," 210.

10.   The Quapaw, Omaha, Osage, Ponca, and Kansa tribes all speak Dhegiha dialects of the Siouan language family and share many other cultural patterns. See C. F. Voegelin, "Internal Relationships of Siouan Languages," *American Anthropologist* 43 (April–June 1941): 246–49.

11.   For examples of early French participation in the calumet ceremony as it was practiced in the Mississippi Valley, see "Of the first Voyage made by Father Marquette toward new Mexico, and How the idea thereof was conceived" in *The Jesuit Relations and Allied Documents*, Reuben Gold Thwaites, 73 vols. (Cleveland: Burrows Brothers, 1896–1901), 59:130–37; and "Memoir of De Gannes (Deliette) Concerning the Illinois Country," in , *The French Foundations 1680–1693*, Theodore Calvin Pease and Raymond C. Werner (Springfield: Illinois State Historical Library, 1934), 389–91.

12.   See William Brandon, *New Worlds for Old* (Athens: Ohio University Press, 1986), esp. 121–22.

13.   Siouan kinship and descent is reviewed in R. H. Barnes, *Two Crows Denies It* (Lincoln: University of Nebraska Press, 1984), 176–185. See also Alexander Lesser, "Siouan Kinship" (Ph.D. diss., Cornell University; Ann Arbor, Mich.: University Microprints, 1958).

14.   Relationships among Siouan clans and moieties are examined in Barnes, *Two Crows*, 50–103. Quapaw clan organization is outlined in James Owen Dorsey, "Siouan Sociology: A Posthumous Paper," *Fifteenth Annual Report of the Bureau of American Ethnology 1893–1894* (Washington, D.C.: Government Printing Office, 1897), 229–30.

15.   Alice C. Fletcher and Frances La Flesche, "The Omaha Tribe," *Twenty-Seventh Annual Report of the Bureau of American Ethnography, 1905–1906* (Washington, D.C.: Government Printing Office, 1911), 261.

16.   See Marcel Mauss, *The Gift: Forms and Functions of Exchange in Archaic Societies*, trans. Ian Cunnison (New York: W. W. Norton, 1967), esp. ch. 1.

17.   Roy A. Rappaport, "Ritual, Sanctity, and Cybernetics," *American Anthropologist* 73 (February 1971), 59–76.

18.   Weddle, *La Salle*, 7.

19.   Henri Joutel, "Relation de Henri Joutel" in Margry, *Découvertes*, 3:222.

20.   In addition to Joutel's relation, two other first hand accounts of this journey are Douay's narrative, printed in *Premier Etablissement de la Foy dans la Nouvelle France*, Christian Le Clercq, 2 vols., (Paris: Amable Auroy, 1691), and Jean Cavelier's account, translated in Jean Delanglez, *The Journal of Jean Cavelier* (Chicago: Institute of Jesuit History, 1938). Delanglez, however, has questioned the authorship of the Douay and Cavelier accounts in "The First Establishment of the Faith in New France," *Mid-America* 30 (July 1948): 187–214, and "The Authorship of the Journal of Jean Cavelier," *Mid-America* 25 (July 1943): 220–23. For a discussion of the Joutel account, see Delanglez, *The Journal of Jean Cavelier*, 11–26.

21.   Swanton, *Source Materials*, 7–16. See also William Joyce Griffith, *The Hasinai Indians of East Texas as Seen by Europeans, 1687–1772* (New Orleans: Middle American Research Institute, Tulane University, 1954) and Herbert Eugene Bolton, *The Hasinais, Southern Caddoans as seen by the Earliest Europeans* (Norman: University of Oklahoma Press, 1987).

22.   Joutel, "Relation," 3:341–42.

23. Ibid., 404.

24. Ibid., 404–6.

25. Ibid., 415.

26. Samuel D. Dickinson, "Historic Tribes of the Ouachita Drainage System in Arkansas," *The Arkansas Archeologist* 21 (1980): 1–11.

27. Joutel, "Relation," 3:416–19.

28. Griffith, *The Hasinai Indians*, 58–68; Bolton, *The Hasinais*, 70–91. The bulk of information on Caddo social and political organization comes from European descriptions of the Hasinai Indians; however, many anthropologists believe that Hasinai social and political forms are at least generally approximated among other Caddoan groups; see for example Don G. Wyckoff and Timothy G. Baugh, "Early Historic Hasinai Elites: A Model for the Material Culture of Governing Elites," *Midcontinental Journal of Archaeology* 5 (1980): 225–88.

29. "Fray Fransisco Casañas de Jesus Maria to the Viceroy of Mexico," translated in Mattie Austin Hatcher, "Descriptions of the Tejas or Asinai Indians, 1691–1722," *Southwestern Historical Quarterly* 30 (January 1927), 206–18.

30. Joutel, "Relation," 3:444–46.

31. In his article "Who were the Ani-Kutani? An Excursion into Cherokee Historical Thought," *Ethnohistory* 31 (Fall 1984), 255–63, Raymond D. Fogelson defines epitomizing events as occurrences, either legendary or real, that encapsulate and dramatize some larger cultural process affecting a group of people. See also Fogelson, "The Ethnohistory of Events and Nonevents," *Ethnohistory* 36 (Spring 1989), 133–47.

ALMOST "ILLINARK": THE FRENCH PRESENCE IN NORTHEAST ARKANSAS

1. Stanley Faye, "The Arkansas Post of Louisiana: French Domination," *Louisiana Historical Quarterly* 26 (July 1943): 633–721; Idem, "The Arkansas Post of Louisiana, Spanish Domination," *Louisiana Historical Quarterly* 27 (July 1944) 1944; González López-Briones, M. Carmen, "Spain in the Mississippi Valley: Spanish Arkansas, 1762–1804," (Ph.D. diss., Purdue University, n.d.); Morris S. Arnold, *Unequal Laws Unto a Savage Race: European Legal Traditions in Arkansas, 1686–1836* (Fayetteville: University of Arkansas Press, 1985); Idem, *Colonial Arkansas, 1686–1804* (Fayetteville: University of Arkansas Press, 1991).

2. Arnold, *Colonial Arkansas*, 138.

3. *Dit* names were nicknames which had more official status than among English speakers and often appeared in legal documents. Thus the records speak of Jean LaBass, Fayas, Jean Fayas, and Jean LaBass *dit* Fayas—all presumably the same person.

4. Morris S. Arnold and Dorothy James Core, *Arkansas Colonials 1686–1804* (Gillett, Arkansas: The Grand Prairie Historical Society, 1986), 5; Arnold, *Colonial Arkansas*, 129, 137.

5. Arnold, *Colonial Arkansas*, 120, 186.

6. Arnold and Core, *Arkansas Colonials*, 20.

7. Arnold, *Unequal Laws*, 38.

8. Arnold and Core, *Arkansas Colonials*, 9.

9. Ibid., 18.

10. González, "Spain in the Mississippi Valley," 76.

11. Arnold, *Unequal Laws*, 81; Arnold, *Colonial Arkansas*, 158. Arnold cites Demasellière to General, 16 June 1770, Archivo General de Indias, Papeles Procedentes de Cuba, *legajos* 107 (hereafter AGI, PC, *leg.*); Brothers Francoeur to Demasellière, 17 June 1770, AGI, PC, *leg.* 107.

12. Arnold, *Colonial Arkansas*, 147.

13. Arnold, *Unequal Laws*, 81.

14. Mrs. Ida M. Schaaf, "Sainte Genevieve Marriages, Baptisms and Burials . . . 1759–1839," Typescript, St. Louis, 23, 41, 54.

15. Sainte Geneviève Baptismal Record B, p. 71, Sainte Geneviève Archives, Western Historical Manuscripts, University of Missouri Library, Columbia, Missouri (hereafter cited as WHM).

16. Ibid., 156.

17. Dorothy Jones Core, ed. *Abstract of Catholic Register of Arkansas (1764–1858)* (Dewitt, Arkansas: Grand Prairie Historical Society, 1976), 20.

18. Arnold and Core, *Arkansas Colonials*, 25, 27, 29.

19. Ibid., 58, 71.

20. Ibid., 87.

21. Ibid., 41.

22. Ibid., 58, 72, 86.

23. W. E. McLeod, "Le Mieux and Janis Families," *Lawrence County Historical Quarterly* 1 (fall 1978): 23–24.

24. Carl J. Ekberg, *Colonial Sainte Genevieve: An Adventure on the Mississippi Frontier* (Gerald, Mo.: 1985), 227–29; WHM: 1805, U.S. WPA Historical Records Survey, Collection #3551, Folder 1851; 1811, Hunt's Minutes of Board of Land Commissioners 5, 437; 1822, U.S. WPA Historical Records Survey, Collection #3551, Folders 18084f.

25. C. W. Alvord, ed., *Kaskaskia Records 1778–1790* Illinois Historical Collections 5 (1909): 239ff.

26. Ibid., 414–20.

27. Schaaf, "Sainte Genevieve," 22.

28. Sainte Geneviève Archives, C 3636, Folder 374, WHM; Rob Beckerman, comp., *Sainte Geneviève County Tombstone Inscriptions*, 3 vols., (WHM, 1982, mimeograph).

29. McLeod, "Le Mieux and Janis Families," 24.

30. Marion Stark Craig cites Lawrence County Deed Book B, pp. 20–21 in Marion Stark Craig, *Lawrence County, Arkansas: Deed Record "B," 1817–1825* (Regional Studies Center, Lyon College, Batesville, Ark., typescript), 3.

31. Arnold and Core, *Arkansas Colonials*, 58, 72, 86.

32. Lucille Basler, *Pioneers of Old Sainte Genevieve* (Ste. Geneviève, Missouri, 1983, mimeograph), 40.

33. L'Abbé Cyprien Tanguay, *Dictionnaire Genealogique des Familles Canadiennes*, 7 vols. (Montreal: E. Senecal, 1871–90), 4:580. I am not able to resolve the contradiction.

34. Natalia Maree Belting, *Kaskaskia Under the French Regime* (Urbana: University of Illinois Press, 1948), 63, 83.

35. Ekberg, *Colonial Sainte Genevieve*, 34f.

36. C. W. Alvord, ed. *Cahokia Records, 1778–1790*, Illinois Historical Collection 2 (1907): xx.

37. Cover, Illinois State Historical Society *Journal* 17 (1924): 221.

38. This account of the beginning of the American period in Illinois is based largely upon Alvord's collection of French documents, and especially upon his detailed essay which introduces the Cahokia volume. See Alvord, *Cahokia Records*, and Alvord, *Kaskaskia Records*.

39. Alvord, *Kaskaskia Records*, 18.

40. Ibid., 86.

41. Alvord, *Cahokia Records*, lxix–lxx.

42. Ibid., ciii–civ.

43. Alvord, *Kaskaskia Records*, 142, 209, 213, 284–90, 340–44.

44. Ibid., 239ff.

45. Alvord, *Cahokia Records*, lxxxiii.

46. Ibid., cxliv.

47. It is difficult to tell when anyone actually made the move, since most of these men had been transacting business and owning land in the western town for years, and the records reflect that business presence.

48. Alvord, *Cahokia Records*, cxxi. Sadly, even Jean Baptiste Janis's attempt to gain a pension for his heroism at the capture of Vincennes turned out badly. He apparently applied in the twilight of his life, and he must have done it incorrectly—he probably just wrote a letter. In 1833 he received from the government agent a copy of the printed Revolutionary War pension rules with a note saying that if Janis wished to obtain a pension, he would have to submit a request by the rules. Three years later Janis was dead at age 87, and the note was left among his effects. Sainte Geneviève Archives, C 3636, Folder 401, WHM. See also the Lyman Draper Collection, the State Historical Society of Wisconsin, Madison: 18J92-93.

49. Arnold and Core, *Arkansas Colonials*, 41.

50. Ibid., 58. The names are given in Spanish, but in this paper I have opted to standardize all the listings of French-speakers in French orthography. While there is the danger of error in retranslating back into French forms, the gain in clarity makes it a reasonable risk.

51. Craig cites Lawrence County Deed Book B, pp. 25–26 in *Lawrence County, Arkansas Deed Record "B,"* 3.

52. Arnold and Core, *Arkansas Colonials*, 72.

53. Alvord, *Kaskaskia Records*, 116, 414–20, 440.

54. Arnold and Core, *Arkansas Colonials*, 86.

55. Record Group 951, First Board of Land Commissioners, 1805–12, Register of Opinions of Commissioners, 1809–12, Box 8, folder 4, New Madrid District, Louisiana, Missouri Archives, Jefferson City.

56. Craig cites Lawrence County Deed Book B, pp. 20–21 in Craig, *Lawrence County Deed Record Book*, 3.

57. Craig cites Lawrence County Deed Book B, pp. 22–24 in Craig, *Lawrence County Deed Record Book*, 3. The name "Charboneaux" is alternatively spelled in documents as "Charbonneaux" and "Carbonneaux." For clarity, I have opted for the use of "Charboneaux" in my text.

58. Board of Land Commissioners, Minutes 5: 84ff, Missouri Archives, Jefferson City.

59. Craig cites Lawrence County Deed Book A: pp. 26–28 in Marion Stark Craig, *Lawrence County, Arkansas: Deed Record "A," 1815–1817* (Regional Studies Center, Lyon College, Batesville, Ark, typescript), 14.

60. Craig, *Lawrence County, Deed Record "A,"* 15.

61. Craig, *Lawrence County Deed Record*, 2–3.

62. New Madrid Land Commission, "Testimony," p. 77, Missouri Archives, Jefferson City.

63. Craig cites Lawrence County Deed Book B, pp. 186f in Craig, *Lawrence County, Arkansas: Deed Record "B,"* 18. Michel's brother-in-law "Piere LeMaux" was a witness.

64. Craig, *Lawrence County, Arkansas: Deed Record "B,"* 21.

65. The original deed is in the Richard Searcy Collection owned by Robert Stroud, with a copy in the Regional Studies Center, Lyon College, Batesville, Ark.

66. Craig cites Lawrence County Deed Book A, 24-25 in Craig, *Lawrence County, Arkansas: Deed Record "A,"* 14.

67. McLeod, "Le Mieux and Janis Families."

68. Ibid., 11.

69. Arnold and Core, *Arkansas Colonials*, 61, 72, 83; Board of Land Commissioners, Minutes 5: 84ff, Missouri Archives, Jefferson City.

70. McLeod, "Le Mieux and Janis Families," 10.

71. Craig cites Lawrence County Deed Book A, pp. 31–34 in Craig, *Lawrence County, Arkansas: Deed Record Book "A,"* 15f.

72. Craig cites Lawrence County Will Book 1817–34, pp. 23–24 in Marion Stark Craig, *Lawrence County, Arkansas: Will Book 1817–1834* (Regional Study Center, Lyon College, Batesville, Ark., typescript), 8.

73. Craig cites Lawrence County Deed Book B, p. 219f in Craig, *Lawrence County, Arkansas: Deed Record Book "B,"* 21. The original deed is in the Richard Searcy Collection, Regional Studies Center, Lyon College, Batesville, Ark.

74. Certificate #1160, in *Early Settlers of Missouri As Taken from Land Claims in the Missouri Territory*, Walter Lowrie, ed. American State Papers, Public Lands (Reprinted by Southern Historical Press, 1986), 2:598.

75. Craig, *Lawrence County, Arkansas: Deed Record Book "A,"* 10–14.

76. Arnold and Core, *Arkansas Colonials*, 25, 41, 49, 55, 57, 71, 82.

77. Certificate #1164, Lowrie, *Early Settlers of Missouri*, 2:598.

78. Core, *Abstract of Catholic Register of Arkansas*, 47.

79. Sainte Geneviève Marriage Record A, p. 164; Deed #116, Collection C 2075), Sainte Geneviève Archives, WHM.

80. Sainte Geneviève Archives, C 3636 Folder 89, WHM; Schaaf, "Sainte Geneviève Marriages," 16, 17.

81. Indians #89, Sainte Geneviève Archives, Collection C 2075, WHM.

82. Ibid., Deed #82.

83. Arnold and Core, *Arkansas Colonials*, 62, 84.

84. Craig cites Lawrence County Deed Book A, pp. 38–40 in Craig, *Lawrence County, Arkansas: Deed Record Book "A,"* 18.

85. For studies of Davidsonville, see Clyde D. Dollar, *An Archeological Assessment of Historic Davidsonville, Arkansas*, Arkansas Archeological Survey Research Report No. 17 (Fayetteville, 1977); Leslie C. Stewart-Abernathy, *The Seat of Justice: 1815–1830* (Fayetteville: Arkansas Archeological Survey Research Report No. 21, 1980); and George E. Lankford, "Town Making in the Southeastern Ozarks," *Independence County Chronicle* 31 (October 1989, January 1990), 1–19.

86. Arnold and Core, *Arkansas Colonials*, 83; Craig cites Lawrence County Deed Book B, pp. 197–99 in Craig, *Lawrence County, Arkansas: Deed Record Book "B,"* 19.

87. Certificate #1161, Lowrie, *Early Settlers of Missouri*, 2:598.

88. Searcy Collection, Regional Studies Center, Lyon College.

89. Belting, *Kaskaskia Under the French Regime*, 60. The name "St. Gem" is also spelled "St. Gemme" in the documents; I have chosen to use "St. Gem" in my text.

90. Goodspeed Publishing Company, *History of Southeast Missouri* (Chicago: Goodspeed Publishing Company, 1888), 243f.

91. Ste. Geneviève Archives, Collection C 3636, Folders 117–18, WHM.

92. Arnold and Core, *Arkansas Colonials*, 40.

93. Ibid., 42, 47, 53, 65; Core, *Abstract of the Catholic Register of Arkansas*, 28.

94. Arnold and Core, *Arkansas Colonials*, 44, 48, 58, 67, 80.

95. Ibid., 40, 42, 47, 53, 65, 77.

96. Ibid., 39, 41, 42, 47, 54, 66, 77, 83.

97. Sainte Geneviève District, Land Record Book B: 116, Collection 2482, Entry 33, pp. 48–51, WHM.

98. Arnold and Core, *Arkansas Colonials*, 8–10, 65–76.

99. Arnold points out that this is not quite correct: "Actually, there was, of course, the huge grant to Law, which, believe it or not, Law's descendants pressed, though unsuccessfully, in the Superior Court of the Arkansas Territory. We also know that as far back as the late seventeenth century (1689?), Tonty made a grant to Jacques Cardinal at Arkansas Post (see Arnold, *Colonial Arkansas*, 27). It is altogether possible that there were some land grants at the various (three) incarnations of the Post during the French period." (Morris S. Arnold: personal communication, 1993.)

100. Arnold, *Colonial Arkansas*, 166; see 163–68 for a detailed discussion of the process.

101. Lowrie, *Early Settlers of Missouri*, 549, for St. Louis and St. Charles.

102. For examples of French settlement strategies around Mobile, see George E. Lankford, *A Documentary Study of Native American Life in the Lower Tombigbee Valley*, vol. 2 of the *Final Report of the Black Warrior-Tombigbee Project*, ed., Eugene M. Wilson (Mobile: University of South Alabama, for the U.S. Corps of Engineers, 1983, mimeograph).

103. See, for example, C. Richard Arena, "Land Settlement Practices in Spanish Louisiana," in *The Spanish in the Mississippi Valley, 1762–1804*, ed., John F. McDermott (Urbana: University of Illinois Press, 1974): 51–60; Ada Paris Klein, "Ownership of the Land Under France, Spain, and the United States," *Missouri Historical Review* 44 (1949): 274–94; Eugene Morrow Violette, "Spanish Land Claims in Missouri," in *Washington University Studies No. 8* (St. Louis: Washington University, 1921): 167–200.

104. Ste. Geneviève Archives, C 3636, folder 299, WHM.

105. Schaaf, "Sainte Geneviève Marriages," 29.

106. Ibid., 39, 43.

107. Ibid., 40.

108. Beckerman, *Sainte Geneviève County Tombstone Inscriptions*.

109. Marion Stark Craig, *Lawrence County, Arkansas: Will Book, 1834–1858* (typescript, 1992), 43.

110. Craig cites Lawrence County Will Book 1817–1834, p. 9 in Marion Stark Craig, *Lawrence County, Arkansas: Will Book 1817–1834* (Regional Studies Center, Lyon College, Batesville, Ark., typescript, 1991), 1.

111. Marion Stark Craig, "1829 Sheriff's Census (Lawrence County, Arkansas Territory)," (Regional Studies Center, Lyon College, Batesville, Ark., n.d., typescript).

112. Craig cites Lawrence County Will Book 1817–34, pp. 231–32 in Craig, *Lawrence County, Arkansas: Will Book 1817–1834*, 39.

113. McLeod, "Le Mieux and Janis Families."

114. Craig cites Lawrence County Deed Book A, pp. 35f in Craig, *Lawrence County, Arkansas: Deed Record "A," 1815–1817*, 16.

115. Craig, *Lawrence County, Arkansas: Will Book 1834–1858*, 21.

116. Craig, "1829 Sheriff's Census," n.d.

BETWEEN A ROCK AND A HARD PLACE: THE INDIAN TRADE IN
SPANISH ARKANSAS

1. Among Arkansas Post's other functions were assisting the convoys and boats that moved back and forth on the Mississippi, helping to safeguard the region, and providing products from hunting. M. Carmen González López-Briones, "Spain in the Mississippi Valley: Spanish Arkansas, 1762–1804," (Ph.D. diss.: Purdue University, 1983), 30.

2. Literature on colonial Arkansas is not extensive. For general works, see Morris S. Arnold, *Colonial Arkansas, 1684–1804: A Social and Cultural History* (Fayetteville: University of

Arkansas Press, 1991); two works by Stanley Faye, "The Arkansas Post of Louisiana: French Domination," *Louisiana Historical Quarterly* 26 (1943): 663–721, and "The Arkansas Post of Louisiana: Spanish Domination," *Louisiana Historical Quarterly* 27 (1944): 629–716; González López-Briones, "Spain in the Mississippi Valley"; and Morris S. Arnold and Dorothy Jones Core, eds., *Arkansas Colonials, 1686–1804: A Collection of French and Spanish Records Listing Early Europeans in Arkansas* (Dewitt, Ark.: Dewitt Publishing, 1986). General histories of Arkansas written by nineteenth or twentieth century specialists usually fail to incorporate any significant information on the colonial period.

3. For a survey of the fort at Arkansas Post in the Spanish era, see Gilbert C. Din, "The Spanish Fort on the Arkansas," *Arkansas Historical Quarterly* 42 (1983): 271–93. Arkansas Post's colonial population is conveniently summarized in Arnold, *Colonial Arkansas,* 179–81. Several of the censuses reveal that the Post had 40 whites and 10 slaves in 1766; 68 whites and 31 slaves in 1768; 114 free persons and 37 slaves in 1791; 283 free persons and 53 slaves in 1794; and in the last census of the Spanish era, 337 free persons and 56 slaves in 1798. The censuses usually omitted the white hunters, who were often away, and their families, few of whom lived near the Post. The reputation of the hunters, particularly outside of Arkansas, was low. They were often described as outlaws, lazy, thieves, and barbarians. Juan Filhiol of Ouachita referred to them as "scum." See in particular Herbert Eugene Bolton, ed., *Athanase de Mézières and the Louisiana-Texas Frontier, 1768–1780* (1914; reprint, New York: Kraus Reprint, 1970), 1:71, 166–68; and Arnold, *Colonial Arkansas,* 156–60.

4. Governors of Spanish Louisiana were Antonio de Ulloa (March 1766 to October 28, 1768); Alejandro O'Reilly (August 18, 1769 to about March 1, 1770); Luis de Unzaga y Amezaga (to January 1, 1777); Bernardo de Gálvez (to March 1, 1782); Esteban Miró (*ad interim* to 1785, proprietary governor to December 30, 1791); Francisco Luis Héctor, Barón de Carondelet (to August 5, 1797); Manuel Gayoso de Lemos (to July 18, 1799); Francisco Bouligny (acting military governor to September 13, 1799); Marqués de Casa-Calvo (*ad interim* to July 14, 1801); Manuel Juan de Salcedo (to November 30, 1803). For convenient sketches of Louisiana's Spanish governors, see Joseph G. Dawson III, ed., *The Louisiana Governors: From Iberville to Edwards* (Baton Rouge: Louisiana State University Press, 1990), 45–79.

5. Spanish commandants at Arkansas Post were Le Gros de Grandcour (1766 to February 1768), Alexander de Clouet (to December 13, 1769), François Demasellière (to December 10, 1770), José Orieta (to April 29, 1771); Fernando de Leyba (to April 18, 1774); José Orieta (to June 16, 1776); Sgt. Lucas García (*ad interim* to September 7, 1776); Balthazar de Villiers (to June 1782); Luis de Villars (to January 7, 1783); Jacobo Dubreuil (to March 1787); Joseph Vallière (to July 20, 1790); Ignacio Delinó de Chalmette (to July 11, 1794); Carlos de Vilemont (to July 22, 1802); and Francisco Caso y Luengo (to March 23, 1804). Arnold, *Colonial Arkansas,* 178; Din, "Spanish Fort," 283, 291.

6. Luis de Unzaga to François Demasellière, New Orleans, October 14, 1770, Archivo General de Indias, Papeles de Cuba, *legajo* (hereafter cited as AGI, PC, *leg.*), 107; Bernardo de Gálvez to Balthazar de Villiers, New Orleans, June 6, 1780, AGI, PC, *leg.,* 190; Esteban Miró to Joseph Vallière, New Orleans, January 28 and May 5, 1789, AGI, PC, *legs.* 16 and 6 respectively; Manuel Gayoso to Carlos de Vilemont, New Orleans, April 24, 1798, AGI, PC, *leg.* 44; Daniel H. Usner Jr., *Indian Settlers & Slaves in a Frontier Exchange Economy: The Lower Mississippi Valley Before 1783* (Chapel Hill: University of North Carolina Press, 1992), 174–75.

7. Although the Quapaws were usually the only Indians mentioned in the documentary literature as living in the area, there probably were other Native Americans residing in what is now Arkansas. The Quapaws have not received much attention. The chief study is David W. Baird's *The Quapaw Indians: A History of the Downstream People* (Norman: University of Oklahoma Press, 1980), which is weak on the colonial period. The Quapaws declined in numbers after European contact. Perhaps there were thirteen hundred warriors in 1687, but by the Spanish era they were far fewer. If the censuses are correct, the Quapaws numbered

509 in 1777 and 708 in 1784. "Denombrement du Poste des Arkanzas et de la Nation Sauvage de ce nom," Balthasar de Villiers, Arkansas, August 3, 1777; "Padrón de las tres aldeas de Indios Arkansas," Jacobo Dubreuil, Arkansas, April 17, 1784, both in AGI, PC, *leg.* 107.

8. For an explanation of Spanish continuation of the French system for dealing with the Indians and Spanish Indian policy, see Bolton, ed., *Athanase de Mézières*, 1:66–75; and Herbert Eugene Bolton "The Mission as a Frontier Institution in Spanish American Colonies," *American Historical Review*, 23 (1917): 42–61.

9. For the Spanish arrival in Louisiana in 1766 and the problems arising from it, see Vicente Rodríguez Casado, *Primeros años de dominación española en la Luisiana* (Madrid: Consejo Superior de Investigaciones Científicas, 1942); and John Preston Moore, *Revolt in Louisiana: The Spanish Occupation, 1766–1770* (Baton Rouge: Louisiana State University Press, 1976). For accounts of the hunters, see Demasellière letter extract of June 16, 1770, to Unzaga, AGI, PC, *leg.* 107; "Judicial Proceeding formed by Ygnacio Delinó against Luison de Rac," Arkansas Post, March 24, 1794, AGI, PC, *leg.* 26; Delinó to Carondelet, Arkansas, April 27 and August 10, 1792, AGI, PC, *leg.* 25A; depositions of Juan Joffre and Luis Daragua, attached to Delinó to Miró, Arkansas, March 24, 1791, AGI, PC, *leg.* 17.

10. "1767—Ulloa Sends an Expedition to the (Spanish) Illinois Country to Establish a Fort and Settlement and his Rules for the Government of the Same," in *The Spanish Régime in Missouri*, ed. Louis Houck (1909; New York: Arno Press, 1971), 1:1–19, with a copy of the original document in AGI, PC, *leg.* 2357; Faye, "Spanish Domination," 632. For trade rules issued by the commandant of St. Louis, see "Regulations made by Captain Rui [*sic*] to Govern the Traders on the Missouri, [1768]," in Houck, *Spanish Régime*, 1:35–36, with the original in AGI, PC, *leg.* 109. For Commandant de Clouet's desire for permission to trade with the Osages and Ulloa's refusal of his request, see de Clouet's letter to Ulloa of February 27, 1768, and (Ulloa) to de Clouet, (New Orleans), June 5, 1768, AGI, PC, *leg.* 107. It later became policy not to permit the Osages to trade in Arkansas.

11. "Ynstrucción que observará exactamente el Theniente Governador del Pueblo de Sn. Luis, Sn. Genoveva, y todo el distrito del Río Misuri, y la parte de los Ylinueses que pertenece a S(u)M(agestad)," O'Reilly, New Orleans, February 17, 1770; "Ynstrucción que seguirá exactamente el Señor De Mézières en el Comando del Puesto de los Natchitoches, que le he confiado," O'Reilly, New Orleans, November 24, 1769; both in AGI, Audiencia de Santo Domingo (hereafter cited as SD), *leg.* 2594. Spanish efforts to control the natives on the Mississippi's west bank are examined in Gilbert C. Din and A. P. Nasatir, *The Imperial Osages: Spanish-Indian Diplomacy in the Mississippi Valley* (Norman: University of Oklahoma Press, 1983); and Bolton, ed., *Athanaze de Mézières*. See also Gilbert C. Din, "Las relaciones españolas con los indios Osage," in *La influencia de España en el Caribe, la Florida y la Luisiana, 1500–1800*, eds., Antonio Acosta and Juan Marchena (Madrid: Instituto de Cooperación Iberoamericana, 1983), 309–29; and Juan José Andreu Ocariz, *Penetración española entre los indios Osages* (Zaragoza, Spain, 1964). For an overview of relations between tribes of the forests and plains, with much on the Indians of the Natchitoches district, see Elizabeth A. H. John, *Storms Brewed in Other Men's Worlds: The Confrontation of Indians, Spanish, and French in the Southwest, 1540–1795* (College Station: Texas A&M University Press, 1975). Morris S. Arnold examines French and Spanish legal systems in Arkansas in *Unequal Laws Unto a Savage Race: European Legal Traditions in Arkansas, 1686–1836* (Fayetteville: University of Arkansas Press, 1985), 1–125, and in *Colonial Arkansas*, 125–70.

12. "Ynstrucción que seguirá exactamente el Comandante del Puesto de los Arkanças," O'Reilly, New Orleans, November 14, 1769, AGI, SD, *leg.* 2594. Commandants were expected to promote peace among the natives, and in late 1791 Arkansas Post commandant Ignacio Delinó achieved it between the Quapaw and Delaware (Abenaki) Indians, for which the governor thanked those responsible. Carondelet to Tomás Portell, New Orleans, January 28, 1792, AGI, PC, *leg.* 18. When the Quapaws received their annual presents, a party was held to mark the occasion. In a 1771 party, 352 Indians consumed a cow, a barrel of flour weighing 280

pounds, and 57 bottles of liquor. Moreover, they all behaved well. Commandant Fernando de Leyba probably paid the expenses. Leyba to Unzaga, Arkansas, June 6, 1771, AGI, PC, *leg.* 107.

13. Balthazar de Villiers to Bernardo de Gálvez, Arkansas, May 20 and 28, 1777, AGI, PC, *leg.* 190; Joseph Vallière to Esteban Miró, Arkansas, January 2, 1787, AGI, PC, *leg.* 13. For the nationalities of the hunters, see González López-Briones, "Spanish Arkansas," 50–77.

14. Vilemont and Catalina were married with royal permission in New Orleans in 1803, but several children had already been born to them by that time. González López-Briones, "Spanish Arkansas," 50–77; Arnold, *Colonial Arkansas,* 166; and Gilbert C. Din, *Francisco Bouligny: A Bourbon Soldier in Spanish Louisiana* (Baton Rouge: Louisiana State University Press, 1993), 237–39.

15. Miró to Dubreuil, (New Orleans), May 25, 1785, attached to Dubreuil to Miró, Arkansas, March 10, 1785, AGI, PC, *leg.* 107.

16. Vallière to Miró, Arkansas, December 31, 1787, AGI, PC, *leg.* 13.

17. Din, *Francisco Bouligny,* 187; Din, "The Spanish Fort," 283.

18. Fernando de Leyba to Unzaga, Arkansas, April 13, 1772, AGI, PC, *leg.* 107; Orieta to Unzaga, Arkansas, March 22, 1776, AGI, PC, *leg.* 189B; González López-Briones, "Spanish Arkansas," 176.

19. John C. Ewers, "Symbols of Chiefly Authority in Spanish Louisiana," in *The Spanish in the Mississippi Valley, 1762–1804,* ed. John Francis McDermott (Urbana: University of Illinois Press, 1974), 272–84.

20. Willard H. Rollings, *The Osage: An Ethnohistorical Study of Hegemony on the Prairie-Plains* (Columbia: University of Missouri Press, 1992), 84–85.

21. Francisco Bouligny to Vilemont, New Orleans, September 6, 1799, AGI, PC, *leg.* 134A.

22. Draft, Casa-Calvo to Delassus, New Orleans, March 18, 1801, AGI, PC, *leg.* 151.

23. Bolton, *Athanase de Mézières,* 1:72-73. On the activities of one trader-merchant, see Carondelet to Ignacio Delinó, New Orleans, February 10 and 29, 1792, AGI, PC, *leg.* 18.

24. "Instructions for the expedition to the district of the Ylinnese, which is in charge of Captain Francisco [Ríu]" in Houck, *The Spanish Régime,* 1:14–15.

25. John Francis McDermott, "The Exclusive Trade Privileges of Maxent, Laclede and Company," *Missouri Historical Review* 29 (1935): 272–78. Licenses issued to Arkansas Post traders by Louisiana governors can be found scattered in the Papeles de Cuba in the Archivo General de Indias.

26. Miró to Dubreuil, New Orleans, April 28 and May 25, 1785, AGI, PC, *leg.* 107; Marcos Olivares to Miró, Arkansas, June 12, 1785, AGI, PC, *leg.* 12; Miró to Vallière, New Orleans, March 6, 1789, AGI, PC, *leg.* 6. Miró granted the license for commerce with the Arkansas Osages at a time when he thought peace with them was possible. Bougard's trade did not last long. He exchanged goods with them during the winter of 1785–86, and returned to Arkansas Post in May. In mid-1786, Miró halted the trade because of Osage depredations. Dubreuil to Miró, Arkansas, May 21, 1786, AGI, PC, *leg.* 12; Miró to Dubreuil, New Orleans, July 5, 1786, AGI, PC, *leg.* 4. Francisco Martin, who was mainly a hunter, was killed by the Osage Indians in 1792. Carondelet to Delinó, New Orleans, September 4, 1792, AGI, PC, *leg.* 18.

27. Morris S. Arnold, "The Significance of the Arkansas Colonial Experience," *Arkansas Historical Quarterly,* 51 (1992): 70. He cautions readers of colonial Arkansas history, "We need to think of the commandants not as government officials who were coincidentally in business, but as businessmen who were coincidentally in the government." Despite Arnold's admonition, it should be kept in mind that not all Arkansas Post commandants shared the same interest in business. They were, first of all, army officers.

28. Leyba to Unzaga, Arkansas, May 10, 1771 and April 13, 1772; Unzaga to Leyba, New Orleans, July 21, 1772; all in AGI, PC, *leg.* 107. On Leyba's debts and trade goods he took with him to Arkansas, see Leyba to Unzaga, Arkansas, November 22, 1771, ibid. On April 13,

1772, Leyba calculated his earnings in trade at Arkansas at 460 pesos. Three months later, he said he had not made money, but had sustained a 553 peso loss, plus interest. Leyba to Unzaga, Arkansas, July 29, 1772, ibid. Ignacio Delinó de Chalmette, commandant at Arkansas Post in the early 1790s, reportedly made a considerable sum of money in the four years he served there. Grace King, *Creole Families of New Orleans* (Baton Rouge: Claitor's Publishing Division, 1971, report), 320.

29. Faye, "Spanish Domination," 631, 647–53; de Villiers to Gálvez, Arkansas, March 22, 1778, AGI, PC, *leg.* 191; legal suits filed by de Villiers' creditors are in the Spanish Judicial Records, Louisiana Historical Center, New Orleans. De Villiers reportedly gave English parties licenses to hunt on the Arkansas River, or at least that was what one party told two French hunters, Paul Martin and Dominque Coco. "Deposition Taken at Arkansas," November 29, 1778, AGI, PC. *leg.* 191.

30. Vilemont to Gayoso, Arkansas, June 15, 1798; Gayoso to Vilemont, New Orleans, July 14, 1798; both in AGI, PC, *leg.* 215A.

31. Delinó to Miró, Arkansas, December 18, 1790, AGI, PC, *leg.* 16; Demasellière to Monsieur, Arkansas, June 27, 1770, and Leyba to Unzaga, Arkansas, January 19, 1773, both in AGI, PC, *leg.* 107. Not only did hunters and traders need licenses or passports to go anywhere in Spanish Louisiana, virtually everybody needed at least a passport to travel there. They were not difficult to obtain, but persons obtaining them needed to have a valid reason for traveling. The licenses helped the Spanish government regulate hunting and trading.

32. As early as 1773 Fernando de Leyba referred to local customs he described "as old as the Post." Dubreuil also commented on them later. Leyba to Unzaga, Arkansas, April 30, 1773; and Dubreuil to Miró, Arkansas, June 1, 1784; both in AGI, PC, *leg.* 107.

33. Gálvez to de Villiers, New Orleans, March 6, April 11, and June 6, 1777, all in AGI, PC, *leg.* 1; Dubreuil to Miró, Arkansas, June 1, 1784; and Dubreuil to Francisco Bouligny, Arkansas, September 1, 1784, both in AGI, PC, *leg.* 107. Over the years Arkansas Post commandants had frequent arguments with François Ménard. De Villiers believed Ménard's character to be unsavory, claiming he had gotten hunters drunk and induced them to gamble or sign certificates for goods they never received. De Villiers stated about him: "The duplicity of this man is remarkable in that he knows how to claim the protection of the laws or ignore them according to his interest." Arnold, *Colonial Arkansas*, 149.

34. Dubreuil to Miró, Arkansas, March 20, 1786, AGI, PC, *leg.* 13. In 1778 an ordinance was made at Arkansas Post giving the outfitter a "first lien on the hunter's catch." Arnold, *Colonial Arkansas*, 149. Jean Diana, a well-known trader at Arkansas Post, was reported missing and presumed dead in February 1791, after an Osage party raided his camp on the White River. He was one of several traders, in addition to numerous hunters, killed in the Spanish era. Delinó to Miró, Arkansas, March 18, 1791, AGI, PC, *leg.* 17; Miró to Manuel Pérez, New Orleans, May 13, 1791, AGI, PC, *leg.* 122A.

35. "Articles de la Convention de Commerçants du Poste des Arkansas," François Vaugine et al., Arkansas, January 16, 1798, AGI, PC, *leg.* 215A.

36. Vilemont to Gayoso, Arkansas, March 31, 1798, AGI, PC, *leg.* 213A.

37. Francisco Vaugine and Joseph Bougi to Gayoso, New Orleans, April 19, 1798, and Gayoso to Vilemont, New Orleans, April 24, 1798, AGI, PC, *leg.* 215A. A copy of Gayoso's letter is also in AGI, PC, *leg.* 44. Gayoso allowed Jardelat to go as a hunter rather than as a trader, but he was not allowed to take or sell alcoholic beverages. Gayoso to Vilemont, New Orleans, April 24, 1798, with Jardelat's attached petition of February (no day), 1798, AGI, PC, *leg.* 44.

38. González López-Briones, "Spanish Arkansas," 194.

39. Vilemont to Gayoso, Arkansas, November 15, 1798, AGI, PC, *leg.* 215A; Gayoso to Vilemont, New Orleans, February 20, 1799, AGI, PC, *leg.* 217A; González López-Briones, "Spanish Arkansas," 194.

40. "Ynstrucción . . . (para) los Arkansas," O'Reilly, November 14, 1769; Faye, "Spanish Domination," 648–49. Governor Ulloa in 1768 proposed only fifteen soldiers for Arkansas Post. Ulloa to the Marqués de Grimaldi, No. 1, New Orleans, October 6, 1768, in *Spain in the Mississippi Valley, 1765–1794*, ed. Lawrence Kinnaird, pt. 1 of 3 pts. (Washington, D.C.: Government Printing Office, 1949), 71–72. In 1769 O'Reilly authorized thirty-two soldiers and one officer for Arkansas Post. O'Reilly to Julián de Arriaga, New Orleans, December 29, 1769, AGI, SD, *leg.* 2583. The post had forty soldiers assigned to it in the 1790s. Vilemont to Gayoso, Arkansas, October 12, 1797, AGI, PC, *leg.* 190.

41. De Clouet to Monsieur, Arkansas, July 14, 1769, AGI, PC, *leg.* 107; de Villiers to Unzaga, Arkansas, December 12, 1776, AGI, PC *leg.* 190.

42. For Anglo-Spanish rivalry in Arkansas in the 1770s to 1783, see Gilbert C. Din, "Arkansas Post in the American Revolution," *Arkansas Historical Quarterly* 40 (1981): 3–30; and for James Willing, see John W. Caughey, "Willing's Expedition Down the Mississippi, 1778," *Louisiana Historical Quarterly* 15 (1932): 5–36. Gilbert C. Din, "Loyalist Resistance after Pensacola: The Case of James Colbert," in *Anglo-Spanish Confrontation on the Gulf Coast During the American Revolution*, eds. William S. Coker and Robert R. Rea (Pensacola: Gulf Coast History and Humanities Conference, 1982), 158–76, differs considerably from D. C. Corbitt's article, "James Colbert and the Spanish Claims to the East Bank of the Mississippi," *Mississippi Valley Historical Review* 24 (1938): 457–82.

43. Quapaw Great Chief to the Louisiana governor, September 12, 1770, AGI, PC, *leg.* 107; Dubreuil to Miró, Arkansas, August 7, 1783, AGI, PC, *leg.* 13; Faye, "Spanish Domination," 693; González López-Briones, "Spanish Arkansas," 148–51. In "Spanish Domination," 693, Faye claims that a *pote* contained two quarts. According to Jack D. L. Holmes, in "Spanish Regulation of Taverns and Liquor Trade," in *The Spanish in the Mississippi Valley, 1762–1804*, ed. John Francis McDermott (Urbana: University of Illinois Press, 1974), 176, a *pote* in French measure was equivalent to two liters. A liter is 1.0567 quarts.

44. Holmes, "Spanish Regulation," 175–76. On page 161 Holmes cites Spanish governors and commandants who prohibited or limited the sale of liquor to Indians, but notes that their laws were rarely observed.

45. Vallière to Miró, Arkansas, June 25, 1787, AGI, PC, *leg.* 13; Faye, "Spanish Domination," 694. See also "Investigation Concerning Sale of Liquor at Arkansas Post to the Abenaquis," [May 19, 1787] in *Spain in the Mississippi Valley*, pt. 2, 203–8, which describes a brawl by a group of Abenaqui (Delaware) Indians.

46. Miró to Vallière, New Orleans, July 19, 1787, AGI, PC, *leg.* 4B; Vallière to Miró, Arkansas, December 31, 1787, AGI, PC, *leg.* 13; Vallière certificate, Arkansas, October 1, 1789, AGI, PC, *leg.* 15A. Two years after Pedro (Pierre) Nitar was accused of introducing liquor, he, Carlos Dauteulle, and two other unidentified whites were killed by the Osages. Nitar was on a trading venture up the Arkansas River. A Big Osage war party returned to its village with ten horses loaded with goods seized from white hunting camps; it also brought Nitar's account books. Two white renegades who had lived among the Osages for years took the books to Arkansas Post. Delinó to Miró, Arkansas, March 24 and August 8, 1791, AGI, PC, *legs.* 17 and 122B respectively; "Depositions of Jean Joffre and Louis Daragua," attached to Delinó's letter of March 24, 1791.

47. Vilemont to Carondelet, Arkansas, January 8, 1796, AGI, PC, *leg.* 212A; memorial of François Vaugine, Andrés Fagot, Joseph Bougy to Gayoso, Arkansas, March 24, 1798, AGI, PC, *leg.* 215A. See also the discussion of alcohol at Arkansas Post in Arnold, *Colonial Arkansas*, 155–56. According to custom, only two taverns could dispense alcoholic beverages at the Post. However, Arkansas seems to have had more of them, if not at the settlement, then in the wilderness surrounding it. Leyba to Unzaga, Arkansas, March 25 and April 30, 1773, AGI, PC, *leg.* 107; Vallière to Miró, Arkansas, July 10, 1788, AGI, PC, *leg.* 14. Commandant de Villiers permitted only two establishments to sell liquor retail, and he condemned the practice of having many taverns. De Villiers to Gálvez, Arkansas, May 28, 1777, AGI, PC, *leg.* 190.

48. Holmes, "Spanish Regulation," 164–65.

49. Studies of the Osages include Carl H. Chapman, "The Origin of the Osage Indian Tribe: An Ethnographical, Historical, and Archeological Study," (Ph.D. diss., University of Michigan, 1959); James R. Christianson, "A Study of Osage History Prior to 1876," (Ph.D. diss., University of Kansas, 1968); Garrick A. Bailey, "Changes in Osage Social Organization, 1673–1969," (Ph.D. diss., University of Oregon, 1970); ibid., "Changes in Osage Social Organization, 1673–1903," *University of Oregon Anthropology Papers* 5 (1973): 1–122; Robert Wiggers, "Osage Culture Change Inferred from Contact and Trade with the Caddo and the Pawnee," (Ph.D. diss., University of Missouri, 1985). For more literature on the tribe, see Terry Wilson, *Bibliography of the Osage* (Metuchen, N.J.: Scarecrow Press, 1985).

50. Lieut. Gov. Zenon Trudeau wrote in 1793 that there were 1,250 Osage warriors. Trudeau to Carondelet, St. Louis, April 10, 1793, in *Spain in the Mississippi Valley*, pt. 3, 148–49. Lieutenant Governor Delassus in 1800 stated that there were 1,500 Osage warriors. This was the highest figure given for their warriors. Delassus to Casa-Calvo, St. Louis, November 29, 1800, Louisiana Collection, Bancroft Library, University of California, and published in *Before Lewis and Clark: Documents Illustrating the History of the Missouri*, ed. A. P. Nasatir (St. Louis: St. Louis Historical Documents Foundation, 1952), 2:622–24.

51. Din and Nasatir, *Imperial Osages*, 59–86.

52. Carl H. Chapman, "The Indomitable Osage in the Spanish Illinois (Upper Louisiana), 1763–1804," in *The Spanish in the Mississippi Valley, 1762–1804*, ed. John Francis McDermott (Urbana: University of Illinois Press, 1974), 287–308.

53. These sentiments were expressed many times in St. Louis. See, for example: Miró to the Marqués de Sonora (José de Gálvez), New Orleans, February 1, 1787, AGI, SD, *leg.* 2587; and Zenon Trudeau to Carondelet, St. Louis, September 28, 1793, AGI, PC, *leg.* 208A, and published in Nasatir, *Before Lewis and Clark*, 1:197–203.

54. Rollings, *The Osage*, 54–58.

55. Miró to the Conde de Campo de Alange, Madrid, August 11, 1792, "Descripción de la Luisiana, 1792," Archivo del Museo Naval, Madrid, 569, folios 178–99. Miró's report did not adequately recount how much harm the Osages inflicted on Arkansas hunters.

56. Din and Nasatir, *Imperial Osages*, 88–119, 385–90.

57. Vilemont to Carondelet, Arkansas, March 8, 1797, with enclosure of goods, AGI, PC, *leg.* 35; Carondelet to Vilemont, New Orleans, June 2, 1797, AGI, PC. *leg.* 24. On the illegal St. Louis trade with the Osages, see Delinó to Carondelet, Arkansas, June 18, 1793, AGI, PC, *leg.* 26.

58. Din and Nasatir, *Imperial Osages*, contains a lengthy discussion of Osage violence. For a different opinion on the nature of Osage violence, see Rollings, *The Osage*.

59. Francisco Cruzat to Miró, St. Louis, November 12, 1787, AGI, PC, *leg.* 13, with enclosure, "Council Held by the Big Osages on October 15, 1787," in AGI, PC, *leg.* 200. In 1793 a Big Osage chief in St. Louis denied that his tribe had ever stolen a horse or even shed a drop of blood in Arkansas. He then asked ingenuously: "It is true that on the Arkansas River some men were murdered and various (people) taken prisoner and robbed; but what nation does not have its delinquents?" Zenon Trudeau to Carondelet, St. Louis, August 22, 1793, AGI, PC, *leg.* 2363.

60. Bolton, *Athanase de Mézières*, 1:304–5, 2:141–47. Rollings, *The Osage*, 138–41, states that Osage-Quapaw relations were generally peaceful. He cites the tradition of "payment or gift-giving as compensation for injury or death" that resolved problems between the two nations. He says the Osages needed the Quapaws as a buffer against the Chickasaws. He also contends that the diminution in game tended to bring the Quapaw and the Osage tribes together. It should be noted, however, that throughout the Spanish era conflict usually went on between the Quapaws and the Osages. Quapaw war parties in the 1770s, 1780s, and 1790s

denounced the Osages and celebrated the taking of their scalps. Din and Nasatir, *Imperial Osages*, 87–254 passim.

61. De Villiers to Gálvez, Arkansas, May 28, 1777, AGI, PC, *leg.* 190. The location sometimes mentioned for trade with the Osages was *El Cuadrante* (Le Cadron), about 180 leagues above Arkansas Post. De Villiers explained that when the trader Andrés López arrived at the Post with permission to commerce freely, he directed him to trade with the Osages. De Villiers to Gálvez, Arkansas, July 14, 1777, ibid. There was a rumor that year that the English had established a blockhouse at *El Cuadrante*. De Villiers to Gálvez, Natchitoches, September 14, 1777, ibid. The rumor appears to have been false.

62. Spanish efforts to obtain Osage hostages are discussed in Din and Nasatir, *Imperial Osages*, 163–64, 166–72, 187, 204–15, 231. For the "head for a head agreement," see "Council formed by Pedro Piernas, Luis de San Ange, Pedro de Volsay . . ." St. Louis, August 21, 1773; Piernas to Unzaga, St. Louis, September 14 and December 13, 1773; all in AGI, PC, *leg.* 81.

63. Miró to Vallière, New Orleans, January 24 and May 27, 1789, AGI, PC, *leg.* 6; Carondelet to Arturo O'Neill, New Orleans, May 5 and November 13, 1792, AGI, PC, *leg.* 18.

64. Carondelet to the Prince of the Peace, New Orleans, April 25, 1797, AGI, PC, *leg.* 2365.

65. Manuel Pérez to Miró, St. Louis, October 5 and November 8, 1791, in AGI, PC, *legs.* 2362 and 17 respectively.

66. Vallière to the governor, New Orleans, February 14, 1792, AGI, PC, *leg.* 1441; a copy of Vallière's proposal is in AGI, PC, *leg.* 18.

67. (Luis de las Casas) to the governor of Louisiana, Havana, May 10, 1792, attached to Carondelet to Casas, New Orleans, February 26, AGI, PC, *leg.* 1441; Carondelet to Delinó, New Orleans, June 29, 1792, in *Spain in the Mississippi Valley*, pt. 3, 56; Delinó to Carondelet, Arkansas, August 7, 1792, AGI, PC, *leg.* 25A. Miró initially rejected the proposal of a fort on the Arkansas River by ignoring it. When he reported on conditions in Louisiana the next year in Spain, he then dismissed the proposed fort. Miró, "Descripción de la Luisiana," fols. 178–99.

68. Delinó to Carondelet, Arkansas, March 24, 1793, with Carondelet's marginal notation, in *Spain in the Mississippi Valley*, pt. 3, 143–144; Carondelet to Delinó, New Orleans, May 8, 1793, AGI, PC, *leg.* 19. When there was talk of an expedition against the Osages in 1786, Commandant Dubreuil of Arkansas reported that he would have several hundred men, both hunters and Indians, ready. Dubreuil to Miró, Arkansas, August 7, 1786, AGI, PC, *leg.* 13. Nothing ever came of it since Miró backed away from war. Again in 1790 there was talk of an expedition, which also fizzled out when Miró decided against it. Miró to Delinó, New Orleans, November 13, 1790, AGI, PC, *leg.* 7.

69. Delinó to Carondelet, Arkansas, April 12, 1793, in *Spain in the Mississippi Valley*, pt. 3, 149–50; Carondelet to Delinó, New Orleans, May 8, 1793, AGI, PC, *leg.* 19.

70. Din and Nasatir, *Imperial Osages*, 239–46. Lieut. Gov. Zenon Trudeau in St. Louis in 1798 summarized Missouri's attitude to the deaths in Arkansas: "It is, therefore, desirable that the Governor-General regard and consider for a moment the prosperity of (Missouri), and the slight evil suffered by the hunters and wanderers of the Arkansas River. That class of people is the scum of the posts." Trudeau, "Report Concerning the Settlements of the Spanish Illinois Country," St. Louis, January 15, 1798, AGI, PC, *leg.* 2365, and published in Nasatir, *Before Lewis and Clark*, 2:534–44, and Houck, *The Spanish Régime*, 2:248–57.

71. Delinó to Carondelet, Arkansas, May 15 and July 18, 1793, AGI, PC, *leg.* 27B.

72. Din and Nasatir, *Imperial Osages*, 255–90; see also William E. Foley and C. David Rice, *The First Chouteaus: River Barons of Early St. Louis* (Urbana: University of Illinois Press, 1983).

73. Vilemont to Gayoso, Arkansas, April 20 and June 18 and 19, 1799, AGI, PC, *leg.* 217; Din and Nasatir, *Imperial Osages*, 290–91.

74. For the poverty of the area, see Francisco Caso y Luengo to Manuel de Salcedo, Arkansas, two letters of August 6, 1802, AGI, PC, *leg.* 77. For attempts to establish trade with Indians, see Vilemont to (Carondelet), Arkansas, January 3, 1796, AGI, PC, *leg.* 34; Din and Nasatir, *Imperial Osages*, 283. For Chickasaw, Quapaw and Choctaw war parties searching for Osages, see Vilemont to the governor, Arkansas, March 2, 1797, AGI, PC, *leg.* 212B.

75. Caso y Luengo to Salcedo, Arkansas, two letters of August 28, 1802, AGI, PC, *leg.* 77. Caso y Luengo either did not know or ignored established policy when he suggested medals for two Osage chiefs. That prerogative belonged to the lieutenant governor in St. Louis.

76. Caso y Luengo to Salcedo, Arkansas, August 30, 1802, AGI, PC, *leg.* 77.

77. Jacques Mackay to Delassus, St. Andrew, April 10, 1803, AGI, PC, *leg.* 220. William Henry Harrison wrote to American Secretary of War Henry Dearborn on March 3, 1803: "I have lately received intelligence from the Arkansas informing me that the Osages have plundered the traders and other inhabitants upon that river to an immense amount." Logan Esary, ed., *Harrison's Messages and Letters* (Indianapolis, 1922), 1:76–84. Possibly the report was not accurate.

78. Din and Nasatir, *Imperial Osages*, 325–26, 328–30. The Osages were not invincible and suffered losses on occasion. See Felix Trudeau to Carondelet, Natchitoches, September 19, 1797, AGI, PC, *leg.* 35; and Delassus to the Marqués de Casa-Calvo, St. Louis, April 24, 1800 and August 3, 1801, AGI, PC, *leg.* 71B.

79. On United States policy to force the Indians out of lands east of the Mississippi in this time period, see Reginald Horsman, *Expansion and American Indian Policy, 1783–1812* (Lansing: Michigan State University Press, 1967).

80. AGI, PC, *leg.* 107 contains a number of documents from Arkansas Post commandants noting the presence of outside Indians in the district. They were Chickasaws, Choctaws, Peorias, and Kaskaskias. For a general article on Indians entering Spanish Arkansas, see Stanley Faye, "Indian Guests at the Spanish Arkansas Post," *Arkansas Historical Quarterly* 4 (1945): 93–108. See also Mary A. M. O'Callaghan, "An Indian Removal Policy in Spanish Louisiana," in *Greater America* (Berkeley, 1945), 281–94.

81. Vallière to Miró, Arkansas, June 3, 1787 and December 22, 1788, AGI, PC, *legs.* 13 and 14 respectively; Rollings, *The Osage*, 185–88.

82. Jean Filhiol to (Miró), Ouachita, June 25, 1789, AGI, PC, *leg.* 202. A discordant note, however, came from Captain Vallière of Arkansas, who attempted to persuade Commandant Jean Filhiol of Ouachita to follow his example and refuse entry to the Miamis and new bands of Delawares. Vallière to Filhiol, Arkansas, September 10, 1789, *Spain in the Mississippi Valley*, pt. 3, 280–81.

83. Summary of Demasellière letters to (the governor), Arkansas, June 2 and 4, 1770, AGI, PC, *leg.* 107; Carlos de Grand-Pré to Carondelet, Avoyelles, July 30, 1796, Bancroft Library; Vilemont to Auguste Chouteau, Arkansas, September 12, 1796, AGI, PC, *leg.* 34; (Carondelet) to Grand-Pré, New Orleans, October 13, 1796, AGI, PC, *leg.* 129; Lawrence and Lucia B. Kinnaird, "Choctaws West of the Mississippi, 1766–1800," *Southwestern Historical Quarterly* 83 (1979–80): 347–70. See also Din and Nasatir, *Imperial Osages*, 178–81; Din, *Francisco Bouligny*, 214n.

84. Dubreuil to Miró, Arkansas, April 20, 1784, AGI, PC, *leg.* 107.

85. Petition of Joseph Bougy to the military governor, New Orleans, March 11, 1801, with Casa-Calvo's marginal notation, and (Casa-Calvo) to Vilemont, (New Orleans), March 19, 1801, AGI, PC, *leg.* 72. Vilemont granted permission to about thirty Loup Indians to settle on the White River in early 1795. Vilemont to (Carondelet), Arkansas, January 5, 1795, AGI, PC, *leg.* 210. In 1800 Arkansas Commandant Vilemont recommended Bougy and Luis Jardelat to the governor for trade with the Osages, but no evidence exists that they acquired the right since Chouteau's monopoly was then in place. However, illicit trade with the Osages went

on from 1799 to 1803, or so an American official reported after Spain lost Louisiana. Vilemont to Casa-Calvo, Arkansas, April 16, 1800, AGI, PC, *leg.* 71B; Arnold, *Colonial Arkansas*, 122.

86. (Casa-Calvo) to Vilemont, New Orleans, March 30, 1801, AGI, PC, *leg.* 71B.

87. Arnold, *Colonial Arkansas*, 172. González López-Briones, in "Spanish Arkansas," 79–81, discusses the extent of farming in Arkansas. William E. Foley, *The Genesis of Missouri: From Wilderness Outpost to Statehood* (Columbia: University of Missouri Press, 1989), 65, notes the presence of Shawnee, Delaware, Peoria, Illinois, Miami, Ottawa, Mascouten, Kickapoo, and Potawatomi Indians in Spanish Illinois (Missouri). He calls them an "ineffective shield" against the hostile Osages.

88. Din and Nasatir, *Imperial Osages*, 357–84. Arnold, *Colonial Arkansas*, 173, blames the poverty of Arkansas on Spanish policy that sacrificed the economic interests and lives of Arkansans to the well-being of St. Louis merchants. While partly true, it ignores the fact that putting pressure on the Osages to behave would only work if they were supplied from one source. It also accepts the Osage excuse that their violence stemmed from not having trade in Arkansas, an excuse experienced Louisiana governors rejected, and they were probably correct. The weakness in Spanish policy was its inability to deal effectively with the Osages because of shortages in manpower and money. The Spaniards also feared that if a war broke out, the Osages would slaughter many whites on isolated settlements in Missouri. By contrast, Arkansas was relatively uninhabited.

THE SIGNIFICANCE OF ARKANSAS'S COLONIAL EXPERIENCE

1. Fontaine Martin, *A History of the Bouligny Family and Allied Families* (Lafayette: Center for Louisiana Studies, 1990), 27.

2. Stanley Faye, "The Arkansas Post of Louisiana: French Domination," *Louisiana Historical Quarterly* 26 (July 1943): 635, 684.

3. Guillermo Náñez Falcón, ed., *The Favrot Family Papers* (New Orleans: Howard-Tilton Memorial Library, Tulane University, 1988), 2:127, 129–30; 3:6.

4. Grace King, *Creole Families of New Orleans* (New York: MacMillan, 1921), 320.

5. Lawrence Kinnaird, ed., *Spain in the Mississippi Valley*, (Washington, D.C.: American Historical Association, 1949), 1:377–82.

6. De Clouet to Governor, 6 October 1768, Papeles Procedentes de Cuba, Archivo General de Indias, Seville, *legajo* 107. [Hereinafter AGI, PC, *leg.*]. But see S. Charles Bolton, *Territorial Ambition: Land and Society in Arkansas, 1800–1840* (Fayetteville: University of Arkansas Press, 1993), 16, where the author makes the interesting suggestion that a common field may have been in operation at the Post in 1765.

7. Vallière to Miró, January 14, 1789, AGI, PC, *leg.* 15A:63–64.

8. On February 23, 1803, Pierre Lefevre, *habitant* of the Post, petitioned Commandant Caso y Luengo for an extension of his grant in order to build a sawmill. Caso granted the petition. Morris S. Arnold, *Unequal Laws Unto a Savage Race: European Legal Traditions in Arkansas, 1686–1836* (Fayetteville: University of Arkansas Press, 1985), 107–8.

9. John B. Treat to William Davy, Letter Book of the Arkansas Trading House 1805–1810, National Archives, Washington, D.C.

10. John Gould Fletcher, *Arkansas* (Chapel Hill: University of North Carolina Press, 1947), 403.

11. *Archives Coloniales, Sous-Série* G^1, p. 404, Archives Nationales, Paris [hereinafter ANC].

12. *Mémoire sur l'État de la Colonie de la Louisiane en 1746*, ANC, C^{13A}30:242, 249.

13. Philip Pittman, *The Present State of the European Settlements on the Mississippi* (London, 1770), 40.

14. De Villiers to Gálvez, Arkansas Post, August 3, 1777, AGI, PC, *leg.* 190.

15. "Memorial of the Heirs of Carlos de Vilemont," in *Miscellaneous Documents of the 24th Congress, 2d Session* (Washington, 1837), No. 89, at 76.

16. François Marie Perrin du Lac, *Voyage dans les Deux Louisianes . . . en 1801, 1802 et 1803* (Lyons, 1805), 360.

17. Fortescue Cuming, *Sketches of a Tour to the Western Country . . .* (Pittsburg, 1810), 273.

18. See, e.g., note 14.

19. Herbert Eugene Bolton, *Athanase de Mézières and the Louisiana-Texas Frontier, 1768–1780* (Cleveland, Ohio, 1914) 1:166–68.

20. Samuel D. Dickinson, "An Early View of the Ouachita Region," *The Old Time Chronicle* 3 (July 1990): 12, 16–17.

21. See letter in note 6.

22. Perrin du Lac, *Voyage*, 360.

23. William Darby, *The Emigrant's Guide* (New York, 1818).

24. David M. Tucker, *Arkansas: A People and Their Reputation* (Memphis: Memphis State University Press, 1985), 18.

25. Bolton, *Territorial Ambition.*

26. Morris S. Arnold, "The Relocation of Arkansas Post to *Écores Rouges* in 1779," *Arkansas Historical Quarterly* 42 (winter 1983): 317, 319.

27. Pittman, *European Settlements*, 40.

28. De Clouet to Governor, October 6, 1768, AGI, PC, *leg.* 107; de Villiers to Gálvez, May 28, 1777, AGI, PC, *leg.* 190.

29. On these matters generally, see Gilbert C. Din and Abraham P. Nasatir, *The Imperial Osages* (Norman: University of Oklahoma Press, 1983), esp. Chapters 6, 7, and 8.

30. There is no complete treatment of Spanish land grants in Arkansas. There is a brief discussion of the Winter grant in Arnold, *Unequal Laws*, 98.

31. Thomas Nuttall, *A Journal of Travels into the Arkansa Territory During the Year 1819* (Philadelphia, 1821), 72–73.

32. Ibid., 78.

INDIANS ON THE LAND

1. Cyrus Byington, "A Dictionary of the Choctaw Language," in *Bureau of American Ethnology Bulletin* 46, eds. John R. Swanton and Henry S. Halbert (Washington, D.C.: Government Printing Office, 1915), 22.

2. Goodspeed Publishing Company, *Biographical and Historical Memoirs of Northwest Arkansas* (1889; reprint, Easley, S.C.: Southern Historical Press, 1978), 605.

3. Père Jacques Marquette, *Voyage of Marquette in the Jesuit Relations 59* (Great Americana, Readex Microprint, 1966), 155.

4. Mildred H. Wright, *A Guide to the Indian Tribes of Oklahoma* (Norman: University of Oklahoma Press, 1951), 219.

5. Stanley Faye, "The Arkansas Post of Louisiana: Spanish Domination," *The Louisiana Historical Quarterly* 27 (July 1944): 87.

6. Pierre Margry, *Découvertes et établissements des Français dans l'Ouest et dans le Sud de l'Amérique Septentrionale*, 6 vols. (Paris, 1878–85), 5:402.

7. Antonio Marinoni, letter to the editor, *Arkansas Gazette*, August 26, 1909.

8. John Pope, *A Tour Through the Southern and Western Territories of the United States of North America*, (1792; reprint, Richmond, Va.: J. Dixon, for the author, n.d.), 26.

9. Robert L. Rankin to author, April 7, 1993.

10. David W. Bizzell, "A Report on the Quapaw: The Letters of Governor George Izard to the American Philosophical Society, 1825–1827," *The Pulaski County Historical Review* 29 (winter 1981): 71.

11. Charles E. O'Neill, *Charlevoix's Louisiana Selections from the History and the Journal* [Pierre F. X. de Charlevoix, S.J.] published for Louisiana American Revolution Bicentennial Commission (Baton Rouge: Louisiana State University Press, 1977), 130.

12. Jean Louis Berlandier, *The Indians of Texas in 1830*, ed. John C. Ewers (Washington, D.C.: Smithsonian Institution Press, 1969), 135.

13. Margry, *Découvertes*, 6:362.

14. Rankin to the author.

15. William A. Read, *Louisiana Place-Names of Indian Origin*, University Bulletin, Louisiana State University and Mechanical Agricultural College, 19 (February 1927), xii.

16. Ibid., 7.

17. Byington, *A Dictionary of the Choctaw Language*, 94.

18. John R. Swanton, *The Final Report of the United States De Soto Expedition Commission*, 76th Congress, 1st Session, House Document No 71. (Washington, D.C.: Government Printing Office, 1939), 53.

19. Frank Schambach and Leslie Newell, *Crossroads of the Past: 12,000 Years of Indian Life in Arkansas* (Arkansas Endowment for the Humanities, 1940), 40.

20. S. D. Dickinson, "Historic Tribes of the Ouachita Drainage System in Arkansas," *The Arkansas Archaeologist*, Bulletin of the Arkansas Archaeological Society, vol. 21 (Fayetteville, 1980), 4.

21. José Antonio Pichardo, *Treatise On the Limits of Louisiana and Texas*, ed. and trans. Charles Wilson Hackett (Austin: University of Texas Press, 1931), 1:86.

22. Clarence H. Webb and Hiram F. Gregory, *The Caddo Indians of Louisiana*, Department of Culture, Recreation and Tourism, Louisiana Archeological Survey and Antiquities Commission, Anthropological Study No. 2 (Baton Rouge, August 1978), 31.

23. Read, *Louisiana Place-Names*, 14.

24. Margry, *Découvertes*, 6:416.

25. Byington, *A Dictionary of the Choctaw Language*, 100.

26. Hiram F. Gregory to author, August 28, 1974.

27. Durbin Feeling, *Cherokee-English Dictionary*, ed. William Pulte (Tahlequah, Okla.: Heritage Printing, 1975), 94.

28. George R. Stewart, *Names on the Land* (Boston: Houghton Mifflin, 1967), 231.

29. Manual Serrano y Sanz, *Expaña y Los Indios Cherokis & Chactas E La Segunda Mitad Del Siglo XVIII* (Seville, 1916), 2, n. 2.

30. Ibid.

31. Louis Bringier, "Notices of the Geology, Mineralogy, Topography, Productions and Aboriginal Inhabitants of the Region around the Mississippi and Its Confluent Waters," *The American Journal of Science and Arts*, 3 (1821): 38–40.

32. Cephas Washburn, *Reminiscences of the Indians*, ed. Hugh Park (Van Buren, Ark.: Press-Argus, 1955), 150.

33. Feeling, *Cherokee-English Dictionary*, 157.

34. Dan D. Flores, ed., *Jefferson and Southwestern Exploration: The Freeman and Custis Accounts of the Red River Expedition of 1806* (Norman: University of Oklahoma Press, 1984), 186.

35. Goodspeed Publishing Company, *Biographical and Historical Memoirs of Eastern Arkansas* (1890; reprint, Easley, S. C.: Southern Historical Press, 1978), 272.

36. Wright, *A Guide to the Indian Tribes of Oklahoma*, 84.

37. Goodspeed Publishing Company, *Biographical and Historical Memories of Northeastern Arkansas* (reprint; Easley, S. C.: Southern Historical Press, 1978), 452.

38. Byington, *A Dictionary of the Choctaw Language*, 82.

39. Bringier, "Notices of the Geology," 25.

40. Wright, *A Guide to the Indian Tribes of Oklahoma*, 98.

41. Dickinson, "Historic Tribes of the Ouachita Drainage," 9.

42. Byington, *A Dictionary of the Choctaw Language*, 114.

43. Joseph Paxton and Thomas Mather to Secretary of War, *Territorial Papers of the United States*, ed. Clarence Edwin Carter (Washington, D.C.: Government Printing Office, 1949), 19:770.

44. John R. Swanton, *Early History of the Creek Indians and Their Neighbors*, Bureau of American Ethnology, Bulletin 73 (Washington, D.C.: Government Printing Office, 1922), 271–72.

45. Zadok Cramer, *The Navigator: Containing Directions for Navigating the Monogahela, Allegheny, Ohio and Mississippi Rivers; With an Sample Account of These Much Admired Waters From the Head of the Former to the Mouth of the Latter* (1814; reprint, Great Americana, Readex Microprint, 1966), 189–90.

46. Raymond J. Martinez, *Pierre George Rousseau Commanding General of the Galleys of the Mississippi With Sketches of Spanish Governors of Louisiana (1777–1803) and Glimpses of Social Life in New Orleans* (New Orleans: Hope Publications, 1964), 58.

47. Delino to Miró, March 4, 1791, in Lawrence Kinnaird, *Spain in the Mississippi Valley*, 3 Vols., Annual Report of the American Historical Association for the Year 1945 (Washington, D.C.: Government Printing Office, 1946–49), vol. 3, pt. 2, 406.

48. Wright, *A Guide to the Indian Tribes of Oklahoma*, 145.

49. Read, *Louisiana Place-Names*, 28–29.

50. William A. Read, "Indian Place-Names in Louisiana," *The Louisiana Historical Quarterly*, (July 1928): 5.

51. Grant Foreman, *The Five Civilized Tribes* (Norman: University of Oklahoma Press, 1970), 398.

52. Samuel D. Dickinson, "The Quapaw Journey to the Red River," *Pulaski County Historical Review* 34 (spring 1986): 16.

53. John E. Shoemaker to author, February 25, 1993.

54. Samuel D. Dickinson, "Colonial Arkansas Place Names," *Arkansas Historical Quarterly* 48 (summer 1989): 148.

55. Thomas Nuttall, *Journal of Travels Into the Arkansa Territory, October 2, 1818–February 18, 1820* (1822; reprint, Cleveland, Ohio: Arthur H. Clark, 1905), 172.

56. Feeling, *Cherokee-English Dictionary*, 196.

57. Byington, *A Dictionary of the Choctaw Language*, 143, 240.

58. Nuttall, *Journal of Travels*, 131.

59. *U.S. Treaty with the Comanches, Wichitaw Nations and Their Associated Bands or Tribes of Indians, Camp Homes, Indian Territory, August 4, 1835.*

60. Robert L. Rankin to author, April 18, 1983.

61. Wright, *A Guide to the Indian Tribes of Oklahoma*, 157.

62. Goodspeed, *Biographical and Historical Memoirs of Northeast Arkansas*, 452.

63. Reed, *Louisiana Place-Names of Indian Origin*, 28.

64. Byington, *A Dictionary of the Choctaw Language*, 111.

65. Sam Dickinson, "Landmark of the Koroa," *Louisiana Folklife* 2 (October 1977): 1–3.

66. Mildred Mott Wedel, *The Deer Creek Site, Oklahoma: A Wichita Village Sometimes Called Ferdinandina, An Ethnohistorian's View*, Oklahoma Historical Society Series in Anthropology, No. 5 (n.p., 1981), 14.

67. Antoine Simon Le Page Du Pratz, *The History of Louisiana Or of the Western Parts of Virginia and Carolina Containing a Description of the Countries That Lie on Both Sides of the River Mississippi* (London, 1774; reprint, New Orleans: J. S. W. Harmanson, n.d.), 109.

68. John R. Swanton, *Source Material on the History and Ethnology of the Caddo Indians*, Bureau of American Ethnology, Bulletin 132 (Washington, D.C. 1942), 16.

69. Bizzell, "A Report on the Quapaw," 72.

70. Samuel D. Dickinson, "Lake Mitchegamas and the St. Francis," *Arkansas Historical Quarterly* 43 (autumn 1984): 197–207.

71. Stewart, *Names on the Land*, 86.

72. Byington, *A Dictionary of the Choctaw Language*, 280, 93.

73. Bizzell, "A Report on the Quapaw," 74, 76.

74. Ibid., 72.

75. Wedel, *The Deer Creek Site*, 10.

76. Bizzell, "A Report on the Quapaw," 72.

77. Wright, *A Guide to the Indian Tribes of Oklahoma*, 189.

78. Webb and Gregory, *The Caddo Indians of Louisiana*, 24.

79. Juan Filhiol, "Sketch of the Ouachita Region in 1786," trans. S. D. Dickinson, *The Old Time Chronicle Folk History of Southwest Arkansas* 3 (July 1990): 12.

80. Frederick Webb Hodge, *Handbook of American Indians North of Mexico*, Bureau of American Ethnology, Bulletin 30 (Washington, D.C., 1907–8), 2:226–27.

81. Edward Palmer, *Arkansas Mounds*, ed. Marvin D. Jeter (Fayetteville: University of Arkansas Press, 1990), 271.

82. Wright, *A Guide to the Indian Tribes of Oklahoma*, 241.

83. Goodspeed, *Biographical and Historical Memoirs of Northwest Arkansas*, 689.

84. Swanton, *Early History of the Creek Indians*, 245.

85. Jeffrey P. Brain, *On the Tunica Trail*, Louisiana Archaeological Survey and Antiquities Commission, Anthropological Study No. 1, Department of Culture, Recreation, and Tourism (Baton Rouge, 1977), 1.

86. John R. Swanton, *Indian Tribes of the Lower Mississippi Valley and Adjacent Coast of the Gulf of Mexico*, Bureau of Ethnology, Bulletin 43 (Washington D.C.: Government Printing Office, 1911), 272.

87. Feeling, *Cherokee-English Dictionary*, 64.

88. Goodspeed, *Biographical and Historical Memoirs of Northwest Arkansas*, 487.

89. Dickinson, "The Quapaw Journey to Red River," 15.

90. Wright, *A Guide to the Indian Tribes of Oklahoma*, 45.

91. Dickinson, "The Quapaw Journey to Red River," 15.

92. Bizzell, "A Report On the Quapaw," 74.

Index

A

Abbott, John S. C.: treatment of
Cofitachequi's kidnapping, 15; account of
de Soto expedition, 15–18; on Ucita, 16;
on christianity of the wrong kind, 15–16;
on preferability of protestant influence, 18;
mentioned, 19
Abenakis Indians, 150
Academy Award, 15
Acansa (Arkansas), 143
Acansas (Arkansas), 143
Acansea (Arkansas), 143
Accancea, (Arkansas), 143
Adams Field, 69
Aiaita (Choctaw Prairie), 142
aiataia, 142
Ak-akan-ze (Arkansas), 143
Ak-akon-ca (Arkansas), 143
Akamsea (Arkansas), 143
Akancea (Arkansas), 143
Akoroa (Tunica village), 67
Alabama, 147, 149, 150, 153, 155, 156
Albornoz, Miquel *(Hernando de Soto, El Amadís
de la Florida)*, 22; on de Soto, 22–23.
Algonquian Indians, 143, 152, 153, 155, 157
Alkansa, 143
Altus, Arkansas, 142
Alvord, C. W., 97, 98, 100
American Revolution, 10, 119, 120, 132, 147, 149
Angaska (Quapaw chief), 120
Anilco, xii
Ani-Yun wiya, 147
Annales school, 22
anthropology: effect on de Soto studies, 24–25
Antony and Cleopatra, 8
Apalachee Indians, xiv
Arcansa (Arkansas), 143
Argentina, 18
Arkansas: origins of name, 143–44
Arkansas Archeological Survey, 63, 154, 156
Arkansas County, 135–36
Arkansas Post: and regulation of trade at,
118–19; and commandants'

responsibilities, 132; and first sawmill, 134;
John Gould Fletcher on, 135; descriptions
of, 137; location of, 139–40; mentioned,
xiv, 54, 55–56, 57, 60, 81, 85, 88, 89, 90, 91,
93, 95, 96, 97, 99, 100–1, 103, 105, 106, 107,
108, 109, 111, 112, 113, 114, 115, 116, 117,
118, 120, 121, 123, 124, 126, 127, 128,
129–30, 132, 137, 141, 143, 148, 152, 153
Arkansas River: archaeological sites, 70; valley,
40, 41, 56, 73, 74, 75; mentioned, xii, 3, 28,
39, 41, 42, 50, 55, 61, 66, 69, 73, 77, 78, 89,
90, 101, 112, 114, 120, 123, 125, 127, 131,
132, 135, 142, 144, 146, 147–48, 149, 151,
152, 154, 155, 156
Arnold, Morris S.: essay by, 131–41;
mentioned, vii, ix, x, xiv, 89, 90, 91, 109
Augusta, Arkansas, 148
Augustin de La Houssaye, Paul, 132
Autiamque, 6
Avila, Pedrarias de, 7, 14
Ayllón expedition, 36
Ayo-Caddi-Aymay (Caddo Supreme Being), 84

B

Badajoz, Portugal, 4
Barbau, Reine Julia, 97
Batesville, Arkansas, 147
Baton Rouge, Louisiana, 119
Baugi, Jean Baptiste, 108
Baugi, Joseph, 100–1, 108
Baugi, Louis, 108
Baugi, Marie du Placy, 108
Bauvais, Antoine, 99, 107, 108,
Bauvais, Jean Baptiste St. Gem: death of, 110
Bauvais, Marie St. Gem, 107–8
Bauvais, Vital St. Gem, 97, 108, 110
Bayou, 145
Bayou Bartholomew, 73, 153
Bayou Chicot, 153
Bayou Colewa, 153
Bayou Macon, 73
Bayou Manchac, 119
bayuk, 145
"bear" state, 138

Beltrán, Antonio, 125
Benoist. *See* Louis Giscard
Benton County, 154
Biedma, Luys Hernandez de: report of, 4–6;
    mentioned, 11, 20, 39, 40
Bienvenu, Pélagie, 97
Bienvenue, Guillaume, 90
Bienvenue, Marianne, 90
Bienville, Sieur de, 154
"Big Knife." *See* Hinma Koapemiche
Billet, Anselmo, 129
Black River, 99, 101, 102, 103, 104, 105, 106,
    107, 109, 111, 156, 157
Blommart, Jean, 55, 117
Bluffton, Arkansas, 145
Boabdilla, Isabella de, 14
Boas, Franz, 25
Bodcaw Bayou, 145
Bogy, Joseph. *See* Baugi, Joseph
Bolduc, Etienne, 97
Bolton, Charles, *Territorial Ambition,* 138
Bonaventure, François Voisin de, 117
Bonne, Michael, 126
Bossu, Jean-Bernard, 146
Bougard, Claudio, 116
Bougy, Catalina, 114
Bougy, Joseph, 114, 118, 119, 121, 127, 129
Bouligny, Francisco, 115
Bowie County, Texas, 146
Bowie Knife ("Arkansas Toothpick"), 138
Bowl, Chief ("The Bowl"), 147
Boyd Hill, 148
Bradley County, 151
Brain, Jeffrey: on De Soto route, 27; and the
    Tunica, 63, 69, 70, 73; mentioned, 74
Branner, John C., 152
Brident, Alexander, 106
Brister, R. C., 68
British West Florida, 117
Brousseau, Simon, 96
Buffalo River, 150
Burnett, Barbara A.: on de Soto expedition
    and epidemics, 36; mentioned, 69
Burnett and Murray: drought as a factor in
    depopulation, 73

C

Cache River, 107, 150
Cadaux-dakioux, 146
Caddodacchos, 146
Caddo Gap, 145

Caddo Indians: hierarchical order, xiv; and
    description of lifestyle, 44–48; and floods,
    46; and trade, 46, 48, 52, 53; Spanish
    policy toward, 53; relations with Spanish
    after Treaty of Paris, 55; erosion of
    position under Spanish, 56; Osage raids
    against, 54, 56, 60, 122, 124; and epidemic
    disease, 57; and La Salle expedition, 76;
    description of, 81; social structure of,
    84–85; greeting ceremonies of, 81–83; and
    symbolic significance of greeting
    ceremonies, 84–85; difference in greeting
    ceremonies from Quapaw, 85–87; territory
    of, 145; mentioned, xii, 35, 38, 39, 41, 44,
    47, 48, 50, 53, 75, 81, 82, 85, 92, 128, 137,
    145, 146, 148, 151, 154
Caddo River, 145–46
Caddo Trace, 146
Caddo Valley, 145
Cadodaquioux, 146
Cadodaquoi, 153
Cadodaquois, 146
Cados d'Acquioux, 146
Cahayhohoua, 146
Cahinnio Caddo, 41, 82, 83, 84
Cahinoa, 146
Cahokia (Mission of the Holy Family of
    Tamaroas), 49
Cajamarca, 28
Calhoun County, 151
Callachee Bay, 150
Callaches (Indian chief), 150
calumet ceremony, 77, 78–79
Camden, Arkansas, 35, 146, 149
Canada, 55, 96, 119, 143
Canadian River, 144
Capac, Huayna (Incan ruler), 7
Capaha (for Pacaha), 71
Cape Girardeau, 128
Carden Bottoms, 68, 156
Carden Bottoms phase, 66
Carmona, Alonso de *(Peregrinación),* 7
Carolina tribes arrive in Arkansas, 60;
    mentioned, 120
Carondelet, Francisco Luis Hector, Barón de
    (governor), 123, 125, 126–27, 128
Carroll County, 150
Casa-Calvo, Marquis de (governor), 115, 129
Casas, Luis de las, 125
Caso y Luengo, Francisco, 127, 128
Casqui, 28, 30, 31, 40, 70
Castilians, 8
Castilla, F. Blanco *(Hernando de Soto, El Centauro
    de las Indias),* 22

Castilla de Oro, 7
Catawba Indians, xiii, xiv
Catawban language, xiii
Cathoochee, 147
Catouch, 147
Caudachos Indians, 146
Cavelier, Jean: and Caddo greeting
    ceremonies, 82–83; calumet ceremony, 85;
    Quapaw greeting ceremonies, 85;
    mentioned, 81, 84
Cavelier, René-Robert, Sieur de La Salle. *See*
    La Salle
Cayas, 28, 40
Cayas-Tanico, 68
Cayoaho, 146
Chaffie Creek, 146–47
Cha-kani-ne, 148
Charboneaux, Jerman (or Germain), 102, 103,
    104, 106
Charboneaux, Meno, 105–6
Charleston, South Carolina: trading houses;
    52, mentioned, 135, 141
Charlevoix, Pére Pierre F. X. de, 144
Charlevoix, Pierre de, 10
Chataugna Mountain, 147
Chattanooga, 147
Chatunga, 147
Cheffie Creek, 146–47
Cheffo, 146
Chenalenne, Anne Catherine, 90
Cherokees, 60, 116, 117, 127, 129, 147–48, 150,
    151, 152, 155, 156
Chicaça, 4, 27
Chickamauga Indians, 147
Chickaninny Prairie, 148
Chickasaw Bluff, 148
Chickasaw Crossing, 148–49
Chickasaw Indians: attacks by, 52, 89; defense
    against, 53; hunting in Arkansas, 54; chal-
    lenge Osage, 57; as English allies, 52–53,
    128; mentioned, xiv, 50, 60, 90, 116, 127,
    145, 150
Chickasawba Mound, 149
Chickasawha, Chief, 149
Chicot County, 141, 149, 156
Chikalah, 148
Chobohollay, 149
Choctaw Bayou, 149
Choctaw Crossing, 149
Choctaw Indians: attacks by, 52, 57; defense
    against, 53; hunting in Arkansas, 54; chal-
    lenge Osage, 57; mentioned, 60, 127–28,
    129, 142, 145, 146, 148, 149, 152, 153, 154

Choctaw Lake, 149
Choctaw Mound, 149
Choctaw Prairie, 142
Choctaw Township, 149
Choctaw Trace, 149
Chouteau, Auguste, 126–27
Chrysler Corporation, 24
Chuckalee, 152–53
Chula, Arkansas, 150
Chula Creek, 150
Clark, George Rogers, 97, 98
Clark County, 145, 154
"Clarksdale Bell," 69
Cleveland County, 151
Clouet, Alexander de, 113, 134
Clover Bend, 104, 110
Coçalla (Simms name for Queen of
    Cofitachequi), 12
Cofitachequi: account of weapons storehouse,
    8, 18; Queen of, Simms treatment of, 12
Colbert, James, 92, 120
Coles, Juan, 7
Coles Creek, 145
Coligua: river, 28; village, 71
Colingua Indians, 41
Colotoches Bayou, 150
Concordia, 120
Conrad, Joseph: on Robert Bontine
    Cunninghame Graham, 18
Consejo de Indias, 5
Conway County, 52, 156
Coulange, Pierre de, 131
Council Bend Lake, 150
Council Island, 150
Couture, Jean, 85, 144
Crawford County, 156
Creek Indians, xiv, 149, 150, 156
Crittenden County, 157
Crosby, Alfred: and the "bardic tradition," 20
Cross County, 31
Crozat, Antoine, 49–50
Cuba, 27, 125
Cumming, Fortescue, 137
Curain, Antoine, 93
Curotte, Charles, 102, 103, 140
Current River, 104
Cuzco, 28

D

d'Abbadie, Jean Jacques Blaise, 116
Dallas County, 151

Daly, Dominick (novel on de Soto), 19
Darby, William *(Emigrant's Guide)*, 138
Dardaine, Baptiste, 126
Dardanelle, Arkansas, 68
Dardenne, Jean-Baptiste, 142
Daughters of the American Revolution, 147
Davidsonville, 107, 110
de Clouet, Louis Favrot. *See* Favrot
Delassus, Carlos Dehault d Luzières, 115–16
Delaware, 60
Delaware Creek, 150–51
Delaware Indians, 57, 60, 114, 1146 125, 128,
    129, 151, 155, 157
Delinó, Ignacio, 115, 125–26
Delino, Juan Ignace, 150
Delinó de Chalmette, Ignace, 132
Delisle, Guillaume, 146
Demasellière, 91, 92
De Monbreun, 99
de Mun and Company, 107
Desha County, 139, 149
de Soto, Hernando. *See* Soto
De Soto automobile, 24
Desruisseaux, Jean Baptiste, 108
de Sueur, Pierre-Charles, 143
Dhegian, 41–42, 66, 70, 78, 79, 80, 143
Diana, Jean, 101, 118
Dickinson, Samuel D.: essay by, 142–56; and
    the Tunican presence in Arkansas, 63;
    mentioned, vii, ix, xiv, x
Din, Gilbert C.: essay by, 112–30; mentioned,
    vii, ix, xiv
Dodge, 100
Dorcheat Bayou, 151
Dorsey, J. Owen, 144, 152
Douay, Father Anastasius, 81
"Downstream People," 143
Dubreuil, Jacobo, 118, 121
Duchasin, Jean Baptiste, 114
Du Lac. *See* Perrin du Lac
Durocher, 97
Dutch, Captain William, 151
Dutch Creek, 151
Duwala, Chief, 147, 155
Dye, David H., 68

ℰ

Early, Ann: on the Hudson route, 34–35
Earth People (Quapaw), 79, 85–87
Ekberg, Carl J., 97, 99
El Cadron, 55

El Cid: mentioned, 8, 22
Emmanuelle. *See* Jean La Fleur
Engels, Frederich: on Robert Bontine
    Cunninghame Graham, 18
English: trade with Indians, 115, 117, 120; and
    the Osage, 122–23, 125, mentioned, xiv, 4,
    10, 89, 120
Ente Nouepa Wattishka, "Bayou of the
    Marshes," 151
Etowah, 142

ℱ

Fagot, Andrés, 118, 121, 129
Favrot, Alexandre de Clouet, 138, 139
Favrot, Pierre-Joseph, 132
Fayas. *See* Jean LaBass
Fayce, John, 102
Faye, Stanley, 143
Fer, N. de, 146
Fihliol, Juan, 137, 138
Fletcher, Alice C.: ethnography of Omaha
    tribe, 80
Fletcher, John Gould: on Arkansas Post, 135
Florida, xii, 3, 10, 11, 12, 15, 40
Fooy, Benjamin, 157
Ford, James, 29–30, 66
Fort Breton, 146
Fort Carlos III, 93
Fort Carondelet of the Osages, 127
Fort Cavanaugh, 53
Fort de Chartres, 88
Fort Malouin, 50
Fort Orleans, 53
Fort St. Louis: established by La Salle, 81
Fort Smith, Arkansas, 149
Foucault, Father Nicolas: killed by Koroas,
    73–74
France: colonial government policy, 139;
    mentioned, 80, 98, 97, 100, 102, 104, 111,
    113, 116, 118, 125
Franciscan, 78
Francoeur, Agnès, 90, 92, 93
Francoeur, Angelique, 90
Francoeur, Anne, 90
Francoeur, François, 90, 93
Francoeur, Jean, 90
Francoeur, Jean Baptiste, 93
Francoeur, Jeanne, 90
Francoeur, Joseph: 89–90; family of, 90; death
    of, 91; account of dispute with Tounoir,
    91–92; mentioned, 101
Francoeur, Marie, 90, 93

Francoeur, Marie Aimé, 90
Francoeur, Suzanne, 90
Francure Township, 90
Franklin County, 142
French: frontiersmen, xiv; American seizure of colonial towns, xiv; interest in North America, 9; colonial expansion, 48; and Quapaw trade, 52; and Caddo trade, 52; and Treaty of Paris, 55; with La Salle, 76; first contact with Quapaws, 77; presence in Arkansas, 88; mentioned, 62, 66, 77, 78, 79, 80, 97
French and Indian War, 55, 97
Frincart, Juan Batista, 93
fur trade, 48, 90, 97

G

Galla Creek, 152
Galla Rock, 151
Galley, 151–52
Galley Hills, 152
Garcilaso de la Vega Vargas, Don Sebastian ("El Inca"): account of, 7–8; author of *La Florida del Ynca*, 7; influence on Grace King's account of de Soto, 18; quoted, 18; Morse preference for his account, 71; mentioned, 7, 8, 11, 20, 38, 39
Garland City, 155
Gayoso de Lemos, Manuel, 117, 119
"Gentleman of Elvas": origins of, 4; report of de Soto entrada, 4; mentioned, 11, 20, 32, 39, 39–40
Georgetown University: Theodore Maynard at, 20; mentioned, 90, 93.
Georgia, 60, 147, 155
Gibson, Robert, 125
Giscard, Louis, 90
Goldsmith Oliver Site 2, 69
Graham, Robert Bontine Cunninghame: life of, 18; reliance on Garcilaso, 18–19; on de Soto, 18–19
Grand Cadaux Indians, 146
Grand Lake, Saint Martin Parish, Louisiana, 156
Grand Prairie, 135, 139
Grappé, François, 151
Graver, Jean Baptiste, 107
Great Britian: growing power of in American west, 49; and Treaty of Paris, 55; and spoils of Seven Years' War, 119; mentioned, 97, 129
Great Council Island, 150
Great Lakes, 49

Greene County, Arkansas, 154
Griffin, James B., 29–30
Grosillion, Charles, 90
Guignolet, Joseph, 103, 104–5
Gulf Coast, 9, 76
Gulf of Mexico, 49

H

Haas, Mary: compilation of Tunica dictionary, 63
Hakluyt, Richard: translation of the Gentleman of Elvas, 10; mentioned, 4
Harvard University, 25, 63
Hasinai Confederacy, 81
Hasinai Indians, 50
Hatchiecoon Bayou, 152
Heckatoo, Arkansas, 152
Heckatoo, Chief, 152
Hempstead County, 145, 149, 154
Herrera y Tordesillas, Antonio de: account of Spanish in Florida, 9; mentioned, 11
Hinma Koapemiche (Caddo chief), 146
Hispaniola, 6
Hoffman, Michael P.: essay by, 61–75; on the Quapaw, 66; and the Tunican presence in Arkansas, 66; mentioned, vii, ix, x, xii–xiii
Hot Springs, Arkansas, 15, 32, 71, 70, 144, 156
Hot Springs Problem, 31
Hudson, Charles H.: introduction by, xi–xv; on the de Soto route, 30–35

I

Iberville River, 119
Illinois Bayou, 152
Illinois Indians: Quapaw/Caddo territorial defense against, 53; move into Arkansas, 57; mentioned, 76, 89, 93, 96, 97, 100, 108, 109, 111, 128, 134, 139, 143, 152
Illinois River, 152
Imbau, Pierre, 90
Iroquois Indians, xiii, 143, 155
Irving, Theodore, portrait of de Soto, 11–12; compared to Simms, 13; mentioned, 15, 20, 37
Irving, Washington, 11
Izard, George, 67, 144, 157

J

Jamestown, 30
Janis, Alex, 101, 103
Janis, Angelique, 96, 102, 103

Janis, Antoine, 93, 95, 96, 97, 100, 101, 102, 103, 104, 105, 106, 107
Janis, Antoine, Jr., 95
Janis, Antoine (Nicholas), 103
Janis, Baptiste, 101
Janis, Catherine, 97
Janis, Elena, 96
Janis, Félicité, 97, 108
Janis, Felipe, 96
Janis, Francis, 102
Janis, Francisco, 96
Janis, François: death of, 110; mentioned, 95, 96, 97, 99, 101, 102, 103, 104
Janis, Hélène, 101, 103, 106
Janis, Jean Baptiste: death of, 110; mentioned, 95, 97, 99, 102, 103–4
Janis, Jo, 102
Janis, José, 96
Janis, Joseph, 101, 103, 106
Janis, Juan Batista, 95, 96
Janis, Louise, 102, 103, 106
Janis, Maria, 96, 101, 103
Janis, Marie Anne, 106
Janis, Maryann, 102
Janis, Meno, 102, 104
Janis, Michael, 102
Janis, Michel, 101, 103, 104, 106
Janis, Miguel, 96
Janis, Nicholas: death of, 110; mentioned, 95, 97, 96, 98, 99, 100, 102, 103, 104, 108
Janis, Philippe, 101, 103
Janis Creek, 110
Janis Mill, 110
Jardelat, Louis, 118, 119
Jaulin, François, 92
Jaulin, Jean Baptiste, 92, 93
Jaulin, Jeanne, 93
Jefferson, Thomas, 39, 60
Jefferson County, 157
Jennings, John (The Golden Eagle), 21
Jeter, Marvin: and the Tunica presence, 63, 67, 71, 72; "maximum Tunican" scenario, 69; on Brain's scenario, 74
Jolliet: exploration of Mississippi River, 76, 143
Joutel, Henri, 71, 81, 83, 85, 144, 146

𝒦

Kadohadacho Caddo, 41, 83, 84, 81, 82, 146
Kadohadacho Confederacy, 81
Kados Indians, 146
Kanoatino Indians, 146
Kansas Indians, 143

Kappa (village), 76, 77, 78, 79, 144
Kaskaskia (town), 95, 96, 97, 98, 99, 100, 101, 107, 108, 109, 114
Kaskaskia Indians, 152
Kaskaskia River, 49
Kealedji Indians, 150
Kentucky, 147, 155
Keshotee Island, 152–53
Kiamichi River, 151
Kickapoo Indians, 152
King, Grace: on Garcilaso, 18; on the Gentleman of Elvas, 18; on the Spanish conquest, 18; mentioned, 19, 20
Kinkead-Mainard site, 69
Know Nothing Party, 13
Koasiti Indians, 153
Ko-ora-too (Cherokee leader), 60
Koroa Indians: and death of Father Nicolas Foucault, 73–74; mentioned, 62, 67, 73, 153
Kuhn, Thomas (The Structure of Scientific Revolutions), 34

𝓛

LaBass, Jean, 103, 106, 107, 110
LaBass, John, 102, 110
LaBasq, Mary, 110
LaCombe, Cola, 106, 107
LaCombe, Louis, 106
Lafayette County, 148, 155
Lafayette River, 151
La Flesche, Frances: ethnography of Omaha tribe, 80
LaFleur, Jean, 90
Lafont, 99
La Harpe, Jean-Baptiste Bérnard de: account of de Soto entrada, 9–10; encounter with Quapaw, 51–52; mentioned, 50, 51, 144, 146
L'Isle, Guillaume de, 29
Lajeunesse. See Pierre Imbau
La Salle, Nicolas de: description of Quapaw greeting, 77–78
La Salle, Robert Cavelier Sieur de: visits Arkansas, 41; and the Tunica prescence, 67, 71; trading concession, 76; and Quapaw greeting ceremonies, 77, 87; returns to France, 80; bypasses the mouth of the Mississippi, 80–81; establishes Fort St. Louis, 81; at Matagorda Bay, 81; murdered, 81; mentioned, xiv, 85, 144, 156
La Source. See Jean Baptiste Taumur
Lake Bistineau, Louisiana, 151
Lake Michigan, 154
Lake Saint Joseph, 156

Lambert, 91
Langlois, 99
Lankford, George E.: essay by, 88–111; mentioned, vii, ix, x, xiv
Lariver, Louis, 106
LaRochelle. *See* Jean Jaulin, 92
las Casas, Bartolemé de: translations of, 10; mentioned, 6
Lasource, 99
Latham, John, 101
Lauratown, 104, 105
Law, John: and the Mississippi Company, 50; Arkansas venture, 136
Lawrence County, 96, 102, 107, 110
Laytanes Indians (Comanches), 125
LeBum (Lebun), Chief, 146
LeCombe, Cola, 106
Lee County, 150
Lee Creek, 156
Lefevre, Pierre, 107
LeMieux, Antoine, 110
LeMieux, Claud, 101
LeMieux, François, 101
LeMieux, Maire Anne, 103
LeMieux, Pierre, 101, 104, 110
LeMieux, Victoire, 101
Lenape Indians, 150
Leni-Lenape Indians, 150
Lepine, Jean François, 90
Les Gallais, 125
Levasseur, 99
Levasseur, Charlotte, 108
Levasseur, Estanislas, 108
Levasseur, Etienne, 108
Levasseur, François, 108
Levasseur, Marie Larose, 108
Lewisville, Arkansas, 148
Leyba, Fernando de, 115, 116, 117
Lincoln County, 149, 152, 155
Little Red River, 149
Little River, 152, 156
Little Rock, 66, 69, 144
Livy, 12
Logan County, 155, 157
López, Andrés, 114, 118
Lorimier, Louis, 128
Lost Prairie, Arkansas, 156
Louis XIV, 48–49, 78
Louis XV, 131
Louisiana, 69, 71, 72, 73, 74, 75, 81, 100, 112, 113, 119, 120, 121, 122, 131, 133, 134, 135, 136, 138, 139, 145, 146, 153, 156

Louisiana Department of Tourism, 28
Louisiana Purchase, 39, 60, 93, 119
Louisiana State University, 151
Loup Indians, 116, 117, 129
Lowery, Woodbury, 25
Luna, Tristán de, xii
Lytle, Andrew *(At the Moon's Inn),* 20–21

M

Madrid, 126
Magdelon, Dame, 120
Mahas, 144
Maine, 155
Malone, Walter: epic poem on de Soto, 19; fictional de Soto, 21
Marion County, 150
Marksville, Louisiana, 63, 156
Marquette, Father: and Tunica presence, and smallpox, 48; 66–67; exploration of Mississippi, 76; mentioned, 41, 143, 153–54, 156,
Martin, Francisco, 116
Mary Louise, 95
Mascouten Indians, 150
Matagorda Bay, Texas, 81
Matis, Jerôme, 106, 107
Mauvila, 8, 11, 18, 27
Maxent, Laclede and Company, 116
"Maximum Tunican," 71, 74, 75
Maynard, Theodore: account of de Soto, 19–20; mentioned, 21
McGehee, Arkansas, 153
McLeod, W. E., 95, 104
Membré, Father Zénobe, 78
Memphis, Tennessee, 107, 148
Ménard, Francisco, 118
Ménard, François, 114, 129, 134
Ménard, Pierre, 114
Menard Complex, 66, 69, 75
Mento Indians, 153, 154
Mexico, 10, 50, 76
Mexico City, 50
Mézières, Lt. Gov. Athanase de, 56; planned attack against Osage, 56; and the Osage, 124; mentioned, 137
Miami Indians: arrival in Arkansas, 57; mentioned, 54, 148, 152
Michigan, 154
Miller County, Arkansas, 156
Minnesota River, 116
Miró, Estevan (governor), 114, 116, 118, 121, 123, 125, 126, 145

Mission of the Holy Family of Tamaroas (Cahokia), 49

Mississippian ceremonial mound, 41

Mississippian culture, 66

Mississippi Company: and French commercial venture, 50; and Claude-Charles Du Tisné, 51

Mississippi County, 149, 152, 155

Mississippi River: de Soto's crossing of, 27; and La Salle, 76; and the liquor trade, 122; origins of name, 153; mentioned, xiii, xiv, 3, 28, 30, 39, 44, 52, 55, 62, 63, 67, 69, 73, 74, 77, 78, 80, 85, 88, 97, 98, 107, 108, 111, 112, 119–20, 139, 117, 120, 125, 128, 135, 143, 144, 148, 149, 150, 153, 154

Missouri, 109, 113, 122, 123, 126, 128, 129, 155

Missouri River, 116, 122

Missouri Territory, 102, 103, 107

Mitchegamias Lake, 153–54

Mitchigamea Indians, 153, 154

Mobile, Alabama, 110, 121, 143

Mobilian trade jargon, 145

Monroe, Louisiana, 137, 146

Montogmery County, 145

Moro Bayou, 151

Morrilton, Arkansas, 52

Morse, Dan and Phyllis: and identification of protohistoric sites in northeastern Arkansas, 71; mentioned, 31

Morse-Hudson route, 68, 70, 71, 73

Moscoso, Luys de, 11

"Mourning War," 122

Mulberry River, 147

Murray, Katherine A.: on de Soto expedition and epidemics, 36

Muscle Shoals, Alabama, 147, 155

Muskhogean dialect, xiii, 148

Muskogee, Oklahoma, 56

𝓝

Nady, Arkansas, 136

Nahua Indians, 146

Narváez, Pánvilo de, 27

Nassonis Indians, 146

Natchez (settlement in British West Florida), 117

Natchez, Mississippi, 132

Natchez Indians, xiv, 62, 73

Natchitoches, 50, 53, 55, 56, 81, 113, 114, 122, 124, 126, 137, 154

Natchitoches Confederacy, 81

"Negro Hill," 93

Neosho River, 41

Netta Boc Creek, 154

Nevada County, 145, 151

New Bourbon, 106

New Brunswick, 155

New Madrid, Missouri, 101, 126, 155

New Madrid earthquake, 104, 147

New Mexico, 55

New Orleans, Louisiana, 18, 51, 88, 113, 115, 116, 117, 119, 121, 123, 126, 129, 131, 132, 135, 137, 139, 143

New Spain, 100

Nicaragua, 7

Niebuhr, Barthold Georg, 12

Niska River, 154

Nitar, Pierre, 114, 121

Nodena points, 74

North Carolina, xiii, 60, 147

Northwest Ordinance, 99

Nuttall, Thomas, 141, 152

Ny-Jitteh River, 154

Ny-Whoutteh-Junka ("Little Muddy River," now the St. Francis), 67, 154

𝓞

O'Reilly, Alejandro, 113

Ober, Frederick: account of de Soto mentioned, 19

Ocllo, Chimpa, 7

Ogálĩpa, 143, 144

Ogaxpa (for Quapaw), 71

Ohio River, 150, 153, 155

Ohio Valley, 54

Oklahoma, 75, 81, 145

Olivares, Marcos, 114

Oliver Complex, 74

Omaha Indians: *He'dewachi* ceremony, 79–80; mentioned, 143

Orieta, José, 115

Osage Creek, 154

Osage Indians: raids against Caddo, 56; drive Wichita from Arkansas Valley, 53–54; territory in Arkansas, 42; dearth of information on, 44; and hunting deer, 44, 47; and trade with Europeans, 46; and French/Indian slave trade, 52; and French access to western Indians, 53; and relationship to Quapaw, 42, 54; raids and depredations by, 54, 57, 89, 91, 117, 127, 122–23, 137, 139–40; relations with Quapaw, 57; challenged by Chickasaw and Choctaw, 57; living on periphery of Arkansas, 60; and trade with, 115, 117,

122–23, 139–40; "Mourning War" ceremony, 122; Delinó's planned war against, 126; peace treaty, 126–27; mentioned, xii, 38, 39, 41, 92, 108, 116, 125, 123–24, 127, 128, 143, 150, 151, 153, 156
Osage Path, 154
Osage Prairie, 154
Osarque Indians, 143
Osarque River, 143
Osceola, 142
Osotouy (Quapaw village), 66, 144
Ouachita County, 146
Ouachita District, 128
Ouachita forests, 46
Ouachita Mountains, 44, 54, 56, 70, 73
Ouachita Post, 137
Ouachita River, 28, 41, 44, 57, 70, 71, 73, 82, 145, 146, 149, 151, 154, 156
Ouyapes Indians, 144
Ovideo y Valdés, Gonzalo Fernández de, 6, 7, 9
Ozark, 66, 143
Ozark Escarpment, 105
Ozark forests, 46
Ozark Mountains, 44, 54, 75, 88, 93, 100, 101, 111
Ozark Plateau, 42, 51, 54, 60
Ozó-tiohi, 144
Ozotoue Indians, 153

℘

Pacaha Indians, 40, 67, 70
Pacific, route to, 48
Paheka, 67
Pahom, Abenazar, 118
Panis Indians (Wichitas), 125
Paracoxi, 4
Pardo era, xiii
Parkin site, 31, 32–33
Parliament, 18
Pawnee Indians, 51, 52
Peabody Museum, 63
Peach Orchard, 104
Pemiscot Bayou, 155
Pemiscot River, 155
Pénigaut, André-Joseph, 143
Pennsylvania, xiv
Pensacola, 55, 121
Peoria Indians, 54, 106 152
Pepper, Lucky Ned, 15
Pérez, Manuel, 125
Perrin du Lac, François Marie, 137, 138

Pertuis, Louis, 93
Pertuis, Pierre, 93
Peru, 7, 10
Peter, Lily (de Soto poem), 21
Petit Barrel, 104
Petit Jean River, 151
Peyroux, Henri, 101
Philadelphia, xiv, 135
Phillips, Philip, 29–30, 66
Piankashaws Indians, 54
Pichardo, Padre José Antonio, 145–46, 157
Pickett, Albert James: on the de Soto expedition, 24
Piernas, Pedro, 124
Pike County, 154
Pine Bluff, Arkansas, 155
Piot, Chritophe, 93
Pittman, Philip, 137, 139
Pizarro, Francisco: campaign in Peru, 14; depicted as a "bad" conquistador by Graham, 19; mentioned, 7
Pocahontas, 142
Poinsett County, 152
Point Remove, 147, 149
pole-striking ceremony (Quapaw), 77–78, 79–80
Ponca Indians, 143
Pontalba, Baron de, 132
Pope, John, 143
Pope County, 152
Portia, 105
Portuguese, 4
Powhatan, 142
Prairie County, 149, 150, 157
Praire du Rocher, 99, 97
Prescott, Arkansas, 13
Prescott, William H.: histories of Mexico and Peru, 10
"Principle People," 147
protohistoric era: defined, xi, 61–62; mentioned, 62, 66

ℚ

Quapaw Bayou, 144
Quapaw Indians: origins of, xii; epidemics devastate, 39, 57; Marquette encounters, 41; dearth of information on, 44; related to Osage, 42, 54; diet, 44–48; and hunting deer, 44, 47; women and gardening, 45; crops cultivated, 46; and floods, 46; abode in Arkansas, 45; and trade with Europeans, 46; and gathering plant life,

46; and wild game, 46, 47; and Catholic
missionaries, 48; and the French fur trade,
48; alliance with French, 48, 52–53; and de
Tonty, 49; encounter with La Harpe,
51–52; and French/Indian slave trade, 52;
and Chickasaw raids for slave trade, 52;
and relations with French, 52; and French
trade, 52, 53; and relations with Spanish
after Treaty of Paris, 55; relations with
Osage, 57; living on periphery of
Arkansas, 60; location of, 61; and protohistoric remains, 66; tradition and the
Tunica, 67, 73; for Ogaxpa, 71; and La
Salle expedition, 76; moieties, 77; as Earth
People, 77, 79, 85–87; as Sky People, 77, 79,
85–87; social organization, 79, 80;
symbolic significance of greeting
ceremonies, 80; pole-striking ceremony,
77–78, 79–80; Sacred Post, 85; difference
in greeting ceremonies from Caddo,
85–87; trade with, 114; and liquor, 120–21;
mentioned, xii, 38, 74, 80, 83, 84, 85, 89,
92, 112, 113, 116, 120, 125, 126, 127, 139,
143, 144, 148, 150, 152, 153, 154, 155, 156,
157

Quapaw Paradox, 66
Quapaw Phase, 66
Quigate province, 40
Quigualtam Indians, 41
Quinguate, 70
Quitsey (Kichais) Indians, 56
Quiz Quiz, 71

R

Ranjel, Rodrigo: report of, 6–7; mentioned, 7,
8, 20, 27, 32, 39, 40
Rankin Robert: and the Tunican presence in
Arkansas, 63–64, 67; mentioned, 70, 144
Read, William A., 151
Red River, 39, 41, 44, 50, 53, 56, 72, 81, 122,
144, 145, 146, 148, 149, 151, 156
Refeld, Charles, 106, 118
Relaçam Verdadeira, 4
Removal Act of 1830, 60
Rio Pánuco, 3
Rivard, Marie François, 97
River of the Cayas (Arkansas River), 68, 70, 71
Rivet, Augustine, 106, 107
Roberts, William, 10
Robertson, James, 20
Robertson, William, 10
Rocky Mountains, 15
Rollings, Willard H.: essay by, 38–60;
mentioned, vii, ix, x, xii

Rome, 12
Roosevelt, Franklin, xii
Rosborough Lake (Texas), 146
Rousseau, Pierre George, 150
Russell, William 102, 103

S

Sabo, George: essay by, 76–87; mentioned,
viii, ix, x, xiv
St. Charles, 95, 99, 100, 109
St. Cosme, Jean François Buisson de, 38, 41,
48
St. Denis, Louis Juchereau de, 50
St. Francis River, 28, 40, 44, 57, 60, 67, 90, 91,
114, 115, 123, 128, 147, 148, 149, 150, 153,
154, 155
Sainte Geneviève, 55, 93, 95, 97, 99, 100, 106,
107, 108, 109, 110, 111
St. Lawrence, 9
St. Louis, 55, 97, 100, 102, 103, 109, 111, 113,
114, 115, 116, 123, 124, 125, 126, 135, 139,
140
St. Marie, Etienne, 101–2
Salas, Alberto, 6
Saline River, 99, 157
San Luis de Cadodachos (Spanish post), 146
Saracen, François, 155
Sarasin, Chief, 155
Sarassa Mounds, 155
Sarrazin, François, 155
Sauer, Carl, 27
Sauk Indians, 150
Schambach, Frank: on the Hudson route,
34–35; on the the de Soto expedition and
Calion and Camden, 35; on Autiamque,
35; Koroan peoples and the de Soto
expedition, 35; mentioned, 29
Scott County, 151
Searcy, Richard, 107
Seminary of Quebec, 49
Seven Years' War, 112, 119, 139
Sevier County, 154
Shaw, George Bernard: on Robert Bontine
Cunninghame Graham, 18
Shawnee, Arkansas, 155
Shawnee Indians: move into Arkansas, 57;
mentioned, 60, 128, 150, 155
Shea, John G. *(Narrative and Critical History of
America)*, 25
Shoal Creek, 155–56
Shreveport, Louisiana, 144
Silvestre, Gonzalo de, 7

Simms, William Gilmore: portrait of de Soto, 12–13; mentioned, 24
Siouan-speaking Indians, xiii, 78, 143
Skaquaw ("The Swan"), 147
Sky People (Quapaw), 77, 79, 85–87
slave trade: Chickasaw selling Quapaw and Choctaw captives, 52; market for, 55; mentioned, 90
Sloan, David: essay by, 3–37; mentioned, viii, ix, x, xi
Smithsonian Institution, 12, 72, 144, 145
Smithsonian Institution's Bureau of American Ethnology, 25
Solgohachia, Arkansas, 156
Soto, Hernando de: expedition of, xii, xiv, 62, 73, 73; route of, xii, 40, 73; article on, 3–37; death of, 6, 14, 18, 23; question of morality, 14; Wilmer's treatment of, 13; depicted as a "good" conquistador by Graham, 19; depopulation following, 38; mentioned, x, 3, 39, 70–71, 145, 156, 157
Souligny, Louis, 126
South America, 9
South Carolina, xiii, 60, 147, 155
"South Wind People," 143
Spain: sixteenth-century expeditions of, 3; and education, 8; Simms treatment of, 12; growing power of in American West, 49; and Treaty of Paris, 55; colonial system, 55, 139; in Arkansas after Treaty of Paris, 55; trade restrictions, 55; posts, 56; restrictions on fire arms, 56; and Indian policy, 115; and trade with Indians, 115–16; and the Osage 122–23, 124, 125; and trade policy, 124; era in Arkansas, 125; mentioned, 10, 88, 95, 97, 98, 99 100, 102, 109, 111, 112, 113, 114
Spanish-American War, 23
Spanish Fort, 54
Spanish land grants, 107, 109, 110, 141
Spanish New Mexico, route to, 48
Spring River, 106, 107, 110
Sulphur River, 57, 144, 151
Sunflower Landing, 30
Swanton, John R.: and the de Soto route, 25–35, 70; and the Tunican presence in Arkansas, 63–64; mentioned, xii, 73, 145

ℑ

Taensas Indians, 78, 156
Tahchee, Chief, 151
Tanico (Tunica), 63, 70, 71, 156
Tanika (Tunica), 63

Tanika (Tunica village), 67
Tanikwa (Tunica), 63
Tascaluza, 8, 13
Taumur, Jean Baptiste, 97
Taumur, Marie Louise, 97
Tawakoni (Wichita village), 50, 51, 54
Tennessee, 60, 147, 148, 155
Tenochtitlán, 30
Tensas Bayou, 156
Tensas River, 156
Texarkana, 50, 146
Texas, 55, 71, 75, 81, 145, 146, 155, 156
Thoriman (Indian village), 144
Three Forks, 41
Thyase, Madelena, 106
Tiller and Hog Lake phases of Bayous Bartholomew and Macon, 72, 73
Tioux Indians, 62
Tisné, Claude-Charles Du: and the Mississippi Company, 51
Toltec, 146
Tongigua (Indian village), 78
Tonguenga (Quapaw village), 144
Tonika (Tunica), 63
Tonnika (Tunica), 67.
Tonty, Henri de, 41, 49, 71, 81, 136, 153
Tounoir, 91, 92
Tourangeau. See Charles Grosillion
Tourangeaux, 90, 91
Tourima (Quapaw village), 78, 144
Treaty of Dancing Rabbit, 149
Treaty of Paris, 55
Trigger, Bruce, 36
Trinidad Poveda, Leonardo de la, 125
Trinity River, 57
Trudeau site, Louisiana, 63, 72, 75
True Grit, 15
Tsalagi (Cherokee Indians), 147
Tukabahohee Creek Indians, 150
Tula (Caddo village), 41, 145
Tulsa, Oklahoma, 50
Tunica Indians: dictionary, 63; and Jeffrey Brain; and the Quiz Quiz; location of, 63; defined, 63; and John Swanton, 63; and Mary Haas, 63; presence in Arkansas, propoponents of, 63–66; presence in Arkansas, evidence of, 63–66; abandonment of Arkansas, 73–74; mentioned, xii, 61, 62, 70, 75, 153, 156
Tuyahhosah Creek, 156
Twain, Mark: on Grace King, 18
Tyronza, 157

U

Ucita, 16
Ulloa, Antonio de, 113, 116, 120
United States, cession to Choctaws, 149
U.S. Board of Land Commissioners, 103, 106, 109
U.S. De Soto Expedition Commission, 145, 156
U.S. Indeminfication Commission, 104
U.S. Land Commission, 109
University of Georgia, 145, 156
University of Kansas, 63
Unzaga y Amezaga, Louis de, 112, 117
"Upstream People," 143
Utiangue Indians, 41

V

Valliére, Joseph, 114, 115, 116, 121, 125
Vasconcelos: A Romance of the New World, 12–13
Vásquez de Ayllón, Lucas, 27
Vaugine, François, 114, 118, 119, 121
Verdigris River, 41
Vilemont, Carlos de: and liquor trade with Indians, 121–22; and Osage trade, 123; Spanish land grant, 141; mentioned, 114, 117, 127, 129, 137
Villanueva y Cañedo, Don Luis (biographer of de Soto), 23
Villasur, Pedro de, 51
Villiers, Balthazar de, 120, 132, 134, 137, 139
Vincennes, 97
Vinseman, Franciso, 129
Virginia, 98, 100, 147

W

Wabbaseka Bayou, 157
Wappanocca Bayou, 157
War of the Spanish Succession, 49
Warr, Lord De La, 150
Washington, Arkansas, 149
Washington County, 152
Wattensaw Bayou, 157
Wattishka Jinka (Little Bayou), 157
Wayne, John, 15
Wazhazhe Indians, 154
West Virginia, 147
Whayne, Jeannie: preface by, ix–x; mentioned, viii, x
White County, 93, 149
White River, 28, 40, 42, 55, 57, 60, 89, 90, 91, 92, 93, 101, 106, 107, 114, 115, 123, 128, 129, 147–48, 150, 154
Wichita Indians, 41, 50, 51, 52, 53, 56, 145, 153, 154
Williamsburg, Virginia, 141
Willing, Capt. James, 120
Wilmer, Lambert A.: book on Spanish in America, 13–15; anti-Catholocism in, 14–15; mentioned, 14–15, 16, 20
Winter, Elisha: Spanish land grant, 141
"Winterville Incised," 69, 72
Woodruff county, 148

Y

Yazoo Indians, 62
Yazoo River, 63, 67, 73
Yell County, 145, 148, 150, 151, 156
Ymvo, Juan Baptista, 118